Texas South Plains
War Stories

Texas South Plains War Stories

Interviews with Veterans from World War II to Afghanistan

LARRY A. WILLIAMS *and* KATHERINE MCLAMORE

McFarland & Company, Inc., Publishers
Jefferson, North Carolina

*All photographs taken or provided by
Larry A. Williams and Katherine McLamore.*

LIBRARY OF CONGRESS CATALOGUING-IN-PUBLICATION DATA

Names: Williams, Larry A., interviewer. | McLamore, Katherine, interviewer.
Title: Texas South Plains war stories : interviews with veterans
from World War II to Afghanistan / Larry A. Williams, Katherine McLamore.
Other titles: Interviews with veterans from World War II to Afghanistan
Description: Jefferson, North Carolina : McFarland & Company,
Inc., Publishers, 2021 | Includes bibliographical references and index.
Identifiers: LCCN 2021021174 |
ISBN 9781476683072 (paperback : acid free paper) ∞
ISBN 9781476642123 (ebook)
Subjects: LCSH: World War, 1939–1945—Veterans—Texas—Biography. |
Veterans—Texas—Interviews. | Veterans—Texas—Biography. | Korean War,
1950–1953—Veterans—Texas—Interviews. | World War, 1939–1945—Personal
narratives, American. | Korean War, 1950–1953—Personal narratives,
American. | United States—Armed Forces—Biography. | BISAC:
HISTORY / Military / World War II | HISTORY / United States /
State & Local / Southwest (AZ, NM, OK, TX)
Classification: LCC D810.V42 U695 2021 | DDC 355.0092/2764—dc23
LC record available at https://lccn.loc.gov/2021021174

BRITISH LIBRARY CATALOGUING DATA ARE AVAILABLE

**ISBN (print) 978-1-4766-8307-2
ISBN (ebook) 978-1-4766-4212-3**

© 2021 Larry A. Williams and Katherine McLamore. All rights reserved

*No part of this book may be reproduced or transmitted in any form
or by any means, electronic or mechanical, including photocopying
or recording, or by any information storage and retrieval system,
without permission in writing from the publisher.*

Front cover images © 2021 Shutterstock

Printed in the United States of America

*McFarland & Company, Inc., Publishers
Box 611, Jefferson, North Carolina 28640
www.mcfarlandpub.com*

Acknowledgments

My first acknowledgment should go to Erin Agee, owner of the Lubbock *Senior Link* magazine. She listened to stories of her grandfather's time during World War II. She had a vision that all veterans' stories should be told. To that end, she recruited Katherine and I to go out and interview veterans. We will forever be grateful for her encouraging us along the way. I also want to thank Jane Bromley, my friend and editor with the magazine. Her suggestions (and gentle corrections) have helped me more than she could ever know. I'd like to thank my writing partner and fellow Veterans Liaison Co-Chair on the Texas South Plains Honor Flight, Katherine McLamore. While I contributed most of the military side of things, she brought the personal touch to each story which I have tried to incorporate in my style of writing. James Bradley (*Flags of Our Father* author) once told me "If you are passionate about a book project, write it yourself." Thank you for that moment of inspiration James. I never forgot it. Author Hampton Sides has also been an inspiration. While I could never approach his status as an author, I have always admired his style of writing and attention to details. A special thanks to my editor, Dylan Lightfoot, who graciously put up with and answered all of my rookie questions about writing a book.

I have a long list of family and friends, too numerous to mention, who have been so kind to indulge me in my writing. You all know who you are. My friends in choir at Westminster Presbyterian were always supportive of my writing, especially 95-year-old Florence Gum, who was always the first to say, "I saw your article" or "I loved your article." Thank you for being one of my biggest supporters Florence. To my mother, Wanda, thank you for believing that I "could always do better" than my early school report cards showed and my sister, Patty, for her love and support. To my children, Jessica and Ty, thank you for being kind to your old man by reading my articles and being supportive in every way. How could I possibly put into words how much my wife, Janet, meant to me during this journey? Her patience has been nothing short of amazing.

She has been my friend, frequent travel partner, part-time editor and full-time encourager. She has put up with my countless hours away from home and watched me sit at the computer day after day like a trooper. I am forever grateful for her love and support.

Last and absolutely not least, are the men and women who we wrote about in this book. They welcomed us, total strangers, into their homes with an easy grace that seems to be a common thread for their generation. We became not just interviewers looking for a story, we became friends. Oftentimes when I would get ready to leave, the veterans and/or their spouses or family members would tell us to "come back and see us sometime." The families of all of these veterans have been very supportive. I have spent many hours visiting, on the phone, emailing and texting them. They have provided a wealth of information to help me "fill in the gaps" for their loved ones' service. Katherine and I salute all of our veterans. We are humbled and grateful that you allowed us to record and write your stories to be preserved for future generations. You truly are what I've always called "Living History." As one World War II POW told me after his liberation from a German POW camp, he shouted, "God Bless America! This is the greatest country in the world!"

—**Larry A. Williams**

I am filled with joy as I recall the people who influenced me on this journey. Writing is a passion of mine, and I thank my sweet Mama, for often refusing to verbalize a word definition as I impatiently asked her to, and she took the high road and pushed the dictionary next to my after school snack plate. I remember her taking my brother and me to the neighborhood library each week, rain or snow, where we would search the baskets and shelves for books, and mom would help us carry our heavy cloth bags, never refusing us even one book. My brother has a vast vocabulary and the best linguistic skills I have encountered, and I feel my imagination and abilities are blessed because mom took the time and made the effort to empower her young children in ways she wished she had as a child. Thank you Stephanie Nash for broadening my view and skills as a writer in her Creative Writing Class at Coronado High School in 1987 when she had all her students "host a birthday party" for their favorite author. Mine, at that time, was Stephen King. He wrote with such vibrant adjectives and plot lines, and his style moved me. Mrs. Nash had each of us students to write our authors and invite them to the party. Each author politely declined and some graciously answered a few questions we included in the invitation. Stephen King wrote me back, thanked me for the invite, and indulged me by answering each question in full. The Coronado High School yearbook department wrote an article about me and me receiving communication from my chosen famous author.

I also owe a great debt of gratitude to W.A. and Charlotte Wheat, from Lubbock, Texas. Welcoming me into their home over the years countless times over a meal or cup of tea, this former pastor and his wife embodied the warm heart of the Lord, and carved out time to encourage me in many writing projects. W.A. would eat with us and then busy himself with fishing or chores, and Charlotte and I would weave the stories together, challenging each other all along the way. These precious times were filled with sweat, tears, and much raucous laughter as we bonded, our ages in years disappearing magically. Kindred spirits and childlike hearts bloomed in deep friendship which will last into eternity.

I attended my first Texas South Plains Honor Flight meeting and gave a brief presentation in 2012. Once I learned what Honor Flight does, I was drawn like a magnet. After becoming a Committee member in 2013, Larry Williams (my Honor Flight Veterans Liaison Co-Chair) asked me to join him in helping him reach out to veterans and families prior to and after the flight. Then Erin Agee, owner of *Senior Link* magazine asked us to help her interview veterans and get their stories for the fall edition of the publication. The veteran stories were so well received by the community who clamored for more, that Erin decided to include at least one veteran article in each of her 5 editions annually, and dedicated the fall edition to highlighting veterans and their families which has continued since that time. Each year the fall veteran's edition grows by leaps, bounds, committed advertisers, and number of pages featuring all ages of veterans and their loved ones.

In summary, my life is full because of the kind people and causes I have been involved with. The deep losses of not having a father or close, positive family relationships have been filled to overflowing by what I know God has brought into my life. Peace and joy flood my heart as I give thanks.

—**Katherine McLamore**

Table of Contents

Acknowledgments v
Preface 1
Introduction: The Cost of Freedom 5

Part I—World War II

1. Alvira Agee: "I Can Do That" 8
2. M.T. Allen: Quonset Hut Expert 10
3. Robert Anderson: Battling on Two Fronts 12
4. Clyde Bearden: "At the Convenience of the Government" 15
5. Stanley J. Bobrowski, Jr.: Son of a Russian Officer 17
6. Bill Boyles: "Straight into Combat" 20
7. James Braxton: A Lifetime of Music 22
8. Roger Britt: "Go, Get 'em!" 24
9. Claude Brown: Life and Death in the Hands of the Parachute Packer 26
10. Lon Colvin: The Liberator Becomes the Prisoner 29
11. Wilma Coon: A Patriotic Calling 32
12. Phil Crenshaw: Finding His Calling 34
13. Robert F. Cummings: Small-Town Navy Veteran 37
14. Jack DuLaney: F4U Fighter Pilot 39
15. Lena Skaggs Duncan: Dedicated to Family and Country 42

Table of Contents

16. Garland Ellis: With the 4th Armored Division 45
17. Thomas Esparza: Tank Commander at Age 19 50
18. Orville Fleming: The Million-Dollar Wound 53
19. Robbie Gill: Lucky #13 and the "Miracle Survivor" 55
20. Carl Gilly: Cobb's War 58
21. Jim Guyton: Dunbar Alum Serves Twice 62
22. Roger Haberer: Normandy, Days after the Invasion 64
23. Bob Hail: Navy Boat Driver Dropped off Marines 66
24. J.W. Hamby: Businessman at an Early Age 68
25. Wallace Haney: A Member of the "Caterpillar Club" 70
26. Ted Hartman: Sherman Tank Driver and Orthopedic Surgeon 73
27. Billy Hendrix: Circling the Globe after World War II 75
28. Ted Hill: P-47 Thunderbolt Pilot 78
29. Charles J. Hoye: Old Newsie Serving with a Pen 81
30. Don Jones: A Life of Service to Country and Community 83
31. Homer Jones: The Long Road Home 86
32. Justin T. Jones: Glider Recovery 89
33. Lamar Jones: Always a Merchant 92
34. R.D. Jones: Sailing the Pacific 94
35. Bob Kiser: Pipeline, Purdue, Petroleum and People Like Us 96
36. Cleatus Lebow: "He Saved My Life Twice" 98
37. George Lewis: Occupied Germany 103
38. Nathan Luger: The Aleutian Islands 105
39. C.B. Martin: Life as a Seabee 107
40. Herschel Martin: One Man, Three Branches of Service 109

Table of Contents

41. John McDonough: The Tall Texan........................111
42. Gene McLendon: A Good Citizen 113
43. Teddy McMillan: A Hero and a Good Man 115
44. Frank Miller: From a Quartermaster to a Headmaster......117
45. Horace Morgan: From the Alcan to the Battle of
    the Bulge 120
46. Frank Odom: On the Front Lines in Europe...............122
47. Vernon Odom: Helping Those Who Can't Help
    Themselves...125
48. Wayne Owen: Smart and Lucky 128
49. R.L. Owens: "Red Arrow Division—First In, Last Out" 130
50. Bill Pasewark: Spreading Freedom's Message 133
51. Marvin Platten: An Artful Journey 136
52. Leon Pope: From POWs to Paradise......................141
53. James Rich: A "Rich Life"—Flirting with Death 144
54. Eugene Roberts: "Hard to Turn Off the Switch"............146
55. Max Robertson: Navy Battles Mother Nature..............149
56. Earl Robinson: "The Good Lord Had My Hand" 151
57. James T. Rodewald: "Hot Meals and a Place to Sleep".......153
58. Eldie Scheffel: "The Coldest Winter I Ever Saw"...........155
59. Harold Schultze: D-Day Remembered by Former
    Higgins Boat Driver.....................................157
60. Charles Sears: Blinded by the Light 160
61. J.L. Slaughter: A Final Mission..........................162
62. Clifford Solomon: "God Bless America"...................166
63. Elmer Tarbox: Texas Tech All-American..................171
64. Dominic Tartaglione: Survivor of Three "Wars" 173
65. Pat Thurman: Twice as Lucky during Two Wars 175

Table of Contents

66. Truett Tyler: Following His Brothers 177
67. Ed Ward: "If You're Not Scared, You're Lying" 179
68. Wayne Webb: Three Years on the Water 181
69. Gene Williams: A World Traveler 184
70. Robert Elton Wilson: "The Good Lord Was Always with Me" 186
71. Andy Winnegar: Naval Aviator Receives the Distinguished Flying Cross 189

Part II—Korea

72. Paul Archinal: From Airman to Admiral 198
73. William Bridge: Korean War Vet Makes a Difference 201
74. James Cathey: The Ghosts of the Korean War 204
75. Jerold Dyess: A Sixteen Year Old Sees the World 207
76. Clyde Fisher: "Finish What I Start" 209
77. Alton Garner: Witness to History 211
78. Gordon Hambright: Naval Postmaster Wins "Best Beard Growing Contest" 214
79. Fred Harvey: "Growing Up" on the USS *Hornet* 216
80. Rodney Manning: From a Policeman to a Preacher 218
81. Cleveland McMillan: Cooking Under Fire 221
82. Gordon Musick: Near the Front Lines in Korea 223
83. Asa Oliver: From Family Farm to Foreign Field to Faithful Follower 226
84. Billy Rudd: A Case of Mistaken Identity 228
85. Curtis Ruff: It Just Wasn't His Day 230
86. Welby Smith: Crew Chief to Two of the Air Force's Fastest Bombers 234
87. Lawrence Walker: Triple "Service" for Lubbock Man 236

88. Fred Watson: Faith Helps Him through Korean War
    Memories..238
89. Charles Williams: Coming Home 240

Part III—Vietnam War

90. George Bradley: "Follow Your Dreams"..................246
91. Charles Brimberry: Danger Was Everywhere in Vietnam...248
92. Doug Foster: The Healing Wall 251
93. Jannie Greenway: Around the World and Back 255
94. Charles Hankson: BBQ and a Slice of Sunshine.........258
95. Bernhard T. Mittemeyer: A Lifetime of Service to His
    Adopted Country....................................260
96. Charles Scarborough: "Recycled for a Reason"............264

Part IV—Additional Stories

97. Various Veterans: "Geezers" Reunite 270
98. Chad and Renee Gross: A Simple Song about a Soldier....273
99. Gary Harber: Lubbock's Southern Brigadier General......276
100. Gordon Musick and Ernest Sears: Two Love Stories
     from the Texas South Plains Honor Flight................279
101. Frances Pierce: Gold Star Wife and Widow...............281
102. Opal Roberts: Living Intentionally 284
103. Wayne Shawn and Justin Jones: Flight into Yesteryear.....286
104. Michael Vasquez: From Combat Casualty to Veteran
     Advocate 289

Veterans' Honor Roll 293
Bibliography 295
Index...299

Preface

As I grew up in Louisville, Kentucky, the 8 × 10 color photo of my uncle always held a place of prominence on my parents' nightstand. My interest in his life and ultimate fate became the seed for this book even if I didn't know it at the time. I became more and more interested in the fate of my uncle, Cpl. Charles Anderson Williams, who was with the Army's Company A, 1st Battalion, 32nd Infantry Regiment, 7th Infantry Division from 1948 to 1950. He was killed on Thanksgiving Day, November 27, 1950, at the Chosin Reservoir in North Korea. I hope the readers will indulge me, as I have included my uncle's story in this book of West Texas and New Mexico veterans. I fully believe that writing his story and follow-up stories is what eventually led me to write this book about our area veterans. It also added some credence to and understanding of what some of them went through.

I joined the Texas South Plains Honor Flight Committee based in Lubbock, Texas, in 2012 and went on the inaugural flight as a guardian and again in 2013 and 2017 as a bus captain. As I visited with our veterans, I recall thinking, "someone should write these experiences down." I wrote articles for the *Lubbock Avalanche Journal* about the flights and some of the veterans. I was approached in the spring of 2015 by Erin Agee who owns the *Lubbock Senior Link Magazine*. She said she wanted to do a fall edition honoring our area veterans with priority given to our World War II–era vets. I began interviewing right away, primarily focusing on the World War II vets, but I also interviewed some Korean War and Vietnam vets. We have taken over 800 veterans on the Honor Flight. To date, I have interviewed over 100 veterans. Being an Air Force veteran helps me understand some of the lingo used and what being in the service means, as all veterans have common experiences.

I searched for the correct questions to ask veterans. I found the Veterans History Project, which is run by the Library of Congress. They have consent forms for the veterans to sign and questions to ask about their service. Since this only covers their service time period, we use another form that has questions about their life before and after the service. We audio-record all of our interviews for further review and clarification as we begin to write up their stories after the interviews are completed.

Due to the advanced age of our World War II veterans, I have a sense of urgency to get to these men and women who gave up a part of their young lives for their country. Out of 16 million who served, fewer than half a million survive, and we are losing about 296 World War II veterans nationwide every day. Once these veterans are gone, so are their stories. In short, their stories deserve to be documented for future generations.

Katherine and I traveled many miles and spent many hours visiting with, recording and writing up these veterans' stories these last five years. It has been both our honor and our privilege to have spent this time with these aging veterans. Many told us stories that (even) their families have never heard and for that we are grateful that they are not lost to history. While reading these stories, some may not agree with the events described by the interviewees. We have worked hard to research each and every story for accuracy, but time and memories don't always agree with what's written in history books or found on a website. While we used the internet extensively to research geography (these men and women served all over the world), camps, airfields, ships, etc., it was used to add additional details to what these veterans told us and add further depth to where they were and what they saw at a specific time in history. We have also listed books that were used to validate, add depth, and give more detail on a particular subject that may be of interest or useful for further study to our readers. These stories are their stories and their unique experiences as they relate to their time in the service. Also, keep in mind, these are their own recollections as they recall them, looking back 50, 60 or over 70 years ago. For continuity and ease of reading, we have organized these interviews and stories into four sections: World War II, Korea, Vietnam and Additional Stories.

—Larry A. Williams

In my home as I grew up were my widowed mother and my older brother. I was told my dad was an Air Force veteran, yet usual reminders through photographs or seeing or being able to touch a medal that he earned were not within my grasp. His second marriage was to my mother, and his first wife had kept everything military. I have seen four pictures of him. One is of him sitting next to my beautiful mother in a meeting with a group of people in a room somewhere. Another is of him holding my brother as a baby, and another is of him leaning against a large metal anchor in the ground, dressed in khaki shorts and tall white socks and a warm smile. He died at only age 43 after suffering several heart attacks. Prior to death as a young father, he and Mom had an agreement that if, while he was on a road trip with his work at a company called Ethicon, he felt chest pains, he would drive himself to the nearest hospital and check in. Connecticut Hospital was where he landed the last time. Mom tells my brother Richard and me that she received a phone call in the middle of the night at our comfortable bi-level home in Doylestown, Pennsylvania. She was told he was in critical condition so she frantically called a neighbor to come sit with us kids while she nervously drove to that hospital. He was dead when she arrived.

 I don't remember having a realization as a child that several of the "good people" in our lives were veterans. This realization came much later in life when I was appointed a veteran liaison by my director at the hospice where I worked. At first I thought, "My ... more work." More contacts to set up, more meetings to attend, more after-hours efforts that I didn't really think I had time for. I am an overachieving people pleaser by nature and I read up on what was required by the National Hospice and Palliative Care Association to completing each "level" of the program. I made Wednesdays my day to focus on the program and soon I had booked a speaking engagement with our branch of the Honor Flight. I attended the meeting, let the attendees know what our program was about in trying to recruit veterans to visit with veterans who were in hospice care, passed out brochures, and answered questions. Then I sat and the meeting continued and my heart began filling up as I listened to first-hand accounts of what it meant for each person in the room to be involved in helping veterans see the memorials built in their honor and the bonding that happened naturally between the veterans on the trip together.

 I got to hear the music my dad liked: Johnny Cash, classical music and Mikado, and the song "Ghost Riders in the Sky." He also enjoyed solitaire, canasta, the TV show *All in the Family,* playing bridge, and football (on TV and radio playing different games simultaneously while he studied for his business administration and chemistry degrees). I have even tried to play his old harmonicas. Mom tells me I got his musical talent. So, as I began getting to know veterans because of work and other volunteer activities I involved myself in, I was permanently drawn into deeper waters than my heart knew how to stay afloat in. I literally have been swept off my feet emotionally as a result of the people God has placed in my life.

Finally having in hand my dad's DD214 has made his sacrifice in the Korean War as a navigator and Morse code operator more vivid to me. So much time and so many connections have been lost, and, at least for my family and me, will not be found in this life. What motivates me is yearning for others to experience more of the connection with veterans, their veterans, our veterans. If we don't take the time to capture their essence, their stories and their values, they will be forever lost.

I have two grown daughters and six grandkids at the date of this writing. My desire is to dedicate my life to loving them and embodying the virtue that has been poured into me by many of these "good people" I have had the opportunity to know. Tears choke me up and fill my eyes as I fight to contain the exuberant richness in my development as a contributor to society being molded by a God that shines through His people, many of whom have served and sacrificed.

In learning about how many veterans cope in life and their stoicism, I have somehow adopted some of these methods unconsciously and it is difficult for me to truly let my guard down. I hope that through these stories your heart can be healed as you read of how we all share the "human condition," yet some rise above and stand on the shore as an example of having navigated the sometimes choppy waters of life to encourage us all to face and conquer our fears and move forward to higher ground.

—**Katherine McLamore**

Introduction
The Cost of Freedom

They are much older now. They don't move as fast as they once did, or see as well or hear as well. You can see it in their eyes and on the walls of their homes, whether they live in town or in rural areas. The men and women that Katherine and I have interviewed over the last several years for the stories in this book have an unwavering love and vibrant sense of patriotism for their country. Whether it was in the cold and damp fields of Europe, the sweltering islands of the Pacific, the frozen tundra of Korea or the rice paddies of Vietnam, all of these veterans gave up a part of their young lives to serve their country. Some were drafted, most volunteered. Without them, we would not enjoy the freedoms that we all seem to take for granted today. Each veteran made an impact and that is why their stories must be told and shared with future generations.

These are the stories of the people who came before us and shaped our country. They are or were our grandfathers, grandmothers, aunts, uncles, fathers, mothers, brothers and sisters. During our country's wars, all gave some and some gave all. They were ordinary people who came from the city streets and farms all over this nation to be a part of something they all believed in—freedom. To a person, the veterans that we interviewed were a humble lot. We heard the same line wherever we went to get these stories—"I'm not a hero. The heroes are the ones who lost their lives and never made it home."

Whether we like to admit it or not, the cost of freedom was paid for in young American lives. The statistics are staggering. By the end of World War II, over 400,000 American service members were killed and today over 73,000 are still Missing in Action (MIA). By the end of the Korean War, over 36,000 Americans lost their lives and over 7,800 are MIA. During the Vietnam War, 58,209 died and over 1,500 are MIA. Thousands of American families lost their loved ones or never learned their fate. Such were the sacrifices of not only the ones killed, wounded or MIA, but their families as well. My family knows about sacrificing for our country. My mother's brother, Private First Class Lloyd J. George, was killed in North Africa on January 30, 1943. As mentioned earlier, my father's brother, Corporal Charles A. Williams, was killed at the Chosin Reservoir in North Korea on November 27, 1950.

Americans are buried in many cemeteries around the United States and around the world. The American Battlefield Monument Commission (ABMC) was established by President Warren G. Harding in 1923. It currently maintains 26 permanent American burial sites and 30 memorials, monuments and markers on foreign soil. The majority of those interred at these sites are from World War I and World War II. Out of the 407,316 Americans killed during World War II, 92,958 are interred in one of these cemeteries. In addition, the names of over 94,000 servicemen and -women who were KIA/MIA are etched in stone in ABMC cemeteries and memorials.

It has been both our honor and our privilege to have spent this time with these aging veterans. Many told us stories that (sometimes) their families have never heard and for that we are grateful that they are not lost to history. Many family members have commented, "I never knew dad [or granddad] did anything like that." We are still in contact with a lot of these veterans and their families and have attended numerous funerals to pay our respects to them and to grieve with the family members.

These veterans are or were ordinary people who had extraordinary experiences. Many had never been out of their local area and were sent to the far reaches of the globe to help preserve not only our freedom but also the freedom of a people they had never met. Many suffered unimaginable hardships that may never be recounted or recorded. That's why this book is so important to us and should be to anyone interested in our country's veterans. Thank you for reading and sharing these stories with others. When you see a veteran on the street (you can usually spot them by the caps they wear), just say "thank you for your service." In most cases, it will mean much more to them than any medals they have or could have been awarded.

Part I

World War II

I was the only survivor out of the twenty men from the two bomber crews.

—Army Air Corps Staff Sgt. Robbie Gill

1

ALVIRA AGEE
"I Can Do That"

After a visit with 90-year-old Alvira Agee, it's easy to see that she could do anything she put her mind to. She was born in 1925 in Brady, Texas. Alvira developed a "can do" attitude, beginning with her childhood on a farm that "raised kids and wheat."

During World War II she recalls collecting scrap iron to donate to the war effort. She said, "After President Roosevelt called it a 'day of infamy,' it was a scary time in our country. Everyone was trying to do their part."

After high school, Alvira became a registered nurse. In 1951 she wanted to "do more" for her country. Going against the conventional wisdom of the time, she joined the U.S. Air Force. She thought, "I can do that" and "I wanted to see the world." After enlisting as a 2nd Lieutenant, she was "put right to work in a hospital at Larson Air Force Base in Washington State."

Her career took her to Ft. Sam Houston in San Antonio after she convinced her commanding officer that she "was interested in Psychiatry." Alvira thought, "I can do that." She was transferred to Sheppard Air Force Base in Wichita Falls for training in neuropsychiatry. Her wish to "see the world" began when she was sent to an air base near Bordeaux, France. Because Alvira wasn't afraid to try anything, she became a "jack of all trades, doing everything from clerical [work] to delivering babies to assisting in surgery."

The young officer was sent to Roswell Air Force Base where she met and married Charlie Agee, a medic and ambulance driver from Rush Springs, Oklahoma. The couple was soon transferred back to post–World War II France. This time she went to Toul-Rosières Air Base and Charlie was stationed at a base 30 miles away, which enabled them to visit many places in Europe. Her service came to an end, however, when she was given an honorable discharge because she was pregnant. She had served her country over 13 years and attained the rank of Major.

The Agees raised three children: Charles Dwayne who was born in Chablais, France; Charlotte Loraine, born in Spokane, Washington; and Robert Wesley, born in San Antonio, Texas.

Her life was bolstered by the strong faith of her uncle, K.C. Bailey, a well-known missionary to India and an Army veteran who devoted his life to serving others. She was also influenced by an older brother who served in the Army during World War II in the Philippines. He is now 91 and lives with Alvira's sister in Wyoming.

This phenomenal woman has overcome many health challenges, including arthritis, gallbladder surgery and a heart attack, but she attributes her full life and abilities to Jesus, her Savior. She has been ambulating by wheelchair since 2008 and has a strong support group, including South Plains Church of Christ and the Lakeridge Ladies from Lakeridge Chapel.

Noteworthy in this well-educated and well-traveled nurse is her whimsical side, which is expressed in the unique gifts she makes for her children and others. She has delighted countless loved ones with her fanciful crocheted creations.

Alvira is deeply thankful for the 2016 Texas South Honor Flight. On that unforgettable trip she was able to spend time at each memorial, appreciating the sacrifices of all veterans. Her gratitude was enhanced by years of wisdom and experience, and it was a truly moving time for her. She treasures the time spent with her daughter, Charlotte, who accompanied her as her Guardian. Getting to hold and lay the wreath that symbolized so many of her brothers and sisters who served in Europe immediately after World War II and in the Korean War was a full-circle moment for her.

When asked what advice she has for future Americans, she unreservedly states, "Determination." She is proud of her military service and ascribes much of her awareness and success to being willing to expand her horizons. Alvira's prayer is for future generations to embrace patriotism and service to their country.

2

M.T. ALLEN
Quonset Hut Expert

Marion T. Allen (known as M.T.), now 97 years young, was drafted and joined the Navy Seabees on April 20, 1943. He had "already graduated from Idalou High School back in 1937." He noted that, "back then, the high school only went through the 11th grade." At the time he was drafted, M.T. was already married to Mary Jane and they had two children. It would be difficult for the whole family to be separated, as it was for millions of young couples during World War II. He noted that "all [he] had known was construction," so he thought the Seabees was the place for him. He had been in construction ever since he got out of high school. M.T. had put those skills to work in California, where he had moved his young family because of the Depression.

While back home in Idalou, he decided to "go to Dallas to be inducted because that was closer to home." He was actually registered in California, but they were "more than glad to accept him into the service in Dallas." After 6 weeks of basic training in Camp Peary, Virginia, M.T. was sent to Endicott, Rhode Island, for advanced training where he was placed with the 97th Construction Battalion. He left on the RMS *Queen Elizabeth* headed for Londonderry, North Ireland. Stripped of their luxury fittings, the *Queen Mary* and *Queen Elizabeth* could carry twice as many passengers across the Atlantic as were normally carried in peacetime.

After doing some work in North Ireland for a few weeks, his battalion was sent to Falmouth and other cities in England to assist with the massive buildup of men and equipment in preparation for the D-Day landing in Normandy, France. His unit's specialty was the "Quonset hut." He noted that "a usual team of 8 men could build these pretty fast once they got the hang of it." His unit arrived on Utah Beach in July 1944, only two months after the invasion. This was M.T.'s first exposure to the war and the destruction of men and equipment. He noted that the "German concrete bunkers and pill boxes had been destroyed by large U.S. artillery, and there were still several dead Germans entombed in them." The Seabees' job in France was to clear the beach, build bridges and tear down the dreaded "hedge rows" that slowed down both the troops and equipment.

One of their jobs in France was to "build signal towers with a light on top." M.T. would "build and move on to the next town" until he received a 30-day leave on December 5, 1944. He received orders that he and his unit would now be needed in the Pacific. He left out of Port Hueneme, California, which was constructed just to supply the needs of the Navy's Construction Battalions (Seabees) operating in the Pacific. The depot received supplies, stored them in huge warehouses and then shipped them overseas as needed. Seabee units came and went through the port, including M.T.'s 97th Battalion, which headed for the island of Okinawa in January 1945. He noted they "had to stay on the ship for 46 days until the island was secured." During this time, M.T. and his unit became even more proficient "building Quonset huts for barracks, mess halls and warehouses and even ... the occasional outhouse." While on Okinawa, M.T. and his fellow Seabees heard about the dropping of atomic bombs on Hiroshima and Nagasaki. He came back to California where he was discharged on November 17, 1945.

Mary Jane and the children were glad to finally have M.T. home, where he was able to find work in construction. He eventually established his own successful construction company and "built over 100 homes and strip shopping centers" in and around Compton and Bellflower, California. The population boom was on and there were plenty of buildings to construct. M.T. and Mary Jane lived most of their adult life in California but were fortunate enough to travel "many places around the world and it was fun," he recalled. "We've had a great life together." They retired in 1993 and moved back to Idalou. They have 2 children, 4 grandchildren and 6 great-grandchildren. M.T. and Mary Jane have now been married for 75 years. Their grandson Taylor Berkstresser said that Mary Jane "doesn't like to talk about the war years much because it took M.T. away from her for 2½ years." That separation and anxiety was endured by millions of families during World War II. We owe a debt of gratitude to the families as well as the veterans.

3

ROBERT ANDERSON
Battling on Two Fronts

Robert Anderson and his future wife, Iris, saw how devastating a world war can be, up close. For Bob, it was surviving the siege on Bastogne in Belgium as part of the Battle of the Bulge. Bob would see the devastation that constant combat and bombardment could do to a city and to the soldiers and citizens who had to endure the onslaught of the German Army. For Iris, it was treating the young wounded men in an Army hospital in Illinois.

Bob was born on June 22, 1924, in Chicago, Illinois. He entered the Army in November of 1942 and did his basic training in St. Petersburg, Florida. He was part of the government's college deferment called the Army Specialized Training Program. He was attending the University of Georgia with "around 800 other men" when the government ended the program in March of 1943 and the unit was called up to active duty. He was assigned to the 10th Armored Division and left New York in September 1944. They were part of the first division to land in Cherbourg, France (and not in England as had been done previously by all troop ships). The 10th Armored "followed General George Patton through France and arrived at the front north of Paris."

Bob was assigned to the 150th Signal Company as a wire man. There were "9 or 10 guys on a half-track," and their job was to "maintain communication lines from the front back to division headquarters." His company moved to Metz, then Thionville, France, where they would become the first division to enter Germany. He noted that "70 years later, the town of Thionville put up a plaque in honor of their liberation by the Americans."

The Battle of the Bulge began on December 16, 1944, and Gen. Patton ordered Bob's signal platoon to Bastogne on December 18, 1944, to establish communication lines. The German Army managed to push American forces back nearly to the Meuse River and surround the town of Bastogne in Belgium. At that time, when ordered to surrender Bastogne, Brig. General Anthony C. McAuliffe famously replied, "Nuts." That same day, reinforcements, food and medical supplies were sent by airdrop, and Allied airplanes began their attack on German tanks. Bob noted that they were "running out of ammo, food and gasoline." He said that he was "sure glad to see the 101st Airborne arrive in Bastogne." The siege was finally halted on December 27, 1944.

On January 7, 1945, Bob came down with hepatitis and was sent first to a hospital in Paris, then Le Mans to recover. He eventually returned to his unit in Trier, Germany, to join the 7th Army push across Germany and ended up on the Austrian border when the war ended on May 7, 1945. During this time, Bob's vehicle "hit a land mine" and he was "blown off but only suffered minor scratches." In September 1945, he was sent to Antwerp, Belgium, where he boarded a Liberty ship bound for home, and he was discharged on January 16, 1946.

Here in Iris's own words is her story of how she and Bob met:

"I met my future husband in a church Bible camp, when we were 15 and 16. There were 20 miles between us in Chicago, where we grew up. He traveled one and a half hours each way, each time we had a date. So, most of our romance was carried on by telephone. I am a year older than he, so that when I started college, he was still in high school. I was teased by the other girls for dating someone still in high school, so we drifted apart for a time.

I was a civilian nurse in training in the Cadet Nursing Program during the Second World War. The year was 1945. I did not have to commit to the program but I did. I received a monthly stipend and a uniform. From my class, only five women signed up for the Cadet Corps. We all roomed together. In the last 12 months of this program, I was sent to Galesburg, Illinois. It was at this time, that Japan surrendered in July and I graduated in September 1945.

The six months I spent in the Army hospital were very traumatic for me. Some of the spinal injuries I saw were so tragic. The attitude of these injured soldiers was bitter and they were desperate. Bedsores were too common. Some of these sores were so large you could put your fist in them! We nurses faced many challenges such as these. This was a very emotional experience for me.

Around this time, penicillin became available. We knew that this was something that would ease the pain and start the healing process, especially with bedsores. We rejoiced over this latest medical discovery.

At about the time the war came along, and after I had become a nurse in the Corps, the mother of my old boyfriend from back home became ill with a brain tumor, which eventually took her life. I was working at a private hospital at the time. I was one of the nurses assigned to her care and realized what a coincidence it was that me and my 'old flame' should see each other again, through the illness of his mother. We began seeing each other and our romance really flourished. We wrote letters all the time, when we were unable to see each other. He arrived home after his discharge in January 1946, became engaged on Valentine's Day and were married in May 1946. We have been married for 70 years. We have two sons.

My husband attended the University of Chicago on the GI Bill and earned his PhD in Psychology from the University of Chicago. We lived in a very small house. He also attended the University of Austin for three years. He was offered a position at Texas Tech and that is how we arrived in Lubbock."

Bob noted that there were 7 PhDs in his family and his wife had a master's degree.

At the conclusion of our interviews, Iris made the following comment about the war: "Bob saw the dead bodies of the soldiers. I saw the dead souls."

4

CLYDE BEARDEN
"At the Convenience of the Government"

Clyde Bearden fully expected to be involved in World War II and quite likely be shipped overseas either to Europe or the Pacific. He was drafted into the Army on March 30, 1945, and would go through basic training at Camp Fannin near Tyler, Texas. It's no wonder Clyde believed he would be sent into combat. From the years 1943 to 1945, over 200,000 young Americans trained at Camp Fannin and became Army Infantry Replacements. Once their training was finished, the soldiers were assigned to serve in the Europe and Pacific Theaters. It's estimated that at least five thousand of these young men lost their lives and twice that many were wounded.

Herbert Clyde Bearden was "born at home 7½ miles west of Snyder in Scurry County, Texas, on July 9, 1926," to Leonard and Ona Ruby Bearden. The second-born of six brothers (five out of the six would serve in the military), he grew up on the farm and attended Snyder High School, graduating in 1943. His favorite subject was World History and in 1945 he would get to see some of the world in the Army. He and his brothers served in nearly every branch of the service.

After 17 weeks of training at Camp Fannin, Clyde was awaiting orders to ship out. However, the war in Europe ended in May 1945 and he figured he would now be sent to the Pacific. He noted that "the atomic bombs were dropped (on Hiroshima and Nagasaki) and the war was over." Clyde received orders for Korea and "shipped out of California on July 28, 1945, on a Merchant Marine ship." The ship needed repairs and stopped in Hawaii for 10 days and then Okinawa for 9 more days. His ship landed at Inchon, Korea, on November 8, 1945, and Clyde was sent to Seoul. The Korean peninsula had been liberated from Japan by the Allies in August 1945. Clyde was now part of the three-year occupation of Korea, which lasted from 1945 to 1948. Situated at the city hall in Seoul, he "worked in public health and sanitation as a sanitary technician." He said, "We needed to clean up the streets as men, women and children all shared the same bathrooms." Clean water and bathroom facilities were badly needed. He recalled that the "Korean people were glad to see the Americans and to be rid of the Japanese."

Clyde would leave Korea on October 23, 1946. He wryly noted that "draftees were not needed any more and were turned loose at the convenience of the government." He landed at Ft. Ord, California, where he was discharged on December 29, 1946. He left Los Angeles via train to El Paso and then to Colorado City, Texas, where his mother and some of his relatives met him at the train station. He was "trying to sneak in and surprise them, but they found out I was coming home through a neighbor." Once home, the only person he surprised was "his grandmother who helped raise him." When he walked in, "she was reading the paper and churning butter."

Using the GI Bill under the Hazelwood Act, he enrolled at Texas Tech and graduated in 1950 with a degree in agronomy, the study of soil. (Named for Amarillo State Senator Grady Hazelwood, the Hazelwood Act enables Texas veterans and children of deceased veterans up to 150 free credit hours at state public universities and community colleges. In addition, unused credits can be transferred to their children.) While working in Spur, Texas, he met and married schoolteacher Wanda Mae Rhine in November 1953. The union produced a son, David, and daughter, Jenne. He would receive a master's degree in 1965 in elementary education and taught 6th grade at Hodges Elementary in Lubbock, Texas, and was the school librarian at Thompson Jr. High and then Coronado High School in Lubbock, Texas, until his retirement in 1990.

When asked what he wanted to be remembered for, he said, "As a man who spent 20 years visiting shut-ins as a member of Highland Baptist Church." Clyde Bearden—truly a man with a servant's heart.

5

STANLEY J. BOBROWSKI, JR.
Son of a Russian Officer

Stanley J. Bobrowski, Jr., of Lubbock, Texas, didn't have the typical family upbringing that most South Plains World War II veterans had. His father, Stanley Bobrowski, was born in Russia in 1881. He served in the Russian Cavalry and came to the United States in 1906. His father, who worked in a steel mill, was active in the Holy Rosary Church in North Chicago and was the bell ringer for the church until his death in 1960. Stanley Jr., one of eight children, was born on January 27, 1923, in North Chicago. His mother, Anna, was a housewife. Four of the boys served in the military during World War II. Stanley joked that, between them, they "served in almost every branch of the service."

Though he had already begun studies at Purdue University on a Math scholarship, Stanley enlisted in the Army on March 3, 1943. Right after enlistment and before basic training, he was assigned to further education studies in Chemical Engineering at the University of Pennsylvania. Having been a former high school track star, during his time at Penn, he was recruited to run in the prestigious Penn Relays (a track-meet competition that first started in the late 1800s). He placed 2nd in the 220-yard dash and was part of the winning relay team.

His basic training took place at Camp Sibert in Alabama. (The camp was named after Major General William L. Sibert, a native of nearby Gadsden, Alabama. A veteran of World War I, Sibert was the first Chief of the Chemical Warfare Service.) Stanley was assigned to the newly activated 93rd Chemical Mortar Battalion, Company C. The Battalion was equipped with 4.2-inch mortars. It was a multipurpose weapon employed in close support of combat ground troops. It had the ability to fire toxic agents, smoke and high explosives. The Chemical Warfare Service saw the mortar as a mobile and flexible weapon that could be placed in and out of action quickly and deliver mass fire in a very short time period. The mortar proved so successful that it was mounted on boats to cover beach assaults in the Pacific.

Bobrowski was a college student when he enlisted. He noted that "everybody went in (the service), so I did too." His major in Chemical Engineering tied in well with the Chemical Warfare Service during World War II. After more training, Stanley's unit was sent to Northern California for more training and then to a camp north of New Orleans. The unit boarded a troop train at Camp Shelby, Mississippi, and headed for Camp Miles Standish near Boston, Massachusetts. The battalion left Boston Harbor on January 18, 1945, onboard the SS *Santa Maria*. They were escorted by an English battleship and DE (destroyer) boats. En route to La Havre, France, the convoy was attacked by German U-boats. Once in La Havre, the battalion departed for Camp Lucky Strike in France. The 93rd joined up with the Fifteenth Army and headed to Germany with its newly motorized equipment.

In one of his many letters home, Stanley described what it was like entering Germany for the first time: "Today I entered Germany—the country of the enemy. My first impression was one of amazement at the contrast. On one side of the Moselle (River) was seemingly untouched Luxembourg and on the other side was war-torn Trier. This horror was at first a welcome sight for it was the result of the Third Army's entry into Germany. There was no waving by the German populace to the passing American troops—only the blank faces of defeat were evident."

Attached to the 87th Infantry Division, and after crossing the Moselle at Trier, France, into Germany, Company C of the 93rd went through the towns of Oberporlitz and Saalfeld, supported an attack on Schleiz with fire, and destroyed buildings in Theuma. Enemy positions were destroyed by the 93rd east of Theuma. Stanley observed the "dark side" of the war upon the 93rd's entry into Laufselden, a "small city unscarred by artillery or bombing." Bobrowski continued: "Being a member of the quartering party, I had to help find and establish quarters for the troops. We located the Burgermeister [mayor] who gave us a note which we showed to occupants of homes we wanted to use. It stated that the occupants were to move in an hour and take all their personal belongings and leave the furniture intact. I met a woman where our platoon was to be quartered. She told me how her hometown of Wiesbaden was bombed out so she moved all she had left including her three-year-old daughter to a room in our house. I tried to act firm but polite and she told her daughter, 'Good American man.' I replied, 'They are all good,' only to be greeted with a blank stare which had me confused but not for long. Our platoon entered the city at 1630 and immediately took over the town. As soon as some of the men entered our building, they began ransacking all the furniture. Not content with looting only our building, they started on other homes by forcing their way in at gun point. I did not participate in any of this—it was against my principles of religion and human nature." The 93rd's last mission was firing on enemy positions at Stockigt. On April 20, 1945, Company C was relieved from the field.

Stanley arrived home in the states on the Fourth of July in 1945. He was transferred to the 506th Battalion at Ft. Bragg, North Carolina, until his discharge on February 5, 1946. He returned to Purdue University to finish his degree. After graduating in 1948, he went to work for Anheuser-Busch in St. Louis as a chemical engineer. While in St. Louis, he met his future wife, Isobel (Susie), on a blind date. They had one daughter, Susan, through adoption after they moved to Matawan, New Jersey. In 1974, they were transferred to Bakersfield, California. In 1978, Susan came to Texas Tech in Lubbock, and Stanley and Susie moved to Lubbock in 1984.

Now 95 years old, Stanley can look back on a long life well lived. When asked what he would like to be remembered for, in an understatement common for the Greatest Generation, he simply said that he would "just like to live and die." We all owe Stanley our thanks and gratitude for his service to our country.

6

BILL BOYLES
"Straight into Combat"

If it had been up to his mother, Lillie Mae, William Boyles's middle name would have been Beauchamp. His father, Henry, said, "That name is much too long for a little baby. Let's just call him William B. Boyles." And that's what it has remained for now 93-year-old Bill Boyles. The middle child of six children, Bill had one brother and four sisters. He was born on October 19, 1945, in Hall County, Texas, close to Quitaque, but his father bought some land south of Sudan when Bill was a young boy and he still lives there to this day.

Bill grew up helping on the farm and attended Sudan High School where he was to graduate in 1944. He was drafted on February 15, 1944, and chose the Navy. His brother had already joined the Navy. He was sent to the Naval Base in San Diego for basic training. After training, he was shipped to Hawaii where he "stayed for about a month waiting on an assignment. I was sent to the Mariana Islands and assigned to the USS *Cleveland*." The *Cleveland* was the first ship built in the Cleveland class of light cruisers. The *Cleveland*, built in by New York Shipbuilding in New Jersey, launched November 1, 1941. The *Cleveland* joined a task force off Bermuda in December 1942 and headed for North Africa where her firepower supported landings at Fedhala, French Morocco. She then headed for the Pacific and joined in attacks on numerous islands before Boyles came aboard. He noted that he "went straight into combat."

"I had to learn how to shoot 5" anti-aircraft guns. This was late in the war and the Japanese were getting desperate. We had the kamikaze planes come over. They came in so low over us that my hair stood up. Ships were hit all around us, but we never had one hole in our ship. We were lucky. I was assigned to radar work tracking enemy ship movements. It seemed like we would get out of one scrape, lose another ship and move on. This went on until the end of the war. We made a lot of landings ahead of the troops being dropped off. All we had was a shovel and a handgun (.45)." Bill's brother, Ellis "Pete" Boyles, was also in the Navy during World War II and was a fighter pilot. Pete was shot down in the South Pacific. Fate would intervene as Bill's ship, the USS *Cleveland*, was in the convoy that picked him up. They had a joyful reunion at sea.

The *Cleveland* sailed to Okinawa in July 1945 and made a series of sweeps against Japanese shipping to ensure Allied control of the East China Sea. The battle would prove to be the last major battle of World War II. It came at a high cost with over 49,000 American casualties including 12,520 killed. Japan suffered even greater losses as about 110,000 soldiers lost their lives. They believed it would bring dishonor to surrender. The end of the war came in August 1945. Bill was aboard the *Cleveland* and said, "We had heard some scuttlebutt and a little about the atomic bomb, but really wasn't sure if the war was over." The *Cleveland* sailed to Japan in September to support the occupation of Japan.

With the war finally over, Bill headed home on a troop transport. Arriving back in San Diego, he was assigned to train other sailors on the use of ship weapons. While still in the Navy, he married his high school sweetheart, Lena Jo Boyles, on November 22, 1945. Lena had been the captain of the high school basketball team. After being discharged on April 16, 1946, Bill returned home to Sudan and farming. He noted that his dad "had a new house waiting for him right down the road from the old homestead." Bill and Jo raised four boys together on their farm southwest of Sudan. They had 9 grandchildren and 19 great-grandchildren. Sadly, Jo passed away on October 13, 2012. Bill and Jo had been married for 66 years. Bill's sons encouraged him to go on the Texas South Plains Honor Flight. He went on the 2013 flight and said he liked all of the memorials and museums and visiting with fellow veterans.

When asked what he would like to be remembered for, Bill thought for a moment and said, "That I was a good neighbor and good to the people I've dealt with." Reflecting on his long life, Bill said, "When you get past 90, you don't feel like doing much. You no longer have the eye of a woman, but you can think of days gone by and realize how lucky you have been."

7

JAMES BRAXTON
A Lifetime of Music

James Braxton grew up loving music. After graduation from Booker T. Washington High School in Tulsa, Oklahoma, James attempted to follow in his father's footsteps. His dad was an alumnus of the Tuskegee Institute (now Tuskegee University), so James started out studying plumbing there. James liked to joke, "If I'd stayed there, I'd probably be a rich plumber now." But his heart was in music, and his destiny was with musical pipes, not plumbing pipes. He left the institute after his sophomore year to travel up and down the east coast performing on his saxophone in places like Atlantic City, New York, and Philadelphia.

After the attack on Pearl Harbor, the United States became embroiled in the world war. James enlisted in the Army on December 14, 1942, and entered active duty on June 5, 1943. He was one of over one million African Americans inducted into the armed services during World War II. After basic training at Ft. Bliss in El Paso, Texas, he was transferred to Ft. Sill, Oklahoma. Thanks to his musical background and training, James's military assignment was as a "Bandsman Saxophone–439" playing in the Army band. He was transferred with other band members to the Philippines where they played for the troops. Something important popped into the veteran's head at this moment, and he noted, "I married Bernice right before I went overseas."

The soldier/musician spent several months in the Philippines. He recalled that on the transport ship back to the States, he and the other band members gave impromptu concerts on the ship for the other troops, which turned into big USO shows. He was surprised when they landed and turned in their instruments. To their surprise, the band members were each given a separate check for playing while on the voyage home. James remembered thinking, "Hey, that's all right." For his dedicated military service, James received the Good Conduct Medal, American Theater, Asiatic Pacific and the Victory Ribbon, and he was discharged March 13, 1946, as a Tec 4.

Back home, James earned his bachelor's degree in music education from Wylie College. While there, he toured with a group called the Wiley Collegians, which included his brother Robert on alto sax and his brother-in-law Roy on baritone sax. He completed graduate work in Colorado and Nebraska, and eventually received his master's degree in music from the University of Nebraska. He returned to Tulsa to teach band at an elementary school near his home, and a long, illustrious career was launched. After teaching band and orchestra in El Paso, Texas, for two years, the Braxtons moved to Lubbock. It was 1960, and James went to work with his brother-in-law Roy Roberts at Dunbar High School as an assistant band and orchestra director. James recalled, "I probably worked at ten different schools in Lubbock over my 30 years in the school system." James primarily played the saxophone and violin, but his role as band director was enhanced by his ability to play many other instruments. His wife, Bernice, was an elementary schoolteacher. The Braxtons were happily married for 69 years until Bernice's passing in January 2014. Not surprisingly, both of their children, Ruby and Thomas, became accomplished musicians themselves.

James Braxton, U.S. Army, World War II.

Mr. Braxton retired from Lubbock Independent School District in 1985, but was coaxed out of retirement by his replacement, a former student named Mary Jo Wilson. Now nearing 98 years old, James continues to volunteer at Dunbar as a mentor and teacher to many students. Countless students have studied under Braxton over the years, and you can hear the joy in his voice as he recalls his days "teaching my kids." He still plays faithfully at his church, Mt. Vernon UMC, where he has been a member for over 50 years.

8

ROGER BRITT

"Go, Get 'em!"

These were the orders issued to Roger L. Britt in Northern France in the winter of 1945. Roger was part of the massive Allied push to defeat the Germans near the end of World War II. His unit, the 87th Infantry Division, was assigned to General George S. Patton's Third U.S. Army. The 87th was part of the Third Army's counterattack during the Battle of the Bulge. It was a highly decorated unit, with over 1,300 medals awarded, including one Medal of Honor and three Distinguished Service Crosses. The unit served 134 days in combat and suffered over 5,500 casualties.

Roger was born on May 26, 1926, to D.L. and Mary Britt. He had two brothers and four sisters. One brother also served during World War II. Young Roger attended school at Amherst, Texas; he did not finish, but he did have a favorite subject—"recess." He moved to Burbank, California, where he helped build B-17 bombers from 1943 to 1944. He also completed high school there by earning his GED. The teenager was drafted into the Army on August 16, 1944, and trained as a combat replacement at Camp Wolters near Mineral Wells, Texas. Audie Murphy, one of the most decorated American combat soldiers of World War II, also received his basic training there.

After basic, Roger's unit was sent to Washington, D.C., then on to Boston Harbor where they boarded a converted troop ship carrying 6,000 men. After six days on the water with their destroyer escorts, they landed in Northern Scotland. The unit then boarded a "blackout train" to Southampton, England. From there they took a ship to France to Camp Lucky Strike, one of several "Cigarette Camps." (A Cigarette Camp was one of several temporary U.S. Army "tent cities" situated principally around the French ports of Le Havre and Marseilles following their respective captures in the wake of the Allied D-Day invasion in June 1944.) It was January 1945, and as Roger recalled, "It was very cold.

8. Roger Britt

We were loaded in box cars headed for the front. It took 24 hours to get to Metz, France, where we were loaded on trucks to go to the front. We were told to get our affairs in order as we could get killed the first day [of combat]. They gave us our ammunition and said, 'Go, get 'em!'"

Roger recounted his combat experience: "I didn't get to sleep in a bed for five weeks. We would fight during the day and dig foxholes at night. The ground was so hard that we used axes to break up the ground and then used shovels to dig our foxholes. Once we walked 20 miles at night to hit the Germans at dawn. I was issued a bazooka and used it on a German half-track. [A half-track is a vehicle with regular wheels at the front for steering and continuous tracks at the back to propel the vehicle and carry most of the load.] It crashed over a hill. We were always afraid of German Tiger Tanks. We couldn't stop them. If we thought one was coming, we'd hit the ditch. We got very little sleep. After 30 days on the front, we were pulled off the front for a warm meal and new uniforms.

"It started warming up in March 1945. We practiced our rowing at night and crossed the Moselle [River] in the morning and captured Koblenz, Germany. We took prisoners along the way. I used a bicycle to herd 15 captured Germans to a POW camp. Coming out of the woods, we came to a meadow where the Germans opened up on us. While running across the battlefield, I was shot in the side by a bullet that passed through my right elbow and in and out of my stomach. I had to lay there in the field for over two hours before a medic got to me. They put me on an old wooden door they found and carried me to an ambulance. I was taken to a field hospital behind the lines and then took a plane to England for recovery." After his recovery, Roger was put on a troop ship back to the United States. He took a train to Birmingham Hospital in Van Nuys, California, for further treatment of his wounds. After recovery, the Army made him an MP, and he "guarded Ft. Mason in San Francisco." Britt was discharged on April 4, 1946, at Ft. Bliss, Texas. He was awarded the Combat Infantry Badge, Bronze Star, Purple Heart, Good Conduct, American Theatre, European Campaign, National Defense and World War II Victory Medals.

After making his way back to Amherst, Texas, he resumed farming. He met his future wife, Ray Lynn Blessing, at a party, and he "bought her a $69 engagement ring." They raised two boys and one girl. Roger continued farming for 50 years, and Ray Lynn was the district clerk for Lamb County, Texas, for 25 years. Roger Britt is a real American hero, but when asked what he would like to be remembered for, he simply said, "Growing good watermelons." Thank you for your service, sir.

9

CLAUDE BROWN
Life and Death in the Hands of the Parachute Packer

It could be said that the best friend of an airplane crew during World War II was the parachute packer/rigger. Lester "Claude" Brown, 97, of Lockney, Texas, was one of those "friends." At least 700 soldiers died during World War II because their parachutes didn't deploy. Proper packing of a parachute is literally a matter of life or death. The job description for a Parachute Rigger and Repairman (620), according to the Military Yearbook Project website, was to "inspect the canopy, rigging, and suspension lines, then to repack and harness the chute every ten days and do any necessary repairs."

Lester C. Brown was born on a farm near Muncy, Texas, on April 2, 1921, to J.M. and Lee Brown. He had one brother and one sister; each died at age 52. His dad was a sign painter and sold insurance for a time. His parents divorced when he was quite young. His step-dad, Tomme, was a barber. By the time Lester graduated from Lockney High School in May 1939, he was known as Claude. After graduation, he went to work at Band-Box Cleaners in Lubbock, Texas. He met Wilma Holcomb "at the dentist office in Tulia," and they were married on April 12, 1942.

Claude and Wilma had barely settled into married life when he was drafted into the Army Air Corps on October 7, 1942. He took six weeks of basic training at Sheppard Field in Wichita Falls, Texas, and then went on to Chanute Airfield in Illinois for the 3½-month parachute packer training. He and a buddy had "applied for jump school but were turned down." His unit was assigned overseas training at Atlantic City, New Jersey. Claude recalled "rigid combat training—we marched up and down the boardwalk and our instructor made us sing before turning in for the night. One night we balked at the singing and he marched us until we started singing." The next stop was New Orleans where his unit was shipped out to South America and then on to Puerto Rico for duty as an observation squadron. "My daughter Ann was born while I was on the way to Puerto Rico."

The 311th Troop Carrier Squadron was transferred from North Carolina to Hawaii in February 1945. While stationed in Hawaii, Claude found the parachutes in a state of disarray. He said he "brought them up to date, got them in good working order and began inspecting them on the required schedule. I think it got me promoted to Sergeant." He was also the manager of the local PX (Post Exchange). Next, his squadron was assigned to Okinawa. While out "on the water [the Pacific], the atomic bombs were dropped on Hiroshima and Nagasaki." He pointed out that "there were still pockets of Japanese soldiers who didn't believe the war was over and had to be rounded up." Claude continued as a parachute packer and managed the PX as he had done in Hawaii. In the fall of 1945, Brown had accumulated enough points to be discharged. He was scheduled to fly out on a plane with other servicemen but "got bumped off the flight by someone else." It's a good thing he got bumped as the plane went missing between Okinawa and Iwo Jima, and everyone on board was presumed killed. "I lost a lot of friends on that flight."

He returned to California in the fall of 1945 and was discharged from Ft. Sam Houston, Texas, on December 21, 1945. "My wife was very glad to see me." Three weeks after his discharge, Claude opened his own dry-cleaning shop in Lockney, Texas. He soon added men's wear, and it became Brown's Department Store. After 48 years, he and his wife closed the store. They were happily married for 66 years until Wilma's death in October 2008. They have two grandsons and four great-grandchildren. Claude has been a prominent citizen in Lockney over the years, including a 16-year stint as the town's mayor. He belonged to numerous boards and was recognized for his many years of service. His daughter Ann likes to tell people that "Dad can hardly walk, but still goes dancing two to three times a week. The women line up to dance with him!"

It's been over seven decades since Claude Brown packed parachutes, but countless men owe him a thank you. A story has been circulating on the internet about a fighter pilot named Capt. Charlie Plumb, who flew jet fighters off the aircraft carrier, the USS *Kitty Hawk*. After 75 missions, he was shot down and spent six years as a POW with the Vietcong. Some years later, he was eating at a restaurant in Kansas City. Charlie says, "A man walked over to my table, and said, 'You're Captain Plumb. You flew jet fighters in Vietnam. You were on the aircraft carrier *Kitty Hawk*. You were shot down. You parachuted into enemy hands and spent six years as a prisoner of war.'" When Plumb asked, "How in the world did you know all that?" the man replied, "Because I packed your parachute." That impacted Plumb, and he continues to tell the story, so that all of us will remember to appreciate the people who do the things necessary to make us successful—the people who "pack our parachutes."

10

LON COLVIN
The Liberator Becomes the Prisoner

Lon Colvin of Lockney, Texas, was close to finishing high school in April 1943 when he was drafted into the Army. Born to James and Sally Colvin on April 28, 1926, he was one of 5 siblings and had three brothers and one sister. Lon was active in football, basketball and baseball in high school and enjoyed living the small-town life. He helped out around the farm like all of his siblings. One brother also served during World War II. Lon took his basic training in Mineral Wells, Texas, and was assigned to the 4th Armored Division, 10th Armored Infantry, Company A. Colvin and his outfit shipped out for Europe on February 28, 1945, arriving on March 9. The 4th Armored had been in combat since landing in Normandy in July 1944, one month after D-Day.

Lon was not in Europe very long when he was assigned to the so-called Task Force Baum. General George S. Patton authorized the highly secretive mission 50 miles behind enemy lines. He had two reasons for doing so. First, his son-in-law, Lt. Colonel John K. Waters, and other POWs were located in a camp near Hammelburg, Germany. Second, he wanted to prove to General MacArthur that he could also liberate POW camps. Lon recalls General Patton telling the troops that "if you get killed, there's another one to take your place." Captain Abe Baum commanded the ill-fated mission. Patton was told that "about 300 POWs were imprisoned there and he wanted no more than 300 or so men to participate in the mission."

The mission got off to a rocky start when, on March 26, an attack was led by Creighton Abrams and Hal Cohen to prepare and secure a route for the task force, clear any obstacles and station a tank at every intersection to protect the task force's flanks so they could get through with as little resistance as possible. However, as one of the soldiers noted, "Old ladies dropped grenades from rooftops and young boys and old men manned machine guns like experienced killers." Many soldiers

Lon Colvin's World War II POW plaque.

were killed but the task force continued to push through towards Hammelburg Lager where the POW camp was located.

Corporal Colvin, a Sherman tank machine gunner, and his unit eventually broke through the barbed wire and into the prison where instead of being greeted by 300 prisoners, there were nearly 1,500. Not all prisoners could be taken out and to make matters worse, Patton's son-in-law, whom they were sent to liberate, was seriously injured and couldn't return with the task force. Although the Germans had initially surrendered, they soon returned with reinforcements to take back the POW camp. The task force split up, but the Germans soon caught up to them and according to Lon, "we were out of ammunition and had to surrender." The liberators had now become POWs themselves. Out of the 300 men of the task force, 32 were killed, 35 made it back to Allied territory and the rest were taken prisoner. The 14th Armored Division liberated the camp on April 6, 1945.

Colvin said after being liberated, he and a buddy "liberated" an old car and drove around Germany and France for a time until they tried to "steal some gasoline from a German farmer." They had to flee when they were caught by the farmer and one of them (Lon didn't recall which one) "shot a hole in the tractor's gas tank when he refused to give them

10. Lon Colvin

Lon Colvin, August 15, 2018.

any gas." He noted that they were "only 19 years old and it was war time." Lon eventually made his way back to an Allied camp where he "was de-loused and had to wait 12 hours to get a shower." He left France on a Victory Ship and arrived back in the states on June 12, 1945. He was separated from the Army on April 28, 1946. He took a train to Ft. Worth and a bus back to Lockney.

Back in Lockney, he went back to farming and would be awarded his delayed high school degree in 1946. During this time he met Lois Morgan. Lois noted, "He used to come out and visit my dad and brother so I knew of him." However, Lois would marry another man and left Lockney. Her husband died at age 38 and she returned to Lockney in 1964. She and Lon became re-acquainted and they finally married in 1967. They have no children. Through the years, Lon worked at the Lockney Gin, the Tye Company and the Lockney Co-op.

As to his short but difficult time in Germany, Lon said, "I was scared from the time I got there until the time I left."

For more information on "Task Force Baum," please see Garland Ellis's story.

11

WILMA COON
A Patriotic Calling

Wilma was born to William L. and Alberta Green on October 5, 1923, in Minglewood, Tennessee. She moved as an infant to New Orleans where she spent most of her childhood. She and her sister Dorothy were instructed in sewing and embroidery and in "all things proper." She and her family enjoyed listening to Bob Hope and Fibber Magee and Molly on the radio. Her grandmother would take them to church.

Wilma attended the Sophie B. Wright School for girls and her favorite subjects were English, literature and history. She had several fictional stories published in the school paper and she graduated in 1941. Wilma had an uncle who was a "soldier of fortune" and who fought in several different countries. She went to Memphis State and Washington University and later studied medicine in St. Louis after she enlisted in the U.S. Navy in 1943, being sworn in on her 20th birthday. She states that her family was very supportive and that the choice of branch was an easy selection for her since New Orleans was a Navy town and she was immersed in the culture.

Basic training and education took place in New York and then she spent 6 months at the Brooklyn Navy Hospital. Long Beach, Long Island, had converted one wing of a summer resort into a sick bay and there she honed her skills on "light cases," including cat fever symptoms. She said that was a short name for catarrhal fever and was easily treated, much like flu.

During her time in the service she also served in Hawaii, where she was when the war finally ended. Wilma remembers her hospital that was located on a mountaintop as being called "Happy Building" because the view overlooking the harbor, open-air ventilation, and long wings with windows on both sides providing natural lighting all lifted the spirits of the patients and staff alike. She recalls one time when she had to work a night shift alone, tending to around 30 patients by candlelight in a hurricane as a very memorable event. She was later commended for her level-headed service to the nervous patients and how she handled the situation bravely and efficiently. She recalls one young Marine patient who was suffering from a bullet wound crying out frantically, "Why did this happen to me? Why am I here?" She visited with him and found out that his panic derived because he had no idea what was happening in the war and truly had no concept of history. She said she was horrified for him and the experience solidified her views that teaching history and geography in schools should be more complete in order to mentally educate and prepare future generations.

While in medical school she married John (Tom) Coon in 1948, and they had one son, John, Jr. They were married 66 years. Working with dogs was a joy to her and her husband and she started dog obedience training at South Plains Kennel Club. In the 1960s Wilma helped start the Lubbock Police Department's Canine Corps.

Wilma went on the 2014 Texas South Plains Honor Flight to Washington, D.C., with her guardian, Betty, who had been her caregiver for two years previously. Camera crews from KCBD followed her and the other veterans around Washington and she was interviewed in the Women in Military Service for America Memorial and spoke of her time as a Navy Nurse. Looking back, she states she especially enjoyed helping to lay a wreath at the Tomb of the Unknown Soldier and spoke of it tearfully, stating what a "great honor" it was to experience.

Wilma Coon with World War II photograph.

12

PHIL CRENSHAW
Finding His Calling

When American sniper Chris Kyle's widow, Taya Kyle, recently came to Lubbock, World War II Army veteran Phil Crenshaw gave the invocation. At the Benghazi Survivor Presentation in 2016, he also opened with a prayer. For occasions like these he proudly dons his woolen dress green World War II uniform and humbly walks to the microphone. His gentle but powerful voice thanks God for freedom, for the people present, and for God's will to be done on earth as it is in heaven. When asked how he can still fit into his uniform after so many years, his face lights up as he names "the five basic food groups: chocolate, vanilla, strawberry, butter pecan and peanut brittle ice cream."

The Pentagon designated Crenshaw as the sole surviving chaplain's assistant of World War II and the Chief of Chaplain's office honored him while on the 2013 Honor Flight with three of his sons. He continues to serve on the Texas South Plains Honor Flight Committee.

After serving his country, doing radio broadcasting for 20 years and operating an employment agency for 40 years, he has gainful employment with Westex Document at Reese Technology Center. Crenshaw writes in his spare time. He has three books in progress: *My Desk Is a Pulpit*, *The Island's Last Call* (about his military service in Okinawa and Korea), and a third that relates to helping young people transition into maturity. He and his family have hosted countless students in their home, earning the title of "the Crenshaw Hotel."

"I love children and am concerned that we have gotten away from where we began in education. Textbooks no longer tell the full story of American history. Students are taught there are no absolutes, and they must be politically correct. My favorite patriotic song is 'America the Beautiful,' because it represents basically my philosophy of life and my love for my country." He calls Southcrest Baptist Church his church home.

"I have made 12 trips with Josh McDowell to Russia. The orphans'

12. Phil Crenshaw

Phil Crenshaw playing the organ for prisoners, Kadena, Okinawa, August 2, 1945.

tears moved my heart. [The children] seeing men for the first time, cried. We gave them teddy bears and lots of hugs.

"Born in Kansas City in 1922, I grew up in Joplin, Missouri, during the Depression. My dad made $2.50 a week as a printer and Mom taught school. At four years of age, I saw a black grand piano for the first time at a revival. It mesmerized me. I went home and told my parents and brother, Loye, that I wanted to learn to play the piano. My parents bartered and sacrificed for me to study music for eight years. I have played in both Protestant and Catholic services and at Grand Central Station.

"Most of my military acquaintances from basic training were sent to the South Pacific, and most were buried there. I was separated from them and sent to the East Coast to study Morse code. I never got a chance to use it. God had other plans for me.

"In a muddy field chapel tent in Okinawa, the chaplain [Capt. V.L. Wuemberger of the Chaplain Corps] learned of my music background and quickly had me transferred to the role of his assistant. Not satisfied to just minister to the Army, Chaplain Wuemberger held services for other branches, schoolteachers and children. When the chaplain learned about the Japanese prisoner of war camp, another chapter in my life opened, lasting 4 months.

"Japanese prisoners were taught to kill and then commit hara-kiri [suicide] for their emperor. Our troops blasted them out of their caves with flame throwers, while many jumped to their deaths off cliffs. At Okinawa, the largest battle in the Pacific, we captured over 7,000 prisoners of war. Chaplain Wuemberger felt an urgency to reach the Japanese prisoners while we could. So we held six or seven services on Sunday. Wherever we went by vehicle, I played music on a little fold-up organ. Everyone on the island knew about [the chaplain] and his passion for God. He dictated letters and I typed them on an old typewriter. He asked for literature for the Japanese, and we received 1,000 Japanese New Testaments from an unknown source. Interpreters assisted us in distributing all but one, which I have to this day.

"I remember hurrying to reach field hospitals to inspire soldiers barely hanging on. Even then, the Lord worked through me. The atmosphere and suffering proved depressing. Yet it encouraged us to see their personal encounters with the Lord brighten their faces.

"My wife and mother to our six children, Ruth, died from Parkinson's disease five and a half years ago. Loving people quickly surrounded her when she needed hospice care. Hospice was wonderful."

When asked what he'd like to be remembered for, Phil said, "Do good. Plant the seed. Be faithful. I have helped plant seeds, and God brought the harvest. As long as we are faithful He will bless our efforts. I would like to know my witness for the Lord touched many lives."

Phil Crenshaw in World War II uniform, September 2016.

13

ROBERT F. CUMMINGS
Small-Town Navy Veteran

Robert F. Cummings grew up in the small Texas Panhandle town of Memphis. Born to Robert C. and Clara Cummings on August 27, 1925, Robert was an only child. Robert Sr. was exposed to mustard gas during World War I and passed away in 1951. As his daughter observed, "Robert F. seemed to have two different personality types depending on which side of the coin you were on. One side of him was proud, private, humble, honorable, dedicated, sincere, etc. The other side of him was ornery, mischievous, stubborn, mean at times, self-centered and high maintenance. He loved his Cadillacs and also pulling pranks." Robert was well aware of the attack on Pearl Harbor on December 7, 1941. He was in the early years of high school and living in a small town; he was involved in boxing, football and tennis. Being a high-spirited young man, he wanted to join the military and help defend our country. He enlisted in the U.S. Navy after his junior year in high school. He was able to complete his GED onboard his ship. His diploma was mailed to his mother's house. Many young men received their diplomas this way while the war was going on.

After being assigned to Norfolk Naval Station, 1st Coxswain Cummings was then assigned to the USS *Saugatuck* (AO-75), which was formerly known as the SS *Newton*. It was renamed the *Saugatuck* on September 16, 1942. Norfolk Naval Station was built on July 4, 1917, as the United States entered World War I. It is now the world's largest Naval Station. The *Saugatuck* headed for the Panama Canal in the spring of 1943 and on to San Diego before heading to the Pacific Theater. Some of the islands that Robert was stationed near were Saipan, Guam, Tinian, Western Caroline Islands, Philippines, Iwo Jima and Okinawa. Robert jokingly called himself a "swab jockey." Always the prankster, he and some buddies snuck a spider monkey onboard the ship. The oilers were frequent targets of Japanese aircraft. On June 18, 1944, the *Saugatuck* was attacked three times. While only one seaman was killed, several others suffered injuries. Robert was one of the injured after an indirect hit on the ship. The blast nearly capsized the ship and he was flung onto the side of the ship where the oil lines were housed. One of his knees became lodged in some of the oil lines, and the impact shattered his kneecap. Crewmates eventually cut Robert out. He had to have surgery later on and had a plate put in his knee. Like many of those injured during World War II, he refused the Purple Heart award.

After his discharge in 1945, Robert headed to Lubbock where he worked at McDonald's Funeral Home. He then attended the Dallas School of Mortuary. He said one of the hardest things he had to do was to go tell a family that their son had been killed. On a tour of Carlsbad Caverns, Robert met Helen Headstream. While Robert grew up an only child, Helen had 7 sisters and 2 brothers. One of the brothers turned out to be one of Robert's high school coaches. After dating for only three months, Robert and Helen were married. Helen affectionately called him "hot lips." They had three children, Kathy, Jan and Kelly. Helen passed away in May 2017. Robert was a mortician and funeral director at McDonald's and then Rix Funeral Home in Lubbock for a total of 43 years.

14

Jack DuLaney
F4U Fighter Pilot

Seventeen-year-old Jack DuLaney wanted to fly. It was July 1942 and Jack had graduated from Shallowater High School and attended Texas Tech for one semester. In the fall of 1943, just two months shy of his 18th birthday, DuLaney enlisted in the U.S. Navy and wanted to be a pilot. He said, "There were 26 of us from Texas Tech and we went down to Dallas to enlist. We took a train to Dallas. Once we got there, they only kept six of us. We were told to go home and they would contact us. They sent us to the University of Alabama to study for a month, then to the University of Texas and then to Kerrville where we learn to fly a Cub. We learned to solo right quick and got to fly on our own. We had a good time chasing coyotes. One of my best buddies, Dalton Teague, was going to go into pilot training with me, but his dad said, 'No, it's too dangerous,' so Dalton went into the Navy. The ship he was on was sunk and he did not survive. His dad would never forgive himself for sending him to the Navy and died at an early age."

Jack was born on October 26, 1924, at home outside of Shallowater, Texas. He first attended Grovesville School, two miles east of Shallowater. During the Dust Bowl of the 1930s, Jack remembers "our clothes were worn and had holes in them, but they were clean. We ate good because of our cattle, chickens, hogs and gardens. We sold eggs, milk, cream and homemade butter for a little cash to get some well-needed things." He played every sport he could at Shallowater: basketball, track, tennis and baseball. He recalled that in 1941, they "played mostly district games because travel was restricted due to the war. I enjoyed all of my team mates." They did not play football because a player was seriously injured a few years earlier and the school decided not to have it anymore.

DuLaney continued his naval pilot training at the U.S. Naval Training Center in Pensacola, Florida. He was appointed as Cadet Lieutenant over other trainees in 1944. About his training, Jack said, "We flew a double-winged airplane with double cockpits, one for the instructor and one for the pilot. You could do flips and rolls with that plane and we learned how to fly. We went out to Barin Field also called 'Bloody Barin' because they trained fighter pilots there and several boys got killed [40 pilots were killed in 2 years of operation, according to the Naval Aviation Museum]. We traveled up north and learned to land on a carrier drawn on the pavement."

Now 19 years old, he received his wings and was assigned to the aircraft carrier USS *Guadalcanal* (CVE-60), which was named in honor of the U.S. Marines' 1942 victory on the island of Guadalcanal in the Pacific.

Jack's squadron was part of the so-called Hunter Killers whose job was to hunt down German submarines in the Atlantic Ocean. The *Guadalcanal* had 28 planes onboard with a mix of Wildcats and Avengers. The Wildcats would strafe the subs, setting up a bombing or depth charge run by the Avengers. By this time, the Allies owned the skies, so the U-boats dared not surface during the day or would be hunted down and sunk by Naval planes. The motto of the ship was "Can do," indicating their willingness to take on any tough job given to them and run with it. DuLaney and his crew shared in this can-do attitude. He noted, "That was our mission, looking for submarines. We used the bombs and depth charges but would also tell the ships where one was. Sometimes there were two or three running in packs."

Continuing, Jack recalled, "One of my flying mates lost his engine on a return trip to the carrier late in the day. I told him to try and start it. He dived down to get more speed, but it just didn't start. He retracted his landing gear and just scooted across the water and stopped. He opened the canopy and I was right above him, watching—he hopped out and I waved at him and headed for the ship. It was too late in the day to go after him, so he had to be picked up the next day after a plane spotted him. While hunting for submarines, we would look for oil which meant we had sunk the sub or it had broken up. But they got smart and if you dropped depth charges, they would just release some oil and make us think we had got them. We did bust some of them and they would come to the surface and blow up little rafts that they would get into."

The *Guadalcanal* had the distinction of capturing a German submarine. Of the capture DuLaney said, "There was an intense effort to capture one of the German U-boats. One day they got one. After it was hit, the aircraft carrier was pretty close so these guys ran out there in a speed boat and the Germans were still coming out of the sub when they got there. The Germans signaled that it was about to blow up but

14. Jack DuLaney

you would think they wouldn't have told the Americans and let it blow them up too! The sailors got in the sub and disconnected all the stuff and they pulled that thing back to port." The capture of U-505 was kept secret in order to gain full advantage of the codes, operational information and equipment obtained. Incredibly, even though over 3,000 men had witnessed the capture, neither Americans nor Germans would learn about it until after the war. All told, 175 U-boats were sunk by Americans during World War II. Today, the U-505 resides in the Museum of Science and Industry in Chicago. After Germany surrendered, Jack said, "We headed to South America and thought we were going to be sent to the Pacific. We found out later we were waiting for orders to ship out to the Pacific. We went round and round in circles. Then we heard that the bomb had been dropped on Hiroshima and soon thereafter, the war was over. There was a lot of cheering. They say it would have cost one million lives to invade Japan."

Jack said, "I left the Navy on December 6, 1945. They wouldn't let trained pilots like me be discharged, so I was put on 8 years of reserves, but I was never called back." Jack returned to Shallowater and started farming with his dad and eventually bought a few acres of his own to farm. He met his future wife, Dorene, at Texas Tech in 1953 where they were introduced by one of Jack's friends. They married on June 1, 1954. Dorene said, "I went to Tech for 3 years and wish I could have finished my degree." She "got busy" and never went back. They now have 3 daughters, 6 grandkids and 5 great-grandsons with another one on the way. Jack still had flying in his blood, so he and his brother Bob bought the Shallowater airport. Manager Norman Teague gave flying lessons. Jack said he "always kept a few planes there to fly." Even Dorene said she learned to fly and even soloed, but never got her pilot's license.

In later years, Jack was very civic minded in Shallowater. He has been the mayor of Shallowater, served on the city council and the Shallowater ISD School Board, and he has been president of the board. He was a member of the Chamber of Commerce, the Shallowater Co-op Gin Board for 29 years and the Shallowater Lions Club for several years and was named "Man of the Year" in 1974–75. He is a Master Mason and has been a Mason for more than 60 years. Both Jack and Dorene have been very active in the First Baptist Church of Shallowater for many years. Jack and Dorene continue to serve the community they love.

15

LENA SKAGGS DUNCAN
Dedicated to Family and Country

Lena "Lyn" Skaggs Duncan (a friend from school didn't like Lena and said "I think I'll call you Lyn" and the name stuck) was born on February 12, 1924, in Derby, Virginia, to Grover Cleveland Skaggs and Carrie Kirk Skaggs. Grover worked as an electrician and wired houses and businesses. She had 4 brothers and 2 sisters. She graduated from Pennington Gap High School in 1942 and attended King College in Bristol, Tennessee, where she said she wanted a degree in "anything if it didn't include taking a foreign language."

Her dad had fallen ill around this time and Lena needed more money to support her family. She was working at a munitions factory in Bristol, Virginia, at the time helping to load 20 mm shells for the war effort. She said she was "only making about $32.00 per week and that wasn't enough." She told her dad she could make more money if she would enlist in the Armed Forces and she was able to send home $78 a month and still have money left over each week. According to the Military Women's Memorial website, approximately 400,000 women served in the armed forces during World War II and nearly 500 of them lost their lives serving their country, 16 in combat. As soon as she turned 20 years old, she joined the Navy waves in March of 1944 and did her basic training in New York City. She said, "New York was quite a sight for a country girl from Virginia"! On her first train ride, as soon as she stepped on, the train took off and she landed in an older man's lap. He told her, "They don't wait for anyone to sit down, so grab the bar as soon as you get on next time." Lesson learned. After basic training she was put on shore patrol for 3 months, manning her post with nothing but her uniform and a nightstick. During World War II women were allowed to do almost any job except carry a firearm.

Lena was then sent to Washington, D.C., with the rank of SPQ 3 Specialist (Communications) Petty Officer 3rd Class. She jokingly said

15. Lena Skaggs Duncan

that she and "about 80 other women in her unit were in 'Q-mmunications.'" While Lena didn't realize it at the time, she was most likely involved in the government's top-secret Venona Project, which attempted to decrypt messages sent by Soviet Union intelligence agencies. All of the other women smoked and liked to drink beer—except Lena. They spent most of their off-duty time "at the Pepsi Canteen across from the White House and it was a lot of fun." Lena would meet her future husband, Almer Doyal Barnes, at a USO dance. He was from Merkel, Texas. He was stationed at Ft. Meade, Maryland, and would see action in the Pacific Theater. He asked her to "not get married until I got back." So she waited and when he returned from Japan, he moved her to Texas where they were married on November 2, 1946. They had four children—two boys and two girls.

Lena's husband, Almer, passed away in January 1988 after 42 years of marriage. Her son, Bobby Skaggs Barnes, was killed in an auto accident in 2006. She remarried on March 15, 1997, to W.L. Duncan of Buffalo Gap, Texas, who was a former Navy Gunner on the USS *Murray* that was in several major battles in the Pacific Theater. W.L. passed away in April 2013.

She soon found out about the Texas South Plains Honor Flight from a friend and was the only woman out of 143 veterans to go on the 2013 Flight. She had not been back to Washington since the end of World

Lena Duncan with fellow vet in Washington, D.C.

War II. She was supposed to be accompanied by her daughter Wanda but she was unable to go and her other daughter Jody accompanied her. She said her favorite stop was the Women in Military Service for America Memorial located at Arlington Cemetery. She couldn't believe it when she was "wheeled in the lobby and there was her picture from World War II staring back at her." She was both proud and grateful to serve her country. Our sentiments exactly, Lyn. Thank you for your dedication to both your family and your country.

For more information on women who served in our nation's military service, please go to https://www.womensmemorial.org. For more information about the Venona Project, see https://warfarehistorynetwork.com.

16

GARLAND ELLIS
With the 4th Armored Division

Private Ellis stopped in a doorway to have a much-needed smoke. His unit, the 10th Armored Infantry, part of the 4th Armored Division, had been fighting their way across France in the early months of World War II from town to town, street by street and house by house. The men were looking for German soldiers left to slow up the advancing Americans. It oftentimes turned deadly. There always seemed to be a sniper lurking around up high, in the shadows. As Ellis bent down to light his cigarette, a shot rang out. Remembering the event vividly, "The shot hit the window frame only a foot from my head," said Ellis. This was warfare in the closing months and days of World War II in Europe. The race to the Rhine River was on and Private Ellis was in the middle of it all.

Garland D. Ellis was born August 2, 1926, at home near Dalhart, Texas, to W.C. and Myrtle Ellis. He had one brother. The Ellis family moved to Ralls, Texas, when Garland was only 4 years old. His dad was a farmer and carpenter and most days were spent helping out on the farm. He played football in school and said "staying in trouble" was his favorite subject in school. In those days, school was over in the 11th grade. Garland made it through part of the 11th grade. He married his high school sweetheart, Dorothy Dillard, in January 1944. He was drafted into the Army on October 4, 1944. Ellis recalled, "I was inducted in Lubbock with some other guys in the area. We were sent to Camp Wolters near Mineral Wells, Texas. At one time, it was the largest infantry replacement training center in the United States." Ellis noted that "infantry training was supposed to be 17 weeks, but we finished in 12. I met Lon Colvin [from Lockney, Texas] there." After the abbreviated basic training, Ellis and other replacements were sent to Camp Shanks in Orangetown, New York, aka "Last Stop, U.S.A." The camp was the largest U.S. Army embarkation camp used during World War II, sending some 1.3 million troops to the European Theater.

Ellis and around 15,000 other replacement troops sailed for Scotland. Continuing, he recounted, "We boarded the *Queen Elizabeth* and zigzagged our way all the way there. We had no destroyer escort. After we landed in Scotland, we took a train to Southampton, England. We took a boat over to Le Havre, France. We were assigned as replacements for the 10th Armored Infantry, 4th Armored Division and rushed to join up with them. I spent the first night on the front lines in a schoolhouse. The next morning the guys were talking about the mortar attack during the night. I was so tired; I must have slept right through it! We were broken down into companies. Lon Colvin and some of my buddies went to A Company. I was assigned to B Company. I used to catch up with them going through other towns." The 4th Armored, unlike other armored divisions, didn't have a nickname like "Old Ironsides." The highly decorated unit spent 230 days in combat from July 17, 1944 (six weeks after D-Day), until the end of the war in May 1945. The unit suffered over 10,000 casualties, with nearly 6,000 troops killed, wounded or MIA (missing in action). After the war, one of their commanders said their record spoke for itself and the 4th Armored was "Name Enough." The inadvertent nickname stuck.

The 4th Armored headed south in March 1945 to Worms, Germany, and crossed the Rhine River March 24–25. Now heading across Germany, Garland said, "We met some resistance as we went from town to town. I carried an M-1 rifle. Later, I became a .30 caliber machine

Garland Ellis, U.S. Army, World War II.

16. Garland Ellis

Garland Ellis, April 12, 2019.

gunner. I had an ammo carrier with me. The squad leader and his assistant took me in, kind of like a brother watching over me. They sure felt like my brothers. We used to ride on the tanks a lot and then get off to fight when we ran into Germans. I got pinned down by a sniper behind a hedge. Every time I would try to see where he was, he shot at me. I was trapped. The rest of the squad spotted the sniper, so they started laying down fire at him and I was able to get away from that hedge. I usually only got scared after it was all over." Garland also recalled the so-called Task Force Baum going through a town that his unit had cleared out for their advance. "I remember seeing them go through the town on their way to liberate the POW camp [Hammelburg] where General Patton's son-in-law was being held prisoner. My buddy Lon Colvin was in on that.* Lon and my buddies were captured on the failed camp liberation raid. I got letters from their folks and they ask me about them. I didn't want to tell them that I thought they had been killed." The Task Force Baum prisoners would be liberated by the 14th Armored Division on April 6, 1945.

Traveling deeper into Germany, Ellis and the 10th Armored Infantry saw the horrors of the Holocaust up close. The 4th Armored Division liberated the first Nazi concentration camp, Ohrdruf, which was a subcamp of Buchenwald. Garland remembered the scene. "We entered the camp and came around a building. We saw about 35 prisoners that the Germans had shot in the head lying dead on the ground. Four or five prisoners had been hiding in the woods and came out to tell us what all the Germans had done to the prisoners. They said all they had to eat for months was turnip soup. They showed us a ditch about 15 feet deep and 60 feet long where they dumped the bodies and bulldozed over it. It was all so horrible that we took the local citizens into the camp to see what was being done to their citizens. They claimed they knew nothing about it." The discovery of the camp led Generals Eisenhower, Patton and Bradley to visit the camp. They were appalled by what they saw and had photographers record the carnage left by the Nazis. In a letter to General George Marshall, Eisenhower wrote, "The things I saw beggar description." Later, in another letter to General Marshall widely published, he wrote, "We continue to uncover German concentration camps for political prisoners in which conditions of indescribable horror prevail."

Always on the move, the 4th captured German cities such as Lauterbach, Creuzburg and Gotha. By April 12, 1945, the Division crossed the Saale River and continued pursuing the enemy. The 4th Armored was racing toward Berlin when they were told to "let the Russians have Berlin." The order came down from General Dwight Eisenhower on April 15 to halt the advance. The Americans were only 120 miles from Berlin. By May 6, the 4th crossed into Czechoslovakia and established a bridgehead across the Otara River. Garland recalled, "We met up with some Russians there. They had vodka in their canteens. We drank with them. It was very strong. We had to drink some water with it to wash it down. I was in Czechoslovakia when we heard the war was over. They gave us some warm beer and everyone was celebrating. We stayed there about a month. I volunteered to go to the Pacific. I was sent to Bremerhaven where I boarded a Liberty ship headed for New York. There was a storm on the North Sea. Everyone got sick. We finally made it into New York Harbor. I was sent to California waiting to go to the Pacific but the war ended there in August 1945. I was assigned as a mess sergeant on troop trains in the states." After additional duties at Camp Chaffey in Arkansas, Ellis was discharged July 22, 1946, at Ft. Sam Houston near San Antonio, Texas.

Ellis took a bus back to Ralls, Texas. He said, "I got in with a construction crew building houses for a while. I then went to work for the post office in Ralls and retired in 1986." He and Dorothy had two sons, Rodney and Val. Dorothy passed away in July 2009. He married Betty Smith, whose husband had also passed away, in July 2010. Garland and

Dorothy used to dance at a senior citizen center as did Betty and her husband. Betty smiled and said, "We were lucky to find each other." She had three girls and they think a lot of Garland and treat him like their own dad. Garland also has 4 grandchildren and 2 great-grandchildren. When asked what he would like to be remembered for, Garland thought for a long while and said he would like to "go down as a good man, husband and father." After meeting with Garland, it was plain to see that he was all that and much more. He also could have included a brave soldier who did his duty all those years ago during the closing months of World War II in Europe.

For more information about the 4th Armored Division and Task Force Baum, please see Lon Colvin's story.

17

THOMAS ESPARZA
Tank Commander at Age 19

"I've been working my whole life. I started at age 9 when I learned to drive an old Model T," said Thomas Esparza of Levelland, Texas. "I was born in Happy, Texas, on September 19th, 1926. I was the 4th child of 6 born to Pedro and Lusina Esparza. My dad worked for the Santa Fe Railroad. Dad got transferred a lot so I went to a lot of different schools. I was always behind in school and wasn't very bright. I finished my schooling at Smyer, Texas. I went to work picking cotton and whatever else I could find. I had two brothers in the service; one was drafted into the Army and was assigned to the Combat Engineers. My other brother was an Army paratrooper." Esparza figured it would be his turn one day.

Sure enough, Tommy was drafted into the Army on November 10, 1944. He continued, "I reported to the Hockley County Courthouse in Levelland, Texas, with about 50 other guys. They loaded us on a bus and took us to Ft. Bliss in El Paso, Texas, for induction. I was sent to Ft. Hood, near Killeen, Texas, and assigned to a tank training battalion. I had 9 weeks of basic and infantry training and 8 weeks of tank training on an M18 Hellcat. The M18 could reach speeds up to 50 MPH and was the fastest of the U.S tanks. We received a 10-day leave to go home and get our affairs in order. They were trying to rush into combat, so we were sent by train to Ft. Meade, Maryland. We were sent to Camp Shanks, New York (the camp was the largest embarkation point for the Army during World War II), and put aboard the SS *Marine Robin*, a Merchant Marine ship that held about 2,000 men. We were part of a large convoy headed for Europe. After 14 days, we landed in Southampton, England. We crossed the English Channel to Le Havre, France, which was a staging area for new troops arriving in the European Theater of Operations and sent to Camp Lucky Strike, one of the so-called Cigarette Camps. We traveled via 6×6 troop trucks to

Verviers, Belgium. Upon arrival, we replaced the 107th Mechanized Calvary Recon Squadron."

With the Battle of the Bulge now over, the push into Germany was on. In March and April of 1945, Esparza's squadron, 43rd Calvary Reconnaissance Squadron, was assigned to the 3rd Army whose mission was to contain enemy forces in the St. Nazaire Pocket and entered Aachen, Germany. It was here that Tommy "saw [his] first German." In late April, the squadron was assigned to the 7th Armored Division under General Omar Bradley and performed reconnaissance and security missions. Esparza continued: "We broke out of the Remagen battle and crossed Ludendorff Bridge and on to the Ruhr (called the Ruhr Pocket). Now promoted to the rank of Sergeant, I was assigned as a tank commander. I had a 5-man crew—a loader (for the 76 mm gun), an assistant driver, a driver and a gunner. We went to Frankfurt, then turned south to Bamberg, Nuremburg and then to Munich. We were covering the right flank of the 7th Army. We were shooting in direct fire supporting the infantry. An L-5 spotter plane would send us coordinates as to where to fire."

Esparza remembered that he "found out the war was over when his company commander told him over the radio on May 8th, 1945. Everyone was really happy that the war was over. There was a lot of celebrating. I saw many German prisoners and they hated us. Even the British didn't like us. They had a saying, 'Damn Yankees, you're overpaid, over sexed and over here' [in England]. The war in the Pacific wasn't over yet, so they sent us to Marseilles, France, where we were fitted with summer uniforms. We boarded a troop ship with orders to Manila and the Pacific Theater. En route, within one day of the Panama Canal, we heard that the Japanese had surrendered and were redirected to Hampton Roads, Virginia, where we landed on 21 August. I signed up for another year and went back to Ft. Meade and taught infantry and tank training. I was discharged at Ft. McClellan, Alabama, on December 21, 1946, and got home in time for Christmas."

Tommy headed back to Levelland and arrived in time for Christmas. He went to work for Loran Tatham Pump as a welder and a machinist on water pumps. He met Hermenejilda "Hilda" Estrada while working for her dad who raised grain. They married in April 1950 and together raised 2 boys and 4 girls. Tommy says he now has 14 grandkids and 26 great-grandkids. Tommy opened up his own machine shop, learned to build water pumps, and taught his son to do machine work. He retired in 1980 and turned the shop over to his son Julian so he could "stay at home and take care of Hilda who was in the early stages of dementia." Hilda passed away in August 2015. When asked about the scariest time when he was in the Army, Tommy said, "I was scared all the time after we left the United States." He said he would like to be remembered for three things: "My service in a tank destroyer during World War II, that I enjoyed my family and that I worked hard all my life."

18

Orville Fleming
The Million-Dollar Wound

World War II was over early for Orville Fleming but he didn't know it at the time. He enlisted in the Army in 1944 in San Francisco, California. Jobs were scarce and he intended on making the Army his career. He was sent to Ft. Ord, California, for sixteen weeks of basic/infantry training. During his training period, the Battle of the Bulge broke out in Europe and the training was reduced to thirteen weeks.

Instead of heading to the east coast and Europe, he was heading west to Honolulu for an assignment in the Pacific Theater. He remained in Honolulu for "one or two months" and finally received his assignment. He was assigned to the 77th Infantry and would be going to an island called Okinawa in early 1945. The 77th made 15 landings on Okinawa and Orville said the battle had "been going on a while" so his company landed on the beach with little enemy resistance and made their way inland.

Orville was the 2nd Machine Gunner. He said all that meant was that he had to "carry the machine gun and it was very heavy!" His company moved up to the front lines the very next night after landing. They were ordered to "take a hill occupied by the Japanese." The Americans were on one side of the hill and the Japanese on the other. His officer told him to "go back and carry as many hand grenades as you can" so Private Fleming took off on the double. As he was returning with his arms loaded with grenades, he saw a Japanese hand grenade coming over the hill right towards him. It exploded and he received shrapnel wounds to his arms and legs and was sent back to a hospital in Guam to recover.

Once Orville recovered, he was ordered to return to his unit on Okinawa. However, he was on his way on an LST (or Landing Ship, Tank) when they received news that the atomic bomb had been dropped on Hiroshima. For Orville, he had received a "million-dollar wound," which quite likely saved his life. His combat days were over. After helping to secure Okinawa, the 77th Infantry moved on to Cebu in the Philippines and prepared for the planned invasion of Japan. Thankfully, the peace treaty was signed on deck the USS *Missouri* in Tokyo Harbor on September 2, 1945. Orville received a Bronze Star, Purple Heart and other medals for his service.

After being in occupied Japan, Orville reenlisted in the Army Air Corps and was sent to Camp Shanks in New York, boarded a troop ship for Le Havre, France, to a "Cigarette Camp," so named after American cigarettes such as Camel, Lucky Strike, Pall Mall, etc. He spent time in Austria and Germany. He left the Air Force in 1949 but re-enlisted after only three months as a civilian. He was stationed at Carswell AFB in Ft. Worth until 1953 when he was sent to Osan, Korea, about one month before the war was over. He got out again in 1954 but reenlisted after 11 months. He finally retired in 1966 after "getting his 20 years in." Orville was married three times and had one daughter, Karen. He moved to "the farm" in Ropesville, Texas, in 1985. He also did air conditioning work for many years. He now lives in Chicago, Illinois, near his daughter.

19

ROBBIE GILL
Lucky #13 and the "Miracle Survivor"

He heard and felt the two B-17s collide in mid-air and Cpl. Robbie Gill knew his crew was in trouble. His plane, the *Black Cat #13*, had pulled up and collided with another B-17 directly above them in low clouds over the North Sea. The collision sheared the *Black Cat #13* in two at the waist of the aircraft. Robbie, being the tail gunner, was now "all alone in the rear of the aircraft." He had struck his head on a crossbar and when he quickly came to, he recalled that "there was absolutely no noise, it was deadly quiet. I looked out and saw the front half of the plane and the rest of the crew falling." Now is when all his training had to pay off as he was rapidly descending into the North Sea.

Like many young men his age, Robbie wanted to "do his part in the war." He didn't want to be in the Army, so he joined the Army Air Corps in late November 1943. He was 19 years old. He completed his basic training in Logan, Utah, then cadet training in Santa Ana, California, followed by gunnery school in Arizona. He then went to bombardier training in Deming, New Mexico, on the Norden Bombsight but was "not coordinated enough," so they sent him to tail gunner school in South Dakota. Robbie said every school seemed to be six weeks long.

He was assigned to the 8th Air Force, 100th Bomb Group, 50th Squadron. He was in a crew with 9 other men and once they "picked up their plane in Arizona, they flew to Maine for deployment." Robbie's crew flew from Bangor, Maine, directly to England where they soon began their first bombing run into Germany. Their first flight was into Merseburg, Germany, and went off without a hitch. The second flight was nearly Robbie's last. En route to their target on July 28, 1944, the two B-17s collided.

Robbie's training and survival instinct kicked in immediately. He recalled, "I quickly put on my 'Mae West' life jacket and my parachute.

I pulled the door off of the tail section and bailed out. By the time my chute opened, I was below the clouds with the tail section spiraling slowly down to the sea. I maneuvered my chute to avoid being hit by the tail of the bomber." He remembered from his training to take his boots off before he hit the water so he "kicked off one of his heavy flight boots to see how far it was to the water, and they seemed to take a long time to get there, so I waited a few seconds and kicked off the other boot. It was time to cut the chute off." The young airman also recalled from his training that you "need to cut your chute off right before you hit the water to keep from being tangled up in the lines, so that's what I did."

Hitting the water, Robbie bobbed up and looked around for other survivors. There were none. "I was the only survivor out of the twenty men from the two bomber crews," he recalled with tears in his eyes. He released some fluorescein dye so he could be spotted by a rescue plane out searching for survivors. The plane spotted him and dropped a dinghy, but he "couldn't catch up to it." He was finally picked up by a rescue boat. However, while pulling him up to the back of the boat, he had to wave at them to stop. He was being pulled toward the propeller!

Robbie flew five more missions after his rescue and then joined several other men on back-up/stand-by duty. Robbie noted that after his ordeal, he was "offered a Purple Heart but I refused. I told them they could call me a miracle, but not a hero."

He then came back

Robbie Gill, Army Air Corps, World War II.

to the states to become an instructor on air/sea rescue in Deming, New Mexico, and Harlingen, Texas.

Robbie and Wanda's eyes met over the Dunlap's Department store's socks display. They chatted briefly and, after Robbie paid for his socks, he invited her to the nearby drugstore café for a coke. The rest is history. God must have known that Robbie would need a kind and nurturing wife, who would walk side-by-side with him through the pleasures and trials (and haunting memories from his time served). He would need the special kind of partner that would give him the freedom to remember and verbalize memories if he so chose, and to stand by her man unconditionally, offering him a safe haven where only he and God were allowed to view and re-live tragedy, defeat, death and loss.

They were engaged in 1946 and as of April 2016, have been on this journey as a married couple for 69 years. They have four children: Stan, Stacy, Stoney and Rhonda, and 39 grandchildren. Robbie was one of 96 veterans to attend the Texas South Plains Honor Flight to Washington, D.C., in 2013. His eyes brim with moisture as he recalls how respectfully his son attended to his needs and witnessed Robbie soaking in and processing the powerfully moving war memorials while his mind revisited the battle scenes. Even though constant waves of emotion swept over him at each memorial, he says now that he stands behind the Honor Flight's mission and encourages all veterans who can physically go, to attend. He feels strongly that they will be blessed. He did not avoid his responsibilities to his country and urges those now serving to "make up their minds before you get in, to fully commit for the greater good." One of his favorite songs is the "Battle Hymn of the Republic."

His strong servant's character was borne out of back-breaking farm work. When asked what hobbies he had back then, he answers seriously, "Hoein' Texas cotton." After graduating from high school in 1940 in Hamlin (Pied Pipers), Texas, he followed in the footsteps of his uncle and signed his military entrance documents, praying he would stay alive, unlike his uncle who gave his life in 1918. Robbie's utilization of the GI Bill helped him gain his secondary education, and he was a good steward of the benefits that opened the door for opportunities to learn the benefits of discipline, commitment to freedom, and loyalty to God and country.

One is forever changed after hearing Robbie's story and is swept to the brink of his memory as the tears roll in, choking him up. When asked if he is a hero (after declining a Purple Heart), he states, "You can call me a miracle, but not a hero. God and I know who truly deserves those awards."

20

CARL GILLY
Cobb's War

Carl Lee "Cobb" Gilly's active duty in the Navy began on October 16, 1942. He said he joined the Navy because he "didn't want to go in the Army as a foot soldier." He was probably thinking he wouldn't see any combat, but he was wrong. Carl was born in Floyd County (Floydada), Texas, on September 16, 1921, to Vince and Ann Gilly. Vince was a cotton and wheat farmer and Cobb learned to work on the farm at an early age. Vince had bought the farm for $1 per acre and it still remains in Gilly's hands 118 years later. He had 2 brothers and 2 sisters. His older brother was in the Army during World War II.

After his induction into the Navy, Cobb was sent to Farragut Naval Training Station. Named for famed Navy Civil War hero David Farragut (the nation's first rear admiral, vice admiral and admiral in the U.S. Navy), the station was at the foot of the Coeur d'Alene Mountains in Northern Idaho. Farragut was the second largest training center in the world behind only the Naval Station in Great Lakes near Chicago. During its 30 months of existence, over 293,000 sailors received basic training at Farragut. After basic, gunner and navigation school, Gilly was assigned to Bombing Squadron VPB-146 on a Ventura PV-1 airplane. In August of 1943, one of the planes piloted by Lt. Commander Ralph Beachum and his crew of 5 were lost in the mountains in Washington State. Inclement weather prevented any search for the downed craft. In December 1943, the squadron moved to the Naval Air Station in Alameda, California, for final training. In December 1943, all aircraft, equipment and men were put aboard the USS *Coral Sea* and shipped to NAS Kaneohe Bay, Hawaii. Additional training was done in the Hawaiian Islands.

In June 1944, Gilly's squadron was sent to the South Pacific area of the Admiralty Islands and conducted combat missions. In December 1944, and now called Patrol Bombing Squadron VPB-146, the squadron was deployed to Morotoi in Southeast Asia to conduct searches and strikes on Japanese shipping. On the U.S. Navy Patrol Squadrons' website (vpnavy.org), Morotoi was noted by one of the men as "nothing but mud, mosquitoes, occasionally a python and frequently a Japanese infiltrator." Gilly remembered "occasional Japanese air raids which destroyed some planes on the ground." He continued, "We got shot at quite a bit from Japanese ground installations on some of the other islands we flew over." By the end of their tour of duty, VPB-146 would lose 9 aircraft and 27 men in combat: 10 officers and 17 enlisted men. One of the crew members, Max Hartman, said, "Some of us matured while others died. Except for those who died, we did not do extraordinary or heroic things, but we all did that we were called upon to do." Gilly was proud to be part of this squadron.

Carl Gilly, U.S. Navy, World War II.

VPB-146 would return to Hawaii in February 1945 and then back to NAS Alameda, California. Cobb was discharged in October 13, 1945, and took a train back to Lubbock. He was awarded the Good Conduct Medal, the Philippine Liberation Ribbon and the Asiatic Pacific Theatre Ribbon. After 52 years, the Navy awarded Cobb with the Air Medal that he earned with the Patrol Bombing Squadron 146. The whole squadron or their widows were presented the medals on the same day all over the country on September 28, 1996. He noted that he married his wife, Lois, "in 1943 in Flagstaff, Arizona, while I was on leave before I went overseas. Lois took the train out with Janette Lackey and met me there. We drove back to Santa Monica where I was to be on duty at 4 o'clock that

Carl Gilly and Wanda Williams, February 7, 2019.

day! I had known her since high school. My daughter Barbara was 18 months old before I ever saw her. I have another daughter named Cathy." Lois passed away in 1995. Returning to Floydada, Cobb went back to farming. "I bought some land near the Cedar Hill community northeast of Floydada and inherited some land." I noticed a notepad near Cobb's phone and the only name and phone number written on the pad was Wanda Williams. She has been his friend for over 20 years. I started thinking about her name and recalled she had gone on the South Plains Honor flight with Carl back in 2012, and we laughed then about her having the same name as my mother. She also lives in Floydada, so Cobb called her to come over and visit. Wanda said Cobb has 3 grandchildren and 4 great-grandchildren.

Wanda remembered one other story that he had forgotten to tell. In October 1994, a local hiker named Charles Eaton was hiking in a remote area on 10,775-foot-high Mt. Baker in northwest Washington. At an altitude of 7,500 feet, he found the remains of an aircraft and crew. He found fragments from the plane and hundreds of rounds of .50 and .30 caliber ammunition. He also found the skeletal remains of 6 crew members who were among over 4,000 Navy fliers lost in accidents in the United States during the war. The Lockheed PV-1 was lost back in

August 1943 and was part of Cobb's Squadron VPB-146. "I remember flying with two of those guys earlier," he recalled. This was to be their last training flight before deployment to the Pacific. The pilot of the plane, LCDR Ralph Beachum, was a Pearl Harbor survivor.

When asked what he would like to be remembered for, I believe Cobb gave me the most honest answer yet. He said, "Lord, I don't know how to answer that one." As I said goodbye to Cobb and Wanda, she said, "Every one of these guys has a great story to tell." I wholeheartedly agree.

21

JIM GUYTON
Dunbar Alum Serves Twice

Lawrence "Jim" Guyton, born April 13, 1927, grew up on a farm in Chapel Hill, Texas. His favorite entertainment was listening to the family radio. Jim remembers being on the edge of his seat during the Boxing Heavy Weight Championship in 1938 when Joe Louis, the "Brown Bomber," fought the German native, Max Schmeling. He also remembers "having great awe and respect for General Patton's leadership." As he observed world events during challenging times, something began to awaken in the young man's spirit. He became aware of an appreciation for determination and patriotism, which served to bolster his own courage throughout life.

When he was 17, he met a young girl named Fanny Lee Lawson at Dunbar High School in Lubbock, Texas. After graduation, Jim wanted to attend Texas Tech but was unable to because Tech was not integrated until 1961. He opted to go to Sam Houston State, and Fanny went to Prairie View A&M. He credits his mother for encouraging him to aim high in school. She would say, "Get an education, boy." The young couple's relationship blossomed throughout college via letters and occasional visits.

Jim was drafted into the U.S. Army in November 1944 and sent to Ft. Sill, Oklahoma, for his uniform and shots. Next up was Ft. Bliss in El Paso, Texas, for basic and anti-aircraft artillery (AAA) training. He didn't have to serve overseas because the war was ending. When he was discharged in August of 1945, Jim said he "needed to finish up his high school education and earned his GED [General Educational Development] diploma." He returned to Sam Houston State in Austin, Texas, and graduated in August 1952.

But now, the United States was in the middle of the Korean War and Jim was recalled to the Army in September 1952. This time he was sent to Ft. Scott (part of the Presidio in San Francisco). He was assigned to Battery A 9th AAA in defense of the west coast and in charge of a 120 mm B1 anti-aircraft gun, which had a range of 26 miles. He said "that gun had to be maintained and loaded at all times. It took 16 men to pick it up." They were on alert 24 hours a day and only received a 3-day pass once a month. Jim achieved the rank of Sgt. 1st Class and was honorably discharged in September 1954. He had served his country during two wars.

Jim and Fanny married in August 1954. They moved to Lubbock. Working with John W. Wilson, Jim helped to establish a Boys and Girls Club in Lubbock. He said it was "hard work rounding up enough kids (they needed 200 to start building) and raising the money." Fanny worked as a substitute teacher. When Jim's job came to an end, he had a hard time finding work. Leaving Fanny in Lubbock, he went to Los Angeles, California, to seek employment. He took small jobs for a while. It was at the U.S. Post Office that opportunity finally knocked. Thanks to his service record, he received extra points and was hired. He said he "learned every street in the Los Angeles area." Fanny soon joined him and finished her education at the University of Southern California (USC) with a master's degree in teaching. Jim and Fanny had two children, first Cassandra and then Lawrence, Jr. Fanny taught in the California public school system for 30 years.

After 35 years, Jim retired from the post office. He and Fanny returned to Lubbock in 1992, but Fanny passed away on January 15, 2004. They'd been married for 50 years and 1 day.

Jim states that Fanny's legacy was that "everything in life is an experience that you can let better you." His own life dictum is "I can't do anything without God. He is involved with everything in your life. He gave us the greatest gift, by giving us Jesus." Jim was an elder at the Church of Christ on Adams Street in Riverside, California, for 50 years. He has attended Church of Christ at 20th and Birch in Lubbock since 2004.

When asked how he would encourage the younger generations of today, Jim replied, "Past generations have made it possible for you to follow their example. Don't give up.... You can make a contribution, too." Just like John F. Kennedy said, "Ask not what your country can do for you, but ask what can you do for your country."

Jim's eyes light up when he talks about the Honor Flight. A man at the VA Clinic saw his World War II cap and asked if he'd ever been to Washington. That conversation resulted in a wonderful experience for Jim Guyton. He proudly displays his cherished mementos from the trip. His favorite part was experiencing the Changing of the Guards at Arlington and the Vietnam Wall. He even knew some of the other Korean War veterans. Jim calls his Honor Flight guardian, Navy veteran Jason Henry, "a wonderful man and helper." For this hero who served his country as a soldier in two different wars, the Honor Flight "was truly a fantastic experience."

22

ROGER HABERER
Normandy, Days after the Invasion

Roger Haberer clearly remembers the day he was picked with a group of men to be dropped off at Normandy, France. They arrived on June 15, 1944, only nine days after the beginning of Operation Overlord, the D-Day invasion that led to the Allied victory in Europe. He said the beach was far from being cleared off from all the fighting. Corporal Haberer had been trained in the Army Air Corps' 9th Air Force, 1st Mobile Photo Supply & Maintenance Division as part of a massive support group for the final push to Germany. The 9th Air Force was by far the largest tactical air component in the European Theater. It had been officially reconstituted in the United Kingdom on October 16, 1943.

Roger was born on December 23, 1921, in Dimmitt, Texas. His dad had been in the Army during World War I but was stationed stateside during that war. He had spent most of his life helping his dad farm. But on November 9, 1942, just before his 21st birthday, Roger enlisted in the Army Air Corps at the Lubbock County Courthouse. He remembered that "all the armed services were set up there to receive enlistees." He did his "limited amount of basic training at Lubbock Army Airfield." By this point during the war, men (and women) were needed on so many fronts that much of the training was shortened to get them assigned as quickly as possible. He said he "and a few other men were trained to ride military motorcycles to deliver messages, but we used them to go to the PX [Post Exchange] and buy beers and give nurses a ride to the hospital." They were soon caught doing this, and "that was the end of the motorcycles."

Six men out of his 1017th Guard Squadron were shipped out to Camp Kilmer, New York, where they boarded a Liberty ship bound for duty outside of London. His ship held around 5,000 troops and took two weeks to cross the Atlantic. He and a few other men from his squadron were picked as "casualty replacements" and were shipped over to

Normandy, France. After spending "a few days on the beach in pup tents where it seemed to rain all the time," Roger and a few other men decided to "move inland and see what was going on." They hitched a ride on an Army Air Corps convoy attached to the 94th Air Depot Group and wound up outside Paris. They had to "find their own accommodations," so they found a house that was "shot full of holes and patched it up as best they could." That stay didn't last long as "a push north was being made to follow the troops through northern France after the retreating German Army." This massive push would require an equally massive supply and re-supply effort. Roger mentioned that there was a "terrible traffic jam of convoys from all different types of Allied units." He recalls using his helmet to "shave, wash and even eat K-rations out of." He said, "The basic helmet was a very versatile piece of gear for all soldiers."

After a time in Cambrai, France, Roger wound up in Liege, Belgium, where he spent the rest of the war. He began flying on C-47 cargo planes back and forth to England to pick up supplies. After one of these trips, when he arrived back in Belgium, his outfit told him how lucky he was, because the Army had just been there looking for casualty replacements for the front line. He was finally able to head for home in September 1945 aboard a Victory ship, but the trip was not easy. They had to "endure a big storm and high seas. A lot of the men got sick and weren't sure if they were going to survive the Atlantic crossing this time."

When Roger returned to Muleshoe, Texas, he contacted one of his buddies and said he "figured he needed to find a wife and settle down." However, his friend told him that most all of the girls he knew had either graduated or left town. He did "know of one schoolteacher" that was available and set Roger up on a blind date with Joy Saunders. They married on March 16, 1946. She had just turned 20 and Roger was 25. They had a son, Davey, and a daughter, Camille. Davey later served in the Army himself. After farming, banking and other jobs, Roger "retired three times and retired for the last time from City Bank in Springlake, Texas, at 85 years old!" Joy Haberer passed away on May 30, 2015. Roger had this to say about her: "It was a blind date that lasted 69 years."

Roger was awarded the Good Conduct, the American Campaign, European–African–Middle Eastern Campaign and World War II Victory medals.

23

BOB HAIL
Navy Boat Driver Dropped off Marines

Navy Coxswain Bob Hail, all of 18 years old, didn't know it at the time, but he was headed into the bloodiest battle of the Pacific War. His job as a coxswain was, as he put it, to be "a boat driver." I submit that he was much more than just a "boat driver." He and his crew's job were to take 26 Marines ashore at Iwo Jima from APA (Attack Transport) # 154 USS *Lowndes* aboard his LCVP (Landing Craft, Vehicle, Personnel). After a "few trips to shore, they would begin bringing back the dead and wounded." The *Lowndes* received and treated 365 wounded from the Iwo beach.

He remembers a "boom with hooks would be lowered over the side of the ship to his boat with four rings to slip over the stretchers and lift the dead and wounded on board." They could lift a man per minute off the boats this way. They could also "carry a Jeep and five men on their boat." The Iwo Jima operation was scheduled to last three days, but wound up taking thirty-six. Bob and his crew would be there for the first eight days of the battle with the *Lowndes*. He said they were "constantly under enemy fire and could see the shells splashing in the water around them from the entrenched Japanese on the island." Getting in the boat was tricky, said Bob. "The Marines had to climb down the netting from the side of the *Lowndes* while he tried to keep his LCVP steady." Out of 26 LCVPs, 8 were lost at Iwo.

Bob was born on March 5, 1927. He joined the Navy on May 24, 1944, and spent his basic training at Naval Base San Diego. He was then assigned to an LCVP as the coxswain and did his training off of the USS *Lowndes*. He recalls the ship having to be "degaussed" (demagnetized) in Oregon so as not to attract enemy mines. In October 1944, the *Lowndes* got underway from California to Pearl Harbor, Hawaii. Once there, they would begin "practicing amphibious landings on several islands." Bob also remembers the beaches were "not pretty at all, but were covered with oil."

23. Bob Hail

In January 1945, the *Lowndes* sailed out of Pearl Harbor en route to Eniwetok Atoll, Marshall Islands. In February 1945, they headed for Saipan to make final preparations for the Iwo Jima invasion. Two to three hours before arriving at Iwo, flares and rockets could clearly be seen on the island. It was hard for the LCVPs to land on the beaches at first because of heavy enemy fire and damaged landing craft, amphibious vehicles and land equipment. After numerous trips back and forth to the beach head, Bob remembers that the *Lowndes* would "take off at 4:00 p.m. every night and head back out to sea to avoid be fired on by the Japanese on Iwo. If you didn't make it back to the ship by 4:00, you would be stuck on the beach overnight until the ship returned the next morning." He said "the Japs would fly planes over at night and their tracers were thicker than stars." They would "use a signal man to steer their LCVP back to the ship via a lantern if it was still dark or flags if it was daylight."

Bob recalled "seeing the U.S. flag on top of Mount Suribachi and it inspired all the men." He would leave Iwo on February 19 on the way back to Saipan but the hospitals were full and the wounded had to be taken to Guam. Next, they were sent from Saipan to land troops from the 2nd Marine Division on Okinawa. The *Lowndes* would win two battle stars.

Bob recalls that he was "out to sea when the men heard that President Franklin Delano Roosevelt had died." He was discharged in November 1946, "received his back pay and mustering out pay and went home to Albuquerque." He worked for a while at Kirkland AFB as a carpenter. He then went into the banking business for many years at various locations. He met his future wife, Joyce Lea, at one of his stops and they would marry in 1959 and have two daughters, Shelley and Stasey. Joyce died May 10, 2016. Bob now resides at Southaven Assisted Living in Lubbock and beamed with pride when he said that "one daughter visits me in the morning and one visits me in the afternoon."

Thank you for your service, Bob.

24

J.W. Hamby
Businessman at an Early Age

Ninety-three-year-old J.W. Hamby of Plainview, Texas, started in business at 17 years old. He "saved and borrowed $110 to buy 1/10th interest in the Plainview Flying Club." His drive to succeed in business would serve him well in later years. He was born at home in Plainview on May 18, 1925, to Buford W. and Eva (Hall) Hamby. He was an only child. His father was "a farmer, day laborer and whatever else he could find to survive the dirty 30s." This was during the Great Depression and Dust Bowl days. Life was hard on the South Plains like the rest of America during that time.

Hamby went to school a half day at Plainview High School in the morning and working a half day in the afternoon in Distributive Education, graduating in the spring of 1942. He was still only 17 years old, and Hamby enlisted in the Army Air Corps because he said, "I wanted to fly. I took basic training at Sheppard Field in Wichita Falls, Texas. In those days, even the Air Corps guys went through infantry training." J.W. Sheppard had just opened as a training facility in October 1941 on a 300-acre tract of land sold by a Wichita Falls cattleman named J.S. Bridwell for just $10. After basic, Hamby was transferred to a college training detachment in San Marcos, Texas, and "took a lot of college courses in 5 months. They needed pilots in those days and were running a lot of men through there," he said. The men were trained to be pilots, navigators, bombardiers and radio and communications experts. After months of training on a B-25, Hamby was ready to put his training to use overseas. However, the war in Europe ended in May 1945. Sent to Lincoln, Nebraska, he "drew a crew to fly a twin engine plane in the Pacific, but our assignment was shot down." In August of 1945, the atomic bombs were dropped on Hiroshima, then a few days later on Nagasaki. The war on both fronts was over.

Hamby was assigned to the 47th Bomb group at Lake Charles,

Louisiana, as the war came to a close and a rapid demobilization began. According to the National WWII Museum website, over 12 million men and women were in the military during World War II, which represented 9 percent of the country's population. By June 1947, only 1.5 million (a whopping 90 percent reduction!) active-duty soldiers, sailors, Marines, and airmen in the armed forces remained. As J.W. noted, "Many men wanted to stay in the service, but we had four Colonels, twelve Lt. Colonels and Majors were a dime a dozen." The service simply did not want or need (they thought) this large of a military force. Americans were tired after over four years of war. Hamby noted that he "had to get a physical exam to fly 100 hours per month and we flew wherever we wanted to go which was fine with me. I loved to fly." He said his scariest time was when he "took off from Pampa Airfield in a B-25 at night and lost an engine. My co-pilot was scared to death, but I tried everything and finally trimmed it up [a means to keep the aircraft level during flight] and was able to land safely back in Pampa."

J.W.'s last flight was from Lake Charles, Louisiana, to Denver, Colorado, in an A-26 Invader where he was "separated from active duty and put on inactive duty where he remained for approximately 9 years" and left the service as a Captain. When asked what he did after the service, he grinned and said, "How much paper have you got?" He tried to recall all the places he worked: Firestone, G.M. Diesel, a plow manufacturer, life insurance, a diesel business and another plow company. All of these jobs led up to what J.W. had always wanted to do, which was start up a wholesale farm equipment and supplies business. He met and married Dorothy Jean Merrifield after he got out of the service and they married on December 21, 1946. They had 1 son and 3 daughters. Dot passed away from multiple sclerosis in 1991.

Hamby's dream of owning his own business came true in 1954 when he started the Hamby Co. He sold to farm equipment dealers all over the South Plains, eastern New Mexico, Oklahoma, Kansas and Nebraska. In 1960, he started to manufacture farm equipment specifically for southwestern U.S. farmers. At the height of his business, he had 140 employees. He sold his highly successful business to Crustbuster Mfg. out of Dodge City, Kansas, in 1989 after 35 years in business. He said he had "been blessed with opportunities in business his whole life." J.W. owns several business properties in Plainview, served on the Board of Lubbock Christian University for 45 years and was named Plainview's Chamber of Commerce 2015 Man of the Year.

25

WALLACE HANEY
A Member of the "Caterpillar Club"

By 98-year-old Wallace Haney's best recollection, he flew around 16 different aircraft during his time in the Army Air Corps. Like a lot of South Plains veterans, it was unthinkable that young Wallace would soon be soaring over the West Texas skies one day. Born in Ira, Texas, to W.A. and Muriel Haney on March 21, 1921, Wallace was part of a farm family that included 3 sisters and 1 brother. He attended nearby Snyder High School where he jokingly said his favorite subject was "chasing girls." The one he "caught" was pretty, young Ellen Larue McCowan. Wallace graduated in May 1939 and attended Texas Tech College for one year.

Haney enlisted in the Army Air Corps on February 4, 1941. This was 8 months before the United States entered World War II. Wallace's brother, William, was an Army parachute instructor in South Carolina during the war. Air Corps training for Haney would begin with 6 weeks of basic training at Goodfellow Field in San Angelo, Texas. Goodfellow was one of numerous bases being built around the country in 1941 as President Franklin Delano Roosevelt began a program of preparedness due to the world aggression across Europe, Asia and Africa. Wallace was in one of the first groups of airmen to be trained at Goodfellow in February 1941. Additional flight training would take him to Hicks Field northwest of Ft. Worth, Texas, and Foster Field near Victoria, Texas. While at Hicks Field, Wallace recalled one scary incident. He was "flying around in a PT-19 trainer above the clouds enjoying the ride. The trainer had 2 seats and I was sitting in the back seat. When I came down out of the clouds, I couldn't find the airfield! The wind had blown me about 30 or 40 miles off course. I had to stand up in the plane and look at the instruments in the front cockpit to get my bearings. I had never flown by instruments before. I finally found Hicks Field on my own. I was sure happy to see that field." Transferred to Foster Field near Victoria, Texas,

25. Wallace Haney

Wallace was commissioned a 2nd Lieutenant and married Ellen on September 6, 1942.

Wallace said, "First, I was assigned to Amarillo Field for about 5 weeks where I was a tow pilot for a one-man glider. I was transferred to Dalhart Field [Texas] and stayed there about a year. I was a tow pilot there for the CG-A glider. I was towing these gliders at night and never really got to see one up close. It could handle a payload of 13 troops; or a Jeep and 4 troops, or 1 75-mm Howitzer, 18 rounds of ammo and 3 troops or 6 litters. Maximum speed of the bulky aircraft was only 150 MPH. I was then sent to Lubbock's South Plains Army Airfield and stayed in the barracks there once again as a tow pilot. Once, I flew a Stinson L-5 plane to Nebraska with a group of guys and then we took the train back to Lubbock. No sooner had we got back then we got orders to take a train back to Nebraska and deliver the same planes to Sheppard Air Field in Wichita Falls, Texas. The L-5 that I flew was a real clunker. It had no brakes; I could hardly start it and stop it. I bent one of the wings after jumping out and trying to stop it."

The plane trouble kept coming for Wallace and seemed to be getting more deadly. He recalled, "I was flying an SB2C Helldiver that we used to pull gliders. I took it up and the oil line busted and my windshield was covered with oil. I had to stick my head out just to see. I had to head back to the airfield and land right away." Haney recalled another SB2C nearly cost him his life. "There was another SB2C that the mechanics and I checked out. We couldn't see anything wrong with it, so I hopped in to take a test run. I was heading down the runway and the plane would not get off the ground. I was nearly at the end of the runway when I decided to try pulling up the wheels. They had taught us that if you had to ditch a plane, to pull up the wheels so you could slide in on the belly of the plane so it wouldn't flip over once you were off the runway. To my surprise, the plane lifted off and I enjoyed flying it around for a while.

"I tried to come in for a landing but every time I would lower the wheels, the plane would want to take a nose dive. I had to keep circling the airfield. I contacted the control tower and the Major wanted to grab another plane and come up and take a look. I told him it was no use. I was going to have to crash-land the plane. I lowered the wheels and the plane started heading down. I ejected too close to the ground and the seams on my parachute burst. I could see the plane right below me explode into a million pieces. I hit the ground going about 30 miles per hour. I landed right in the middle of all the wreckage. There were some workers hoeing cotton close to where I landed and one of them came running up and asked, 'Hey mister, is this your hat? He had my flight cap that had blown off and was tore down the middle and full of holes. The Major came flying up in a car and ran through a barbed-wire fence and part of it was stuck on the front of the car. He jumped out of the car yelling, 'Oh my God, I've just killed a pilot.' He had a little fire extinguisher he was spraying around. He kept saying that until I stood up and told him I was all right. He was sure surprised to see me alive! I had a death grip on the rip cord."

Later, Haney found out that a woman in Slaton also named Haney had packed his parachute. Wallace tracked her down in Slaton and thanked her for saving his life. Soon after his near-death experience, Haney found out he was now a member of the "Caterpillar Club." According to *Atlas Obscura*, "The sole requirement for joining the Caterpillar Club [a reference for the silk threads used in parachutes recognizing the silkworm's contribution] is to make an emergency escape from a failing aircraft, then plummet to earth with the aid of a parachute. Should you survive, you automatically become a member." The club dates back to October 1922 when an Army test pilot lost control of his aircraft and deployed his parachute for the first time. He was quite shaken up after landing, but alive. Two *Dayton Herald* reporters realized more jumps would follow and suggested the idea of the Caterpillar Club. The Warfare History Network website states that, by war's end, more than 13,000 American aviators lost their lives in training accidents at home and never faced the enemy. One more "cost of war" all but forgotten.

Many more flights would follow for Wallace. He said, "I stayed in Lubbock and took planes all over the country. I was checked out on a B-29 and sent to Seattle where I had orders to go bomb Japan. The war ended in August of 1945 and I've never seen such a drunken bunch of happy men! I was discharged on February 4, 1946." Spending 5 years in the service, Wallace is one of the few surviving non-career military men who went in before World War II and was discharged well after it was over. Wallace's mother kept a poster in her window with two blue stars denoting that her two sons were in the service during World War II. During the war, the Blue star and Gold star flags (families who had lost a service member) could be seen in windows all across the country.

After his service, Wallace attended Baylor Dental School in Waco, Texas. Wallace said, "I was a left-handed dentist and we only had one chair for 4 or 5 left-handed people. We always tried to be the first one to get that chair!" He returned to Lubbock and set up his practice. Wallace joked that he "worked for 30 years" and now "has been retired for over 35 years. I didn't intend to live this long!" He and Ellen had 2 sons and 1 daughter. Ellen passed away in February 2019. She and Wallace were married 67 years. When asked what people would say about him when he was gone, he smiled and said, "Good riddance," and laughed at his own joke. Wallace Gerald Haney: a survivor and one of a kind.

26

TED HARTMAN

*Sherman Tank Driver
and Orthopedic Surgeon*

Dr. J. Ted Hartman was born in DeRidder, Louisiana, on June 13, 1935. Shortly thereafter, his family moved to Ames, Iowa. He was the last of three siblings. His father was a professor of forestry on the faculty of Iowa State University. Dr. Hartman is 91 years old and has written a book titled *Tank Driver*.

Ted graduated from high school in 1943, and started college, but was drafted shortly thereafter. The Army sent him to basic training in field artillery at Camp Roberts, California. He was assigned to the 11th Armored Division at Camp Cooke, California. Once his training was complete, he drove a tank under the command of General George Patton. A year later, the division was shipped to the east coast by sleeper trains. They boarded troop ships in the New York Harbor. His ship was in the largest convoy of ships to cross the Atlantic Ocean up to that time.

After a two-week crossing, his division landed in Liverpool, England. The 11th was moved by train to southeast England to an armored training camp. After five months, his division drove their tanks to the English Channel and boarded ships called LSTs (Landing Ship, Tanks) and transported to Normandy, France. The 11th then engaged in a forced march across Northern France.

Dr. Hartman said, "We left for Belgium where the Battle of the Bulge was being fought. We steadily gained ground and by mid–March 1945, we reached the Rhine River. The Rhine was ¼ of a mile wide in that location. The engineers had built a pontoon bridge for us to cross. A pontoon bridge consists of air-filled tanks attached to each other with tread ways for the tracks of our tanks to roll on. As soon as we were across, we headed across Germany at full speed, gaining 35 to 40 miles per day. We headed to the eastern border of Germany and turned south to the Austrian border. We crossed the Danube River into Austria. At this point, the war in Europe ended on May 8, 1945. We were 100 miles from the Russians. There were 20,000 German soldiers trapped between the Russians and us. The German soldiers fled and we set up a camp to hold them until we could march them back to the Russians. In order to march them back, we had a tank in front facing forward and a tank facing backward and repeated this process with more tanks until the Germans were surrounded. The Russians were already punishing the Germans angrily."

Dr. Hartman continued, "There were five men assigned to each of these massive Sherman tanks. They weighed 33 tons and consumed two gallons of gas to drive one mile! In Belgium and France, I drove a tank in a foot of snow many times with no heat in the tank. It was designed to pull in the air through the front and push the air through to the back, so in the summer it was hot and in the winter it was cold. My feet were cold so much of the time that they froze. The doctor told me the blood flow had been constricted for so long during the freezing weather that my feet would never function normally again. My feet still bother me when it is cold.

"Upon my arrival home, I enrolled in Iowa State to complete pre-medical studies. I was accepted to Northwestern University Medical School, after which I acquired training as an orthopedic surgeon at the University of Michigan. I was granted a fellowship at Oxford University, England, where orthopedic surgery first started.

"I met my wife, Jean, in a cafeteria. She had been educated in dietetics, and that was her first assignment. I introduced myself and we began dating. After about a year, we married in her hometown of St. Louis, Missouri, in 1954. We have been married for 61 years and have three children and four grandchildren.

"We have been back to Europe and met an orthopedic surgeon from Belgium who invited us to the 50th anniversary of the Battle of the Bulge. When we visited Germany, we were treated nicely and even thanked by some Germans, who said they would never have gotten rid of Hitler if the United States had not been involved!"

For a more detailed account of Ted Hartman's story, please see his book "Tank Driver: With the 11th Armored from the Battle of the Bulge to VE Day" (Indiana University Press, 2003) or http://tankdriverstory.com/.

27

BILLY HENDRIX
Circling the Globe after World War II

Growing up on a farm outside of Goree, Texas, sailing around the world was the farthest thing from young Billy Hendrix's mind. He was too busy helping around the farm with chores to have such thoughts. That all changed in 1944. Billy's older brother was already overseas with Patton's 3rd Army as they raced across Europe to help clinch the Allied victory over Germany. Billy tried to convince his dad to let him sign up for officer training in the Navy. They went to sign up but his dad hesitated signing the documents and took Billy back home. "In those days, you did what your father told you to do. End of discussion." Billy said it took three more months to convince his dad to let him sign up in December 1944 as inactive.

Billy was born on February 4, 1927, on a farm to L.L. and Ida Mae Hendrix. Besides being a farmer, Billy's dad was also a house builder and worked at a lumber yard. He had an older brother and a younger sister. He attended school in Goree, a small town southwest of Wichita Falls, Texas. In those days, the end of school was the 11th grade. Billy wanted to do his part for the war effort and wanted to join the Navy because he "didn't want to join the walking Army." After interviewing numerous Navy and Army Air Corps veterans, I have heard some version of this saying several times. They all believed that a warm bed had to be better than a cold foxhole.

Orders for basic training arrived and Billy headed to Naval Training Center in San Diego, California. In those days, basic training was either 6 or 8 weeks depending on the needs of the Navy. After the usual round of shots and buzz haircuts, the "boots" discarded their civilian clothes and issued Navy uniforms and a sea bag to neatly put the clothes in. The boot camp Chief Petty Officer assigned to a Boot company would bark out orders and lead the men on grueling 10-hour days of marching, calisthenics, washing clothes, pulling oars in a boat, rifle drills, and so on.

Men were needed quickly for the Pacific War and Billy was assigned to the USS *Mustin* (DD-413), a Sims class destroyer.

Arriving in San Francisco, California, Hendrix recalled, "The harbor was full of ships of all kinds. We were loading up troops to head to Japan. I drove the boat under the Golden Gate Bridge and out to sea. Not long after we got underway, we heard the A-bombs had been dropped on Hiroshima and then Nagasaki. The war was over. We headed for Alaska and made port at Kodiak, Alaska. We then headed past the Aleutian Islands headed for Northern Japan." The Japanese Army occupied Attu and Kiska during the early part of World War II. Allied forces liberated the islands in 1943. After "refueling in the ocean, we sailed to and anchored in Sasebo, Northern Japan. We unloaded wave after wave of troops which would become the Army of Occupation. We didn't see anyone after landing onshore. As soon as the Japanese surrendered, it was as if they had disappeared. We didn't even see any women and children. Slowly some children would come out and we would give them candy bars and eventually the women and older men would come out.

"We left Sasebo and sailed to Yokohama. Everything onshore had been leveled by our bombers. There was nothing to see. I was transferred to the USS *Hamlin* (AV-15), which was anchored at Yokosuka and was an airplane tender [a tender was a ship that supported sea planes and were often considered the first aircraft carriers]. We had a little boat to look after the sea planes. Hunter and I checked the planes daily. There were a lot of logs floating in the harbor and we had to keep the harbor clear for the sea planes to land. We missed one log. One of the planes came in and hit the log and started to sink. We tied our hawser line [large rope] to the sinking plane and tried to drag it back to the Hamlin but it was sinking. We had to cut the rope with my knife and helped rescue some of the men from the sinking PBY [an American flying boat Patrol Bomber].

"We sailed from Japan headed for China. I was assigned as Captain Hopkins's 'boy.' It was my job to sit outside the Captain's quarters. Everyone had to go by me to see the Captain, even officers. One day he told me he didn't want to be disturbed so when a radioman came by with a note for the Captain, I told him he didn't want to be disturbed. The radioman showed me a tape that said Admiral so and so was coming onboard. I had to go and wake up the Captain. He said, 'I told you I didn't want to be disturbed' but once he saw the Admiral was coming onboard, he jumped up in a hurry!"

Bill recalled sailing around the world from China to the tip of India past Sri Lanka. "I was initiated as a Shellback [crossing the equator]. They held a ceremony and would feed you terrible stuff and grease you down. I don't remember what all they did to us, but it wasn't good!" Bill remembered going through the Suez Canal and into the Mediterranean Sea. He was looking forward to seeing the Rock of Gibraltar, but they "went through at night and we missed seeing it. I remember stopping in the Azores [in the North Atlantic Ocean]. We finally arrived back in the United States at Norfolk, Virginia. We had picked up sailors all over the world and brought them back to the States. I was discharged at Ft. Sam Houston near San Antonio, Texas."

Bill said he "got on a bus to Houston to visit my Uncle Frank who was a World War I Navy veteran. He was in John Phillip Sousa's band. The band would play for troops being hauled back and forth to Europe during World War I. I took another bus to Goree and then to Lubbock. My dad had moved to Lubbock in 1944 and established the L.L. Hendrix lumber yard on the Clovis Highway. I attended Texas Tech and graduated in 1950 with a degree in electrical engineering. I went to work for my dad. I met my future wife, Eleanor McCraney in Lubbock, Texas. She came to work for an uncle in Lubbock who was a doctor. Her aunt was a cousin to my mother. She came by to see my mom and I saw her sitting in the car outside. I decided to go see the doctor (actually just to see Eleanor). We married on September 20, 1950, and had 2 boys and 2 girls." Eleanor passed away in May 1998. Bill married Charline Langley in January 2000. Charline is known as the "cake lady" in Floydada, Texas, as she bakes cakes for numerous events in the area. When asked what he would like to be remembered for, Bill said, "I'd like to be remembered for being a good guy and a free American."

28

TED HILL
P-47 Thunderbolt Pilot

In the spring of 1945, Lt. Ted Hill and his P-47 Fighter Group were returning from a mission over Germany to their base in Kelz, Germany. The Thunderbolts flew support missions patrolling roads for concentrations of enemy troops, strafing German military trains and vehicles, and dropping bombs on gun emplacements. Once, their squad leader dropped down through the clouds over what he thought was their home base. Unfortunately, he guessed wrong, and they quickly realized they were actually over Cologne, Germany, where 1,800 (88 caliber) anti-aircraft guns ringed the city and all were seemingly firing at them. Ted said, "The sky turned black from all the flak." All the pilots had to quickly get back above the clouds and out of the range of the 88s. Surprisingly, every one of the planes made it back safely to their home base.

Ted Hill was born September 18, 1924, in North Andover, Massachusetts. He remembers walking home from church when he heard the news that Pearl Harbor had been bombed on December 7, 1941. He enlisted in the Army in October 1942 but was sent home. He was recalled to active duty in November 1942. He spent his basic training "on the boardwalk in Atlantic City, New Jersey." He had always wanted to be a pilot and signed up for the Army Air Corps. He was sent to Butler College in Indiana to "take cram courses in math, physics, etc." He spent the next year or so getting trained as a pilot in San Antonio, Texas; Cimarron Field, Oklahoma; Enid, Oklahoma; Moore Field, Texas; Wendover Army Air Base, Utah; and finally Abilene, Texas. While completing his training at Moore Field, Ted said he "was discharged as a Private and commissioned as a 2nd Lieutenant the same day."

It was here that Ted learned to fly first an AT-6 and then a P-47 aircraft. The P-47 was one of the most durable and best armed fighter planes of its time. It was mounted with eight .50 caliber machine guns and was very fast, with a massive 2,300 horsepower engine, and it could

28. Ted Hill

reach speeds of up to 433 miles per hour and had a range of 449 miles. Ted mentioned that the "atomic bomb played an important role" in his personal life. During P-47 training in Wendover, Utah, everyone was ordered to "evacuate the base—no explanation was given." It wasn't until after the war that they found out that the base was being used to fit B-29s with the atomic bomb.

His class was "broken up in groups of 4 or 5 and was sent to various bases to resume training." Ted was sent to Abilene Army Air Base in Texas. It was here that he was set up on a blind date by one of his buddies with a local girl, Doris, who was a student at Hardin-Simmons University. After only three dates, Ted was sent to Harding Air Base in Louisiana. He gave her a silver dollar on their last date and said he would be back for it after the war. He was unable to tell Doris, as she had gone home for Thanksgiving. Later, he was sent to Camp Kilmer, New Jersey, where he boarded a British Liberty Ship and arrived in Liverpool, England. He was assigned to the 404th Fighter Group and was sent to Paris, where his unit was put up in tents at a chalet. He was in a group of 20 or so pilots awaiting assignment.

Ted Hill, Army Air Corps, World War II.

Ted's first mission would be "ground support for troops in Belgium at the tail end of the Battle of the Bulge." Ted said, "The P-47 was one tough plane. It could take a hit and still make it back to base." He would eventually fly 41 missions. Ted's group wound up at a liberated base in Fritzlar, Germany, when Germany surrendered in May 1945. Ted said that "set off some pretty wild celebrations. Guys were firing flares and whatever they could find." His Fighter Group was sent to Antwerp, Belgium, where they were put in a staging area to be sent to the Pacific to fight the Japanese. During this time, the atomic bombs were dropped on Hiroshima and Nagasaki. Following this news, his Fighter Group was sent to Tampa, Florida, where they were disbanded.

During his 45-day terminal leave, Ted went back home to Massachusetts and asked Doris to come and meet his parents. Shortly after the visit, Ted made good on his promise to return from the war and married Doris on November 18, 1945, at the Drew Field Air Base Chapel in Tampa, Florida. He applied to be a pilot at Eastern Airlines, but they told him they "would not take fighter pilots." He checked on being a dentist, but that had a two-year waiting period. He went to pharmaceutical school in Boston for 4 years and graduated in 1950. He spent 39 years as a pharmacist in various locations. He and Doris moved to Abernathy, Texas, in 1956 and owned and operated Hill's Pharmacy. He retired from Hi-Plains Hospital in Hale Center, Texas, in 1989 after a 20-year stint.

Ted and Doris had 3 sons and 6 grandchildren. Sadly, Doris passed away in March 2013 after what Ted said was "67 years, 3 months and 12 days until death did us part."

29

CHARLES J. HOYE
Old Newsie Serving with a Pen

Charles J. Hoye can look back on a long life, well lived. Charlie was born on June 14, 1923, in Taunton, Massachusetts, 40 miles south of Boston, to Joseph and Annie. His father was a butcher, then a World War I Army soldier and lastly a U.S. Postal Service employee for 48 years, rising to the position of Assistant Postmaster in Taunton. Charlie had two siblings, Paul, a sailor and 25-year editor of *Aramco World* magazine, and Margery, a radio singer and registered nurse. Charlie was a 1941 high school graduate, a correspondent for the *Taunton Daily Gazette* and a gas station attendant before World War II. On Pearl Harbor Day, and because of his part-time newspaper experience, he was drafted that night to do phone interviews with parents of men who were serving at Pearl Harbor.

Inducted on March 13, 1943, he failed the Army eye test because of weak eyes. Wanting to help in the war effort, he ignored rejection and "enlisted on the spot" for limited service because his high school English and bookkeeping studies could prove to be valuable eventually. Soon after, a train took him to Ft. Snelling, Minnesota. Upon arrival in a blizzard, a burly sergeant shoved him off into a snow bank, breaking an ankle and curtailing much of his basic training. The Historic Ft. Snelling website indicates that over 300,000 men and women passed through Ft. Snelling after being inducted into the armed forces. As part of the 444th Engineer Base Depot Company, he went to Ft. McCoy in Wisconsin ("bitter cold it was") for rifle training. Next, it was on to Ogden, Utah, where he spent eight weeks learning the "Army way" of doing inventory, supply and bookkeeping.

The 444th shipped out of New York Harbor on a converted cruise ship and headed for England via Scotland. Charlie noted that "they had destroyer escorts, and several German U-boats were spotted on the way over." After landing in Scotland, that cruise ship was torpedoed outside the harbor and sunk with other troops still aboard, destined for Africa. His unit was sent to Thatcham, England, where the unit lived in "the Hut Camp," which consisted of wooden barracks and metal Nissen Huts (like a U.S. Quonset hut). Hoye and his unit helped supply the massive war effort in Europe for three years. According to the Warfare History Network website, items like a "Bailey bridge built right there in England" were provided to help the Allied troops cross the many rivers in Europe while fighting the Germans. He also wrote occasionally for the *Stars and Stripes*, the Army's newspaper. He remembered that "V-2 rockets and the occasional German plane would fly over the camp, and one of the cooks actually shot down one of their planes."

While in England, Charlie went to some London dances and met Joyce, a "WREN in the British Navy who was doing top-secret work" and couldn't tell Charlie what she actually did. She "became my three-year dance partner." Although the 444th had a large number of war brides, and even though Joyce and Charlie became close, he "was engaged to future wife Loretta back home in Taunton." He said Loretta "didn't like him in high school, but he was persistent." Joyce, who no doubt secretly hoped she might be Charlie's bride and go to Taunton with him, traveled to Southampton when he sailed home. Waving at him while crying dockside, she gave a wrapped package to a British seaman and had him deliver it to Charlie. It was a diary, and on the inside cover, she wrote, "To dear Charlie, Bon Voyage and a happy landing. Love, Joyce." Charlie and Loretta wrote to Joyce and sent her care packages for a while but lost track of her when she married.

He was discharged on February 3, 1946, at Ft. Devens, Massachusetts. Charlie and Loretta had five children, two girls and three boys, but the last, a boy, died a day after his birth. Charlie worked several jobs and later landed a job at the *North Adams Transcript* in Massachusetts. He stayed there for 17 years. His wife's health was declining, so he took a job in Truth or Consequences, New Mexico. He eventually moved to Hobbs, New Mexico, where he retired in 1985 as City Editor of the *Hobbs Daily News-Sun*. Loretta passed away in 1991. Her friend, Bernice Wisdom, a widowed schoolteacher, and Charlie, who were both members with Loretta in a genealogy society, "somehow drifted together" and married in 1993. Charlie offhandedly mentioned that, during his many years as a newspaperman, he met such famous people as Franklin D. Roosevelt, Harry Truman, John and Jackie Kennedy and many more. As the "pen is mightier than the sword," Charlie was a genuine warrior.

30

DON JONES
A Life of Service to Country and Community

Don Jones knows about service. Now 89 years old, he can look back on a long distinguished career and say, "I have been blessed." Don started life on a farm in Panola County, Texas. His father died when he was one year old and his mother had to raise two girls and four boys by herself for a time before remarrying. Don went to Prairie View A&M to begin college, but World War II and the selective service came calling on him and he was "drafted" into the Navy in 1944. The National WWII Museum has documented that, by the end of the war in 1945, 50 million men between 18 and 45 had registered for the draft and 10 million had been inducted into the military.

All three of Don's brothers served during World War II. Casey was a Medic, Albert an M.P. (Military Police) and Robert was in Field Artillery. He said Robert saw the most combat of the group. Don took his basic training in Bainbridge, Maryland, then on to New London, Connecticut, for submarine training. He then shipped out of California for the Pacific and docked in Pearl Harbor. He said it was very difficult to get used to military traditions. He served on the USS *Ronquil* (SS-396), which was later used in the movie *Ice Station Zebra*. Don was the only black man out of 92 men serving on the sub. They "would go out on patrols into enemy waters and knew they were close to the enemy when they had to endure depth charges." Sonar was now in use by Naval combatants and Don said, "You had to be very quiet on the sub at times to avoid enemy detection. We would put on thick socks to wear and no one was allowed to talk or move much while an enemy ship was in the area."

Don's job as a Steward onboard was to "take care of three officers," with such chores as getting them the correct "uniform of the day," bring them coffee and meals, tidy up their quarters and any other jobs

Don Jones (2nd from right with Honor Flight cap) and brother Robert Jones (left with Honor Flight Cap) shake hands with well-wishers at the World War II Memorial in Washington, D.C.

they deemed necessary. Don's quarters consisted of a bunk or "sling near the forward torpedo tubes." His Captain called him up one day and "proceeded to call him every vile name in the book" and made sure the rest of the crew heard all of this over the intercom. Don was rattled and "the tears began to flow." The Captain then surprised him by saying, "Don, are you a man?" To which Don answered, "Yes sir!" "Then don't let anyone on this ship talk to you like I just did!" Don then had a lot of respect for his Captain and his "attitude changed." However, being in such tight quarters, tempers flared among the men and Don had his "fair share of fights" with the other sailors. He remembered that in one of these, he got hit so hard by one of the sailors that his "tongue even hurt the next day." The USS *Ronquil*'s official website indicates that, during her five war patrols, the *Ronquil* damaged 10,800 tons of enemy shipping and sent 21,600 tons to the bottom. She was awarded the Submarine Combat Patrol Insignia, six engagement stars on the Asiatic-Pacific Area Service Ribbon and the Navy Occupation Service Medal, Pacific.

Don heard about the end of the war while stationed in Pearl Harbor and was eventually discharged from the Navy at the University of Oklahoma campus in 1945. He hitched a ride to Dallas and took a bus to Longview where his brothers picked him up. He said his mother was "so happy that all four of her sons returned home safely." He married Dorothy in 1947, and they had two girls and a boy. Both girls graduated from college and his son and grandson graduated from the Naval Academy. Dorothy graduated from Texas College in Tyler, Texas, and spent 35 years teaching in the Lubbock Public School System. Don finished his degree in education from Bishop College in Marshall, Texas, then obtained a master's from Texas Tech and spent over 50 years as a special education teacher at various schools, including Dunbar and Estacado High Schools in Lubbock.

31

HOMER JONES
The Long Road Home

Homer Jones was born "on the farm" near Slaton, Texas, on April 23, 1923, as one of nine children. He graduated Slaton High School in 1941. He enlisted in the Army Air Corps in December 1942, because he "wanted to learn to fly." His basic training was at Kelly Air Field in San Antonio, Texas, where he trained on a PT-19 (Primary Trainer). Due to depth perception issues, Homer "washed out" of flight school but wanted to remain in some flight capacity. Next, he trained at Ft. Stockton Field, Texas, then Scott Field, Illinois, for radio and Morse code. Then it was on to Yuma, Arizona, for gunnery school and Tucson, Arizona, for combat and crew training. This is where Homer found out he would be flying in a B-24 with a crew of 10 airmen.

Homer's war began with a flight from Tucson to Lincoln, Nebraska, with other crew members to pick up a new four-engine B-24 bomber they called "Cameron's Crew," named for pilot James Cameron. It was on to Bangor, Maine, where the crew then began the long trek to Europe. They flew over Newfoundland, the Azores, Casablanca, Morocco, North Africa and finally on to their base in Foggia, Italy. His first mission was in September 1944, where they flew to bomb a railroad yard in Yugoslavia. They flew 21 straight missions, one every night for three weeks. While the allies "owned the skies," they were still subject to flak on every mission. Homer said that "when the flak hit your plane, there was shrapnel flying everywhere." Their luck finally ran out on September 24, 1944, when they were shot down over Saloniki, Greece. All the crew, except the pilot, parachuted out together. Homer said this was his scariest moment in the war. He said he "didn't like jumping six feet, much less jumping out of a spiraling plane going down!" His crew was taken prisoner by the Germans upon landing. They later found out that the pilot of the plane, James Cameron, had jumped out later and was being hidden from the Germans by Greek mountain people.

31. Homer Jones

Homer and his crew were interrogated by the Germans immediately upon capture. Their primary mission was to bomb the ports and railroad yards to disrupt supply shipments to German troops. They were then loaded on a train and headed to Germany. Even this was a harrowing trip as the train was being bombed by Yugoslavian troops and to add insult to injury, they were even strafed by American P-51s. They finally made it to their prison camp just inside the Austrian border. The camp held 3,000 Russian soldiers and only 56 American and British. He stayed in this camp until him and one of his crew, Wilson Leon, the engineer, escaped by climbing over an 8-foot barbed-wire fence at 2:00 a.m. in a blinding snowstorm. They were aided by Chetnik guerrillas, led by General Draza Mihailovich, who had killed all 30 German guards and then led the prisoners into the hills.

Homer and Wilson were led back to Yugoslavia and began a long trek through Europe to try and get back to an Allied occupied area. They went into Hungary, across Romania and into Bulgaria, where they ended up in the capital, Sofia, where they stayed in an American Mission about 6 weeks and were finally flown back to their base in Italy on April 10, 1945. Homer said that he sometimes went as much as 2 or 3 days without food. That and the constant fear of being recaptured was always on their minds.

Not long after Homer and his crew were shot down, his parents received a telegram from the War Department that his plane had "been shot down, that he was MIA [missing in action] and no parachutes were seen being deployed." They immediately thought the worst—their Homer was gone. Sometime during their imprisonment, the pilot of their B-24 who had been in hiding with the Greek mountain people came across a German magazine and saw a picture of his crew being paraded down a street by German troops. He immediately sent this information to the War Department and they sent the picture of the crew members to the families to let them know that their loved ones were in fact still alive and probably in a German prisoner of war camp. This was the first time they knew that Homer survived the crash and might still be alive.

Homer's war in Europe was finally over when he departed Italy for the United States on June 17, 1945, aboard the USS *West Point* (AP-23). He arrived on June 23, 1945, and after rehab in Florida, was discharged November 6, 1945, in Roswell, New Mexico. He met and eventually married Jo Pruitt from Wilson, Texas, on June 1, 1946. He then enrolled in Texas Tech in 1946 and received his bachelor's degree in 1948. He said he "went straight through and graduated in 3 years." He also earned his master's degree in 1960. He retired from Wellman ISD after 35 years as an agriculture education teacher. He then worked for Wellman Gin as a bookkeeper for 18 more years and did not retire again until he was 80 years old. Homer and Jo had 5 children, including twin boys. Sadly, one of the twins was killed in a car accident. Homer said that was "the hardest thing Jo and [he] ever went through."

While searching a World War II website, Homer's son Rick came across a photo of his old crew and eventually found Homer's good buddy Wilson Leon living in Florida. Rick said he "nearly fell out of the chair" when he found out it was the same guy that escaped with Homer back during World War II. They met in Florida in May 2009, after not seeing each other for 64 years and the tears and memories flowed freely. Mr. Jones went on the 2011 Texas Panhandle Honor Flight. He said he still likes to tell schoolchildren about his experience during the war and he tells them that he "learned when his freedom was gone as a POW that we [the United States] are more free than any nation under the stars."

32

JUSTIN T. JONES
Glider Recovery

Captain Joseph DeDera received his orders from his commander, Colonel Albert Price, in late September 1944 in Aldermaston, England. His mission was to recover gliders used in the invasion of Holland. Just days before, the 1st Allied Airborne invaded Holland in an effort to seize the bridges over the Rhine and make an end run around the Siegfried Line. It didn't work. The Nazis were prepared for the move, and the Allies were stopped just short of the Rhine. The Holland landings were successful, however, and several cities were liberated. Lubbock resident Justin T. Jones took part in the glider recovery effort. A little-known but critical mission during World War II, it was a highly dangerous assignment.

Justin was born in 1921 to Clyde and Dora Jones. His father was a farmer and his "mother and grandmother ran the whole family." During his rare time off, he loved fishing "with a willow pole, using grasshoppers as bait." He graduated from Byers High School in 1938. He moved to Lubbock, planning to attend Texas Tech, but said he "found out how much money I didn't have!" Instead, he landed a job at Coca-Cola. On December 7, 1941, the attack on Pearl Harbor stunned all of America. Justin saw an ad in the *Lubbock Avalanche-Journal* to join up for Lubbock Army Flying School. He and 152 West Texas men signed up on December 12, 1941. The men were sent to Ft. Sill, Oklahoma, to "get shots and uniforms." Then it was back to the Lubbock Airfield. There were only 39 enlisted men and three officers stationed there when they arrived.

After very little training, they were "on the flight line working with PT-19 trainers." After two months, they moved up to AT-6s, then AT-9s and finally AT-11s. Justin was unable to make cadet because of poor eyesight. His next stop was Will Rogers Field in Oklahoma City where the 458th Air Service Squadron was formed. The squadron was reorganized at Barksdale Army Air Field and sent to Ft. Dix, New Jersey, shipping out on a troop carrier to Liverpool, England. The squadron had been at Aldermaston, England, for several months when they were ordered on the glider mission to Holland. On October 2, 1944, more than 100 mechanics and four officers were airlifted to Eindhoven, Holland, with lots of equipment, including jeeps and trailers, to load into 20 C-47 aircrafts. This was part of mission Operation Market Garden.

The retrieval zone was called the LZ-W at Zon, Holland. There were hundreds of CG-4A gliders (707 to be exact) scattered all over the countryside. The three detachments on the field soon realized that Zon was a hot zone, where British and German artillery units were shelling back and forth. The men did not get much sleep here as the shelling could commence at any time. The work was tedious, and many gliders had been damaged. The gliders were made by three different manufacturers, and some of the parts were not interchangeable, complicating the mission. The men also had to watch out for land mines left by the Germans. Some of the gliders themselves were even booby-trapped. The gliders were taken back to an air strip, repaired and picked up by transport; some were even picked up by a tow rope that would "snatch the glider off the ground."

The next retrieval zone had 60 gliders. At this location, the squadrons were bombarded by German 88-millimeter artillery. One airman was killed by a direct hit, and three were wounded. The V-1 and V-2 rockets launched by the Germans were visible from their bivouac area. The Battle of the Bulge was about to begin, and the men could also see British Spitfires and German FW-190s dog-fighting at tree level. Early in January 1945, their mission completed, they returned to Reims, France, where the squadron was deactivated (it was in Reims where German Marshall Alfred Jodl signed the German surrender on May 7, 1945). On March 24, 1945, 906 reconstituted CG-4A gliders joined the Allied air armada and descended into Wesel, Germany, and "helped deliver hundreds of fighting men and air power due to the ingenuity, resourcefulness and hard labor of aircraft mechanics in Holland several months before." This was the mission called Operation Varsity.

Returning to the United States from Le Havre, France, Justin was discharged at Ft. Sam Houston on October 19, 1945. He was awarded numerous medals for his service, including the Bronze Star. Returning to Lubbock, he went back to Coca-Cola and worked as a manager for several years. He met and married Winona Cawthorn in 1948. They had four daughters, four grandchildren and seven great-grandchildren. After leaving Coca-Cola, Justin bought a Curtis Candy franchise, then a Borden's distributorship in Levelland, Texas, where he spent 17 years.

Gliders played a significant role in the war. The Military History Now website provides the following interesting information: "Troops dropped by parachute risked being scattered over vast areas, while gliders could land hundreds of infantry with a much greater degree of precision." Because they were quiet, "they also afforded a better chance of surprise ... often landing undetected.... More than 5,000 glider pilots were trained by the United States military alone in World War II. The aircrews suffered casualty rates exceeding 30 percent. Most of these aviators were trained in Lubbock, Texas. Today, the city is home to the Silent Wings Museum, which is dedicated to preserving the memory of these brave fliers."

Justin Jones's role in glider retrieval helped fill the skies with American air power, helping the Allies secure victory in Europe and earning his place among the Greatest Generation.

33

LAMAR JONES
Always a Merchant

It seems that Lamar Jones was destined to be a merchant in more ways than he ever realized. Born to W.A. and Dorothy Jones in Bokchito, Oklahoma, Lamar's father was a merchant who owned a dry-goods store in the small town of Odell, Texas, before moving to Plainview, Texas, in 1930 during the Depression. Lamar said he "started working in his dad's stores when he was 12 or 13 years old." He graduated from Plainview High School in 1944 where he "played football and was a good student." He attended Texas A&M for two semesters. Many young men and women were still signing up to serve their country during World War II, and Lamar wanted to do his part. He was also inspired by his older brother who was serving as a navy pilot.

Lamar tried to sign up to be a commissioned officer in both the Army Air Corps and the Navy, but both had closed their enrollment by the time he applied. It was suggested that he try the Merchant Marine. During peacetime, the Mariners (they were not Marines) carried imports and exports. However, during World War II, the U.S. Government determined the cargo and destinations, contracted with private companies and put guns and Navy personnel on board. After signing up for the Merchant Marine in Kansas City, Lamar reported to basic training in Sheepshead Bay in Brooklyn, New York. The U.S. Maritime Service Training Station, which opened on September 1, 1942, and closed on February 28, 1954, was the largest maritime training station during World War II and could train up to 30,000 merchant seamen each year. He was supposed to attend a 13-week radio school on Gallups Island in Boston Harbor, but the program was cut after 12 weeks, so it was back to Sheepshead Bay for a time.

Lamar's first voyage was on the auxiliary patrol vessel *Aloma Hills* in December 1945. In May of 1946, Jones also served on a coastal tugboat up and down the eastern seaboard. His next voyage was "as a Junior

3rd Engineer on the tanker SS *Elk Basin* in July 1946 from Baytown, Texas, to England, which then crossed the Dutch Netherlands on a very small canal, where it looked like you were sailing on land." They docked at Danzig by the sea as the postwar effort began. This was an important port to the Germans during World War II and to the Americans afterward. While on shore, Lamar couldn't help but notice the "total devastation of the town and the haunted look of fear on the local residents' faces." He saw the results of war, and it stays with him still.

After a trip to the Caribbean, it was back to Galveston, Texas, where he was discharged after two years of service. He headed back to Plainview and began working in his father's mercantile stores again. He met his wife of 66 years, Bettye, on a blind date where they "went to a Texas Tech football game and then to the HI-D-HO Drive-In, where I always ordered a lot of food." Always a heavy eater, Jones recalled that "my mother said that when I married Bettye, she gained a daughter and lost a grocery bill." Lamar and Bettye had four daughters. Lamar bought the Vogue Dress Shop in Lubbock in 1954 and owned it for 50 years. His wife ran another shop on 34th Street for 17 years. All four girls worked at the shops growing up, and Lamar noted with pride that "all the girls graduated from Texas Tech." Lamar and Bettye were active in their community, church, and volunteer service organizations. Bettye, the love of his life, passed away in November 2016.

Still active, Lamar is an avid bridge player, playing three times a week at various locations in Lubbock. He even played tennis until he was 87 years old. While reflecting on his life, he noted that he "had several nice friends while in the service and many good friends all through his life."

Merchant Mariners like Jones had to wait a long time to be recognized for their service. This excerpt from the *Los Angeles Times* in January 1988 explains:

> *The Defense Department, yielding to pressure from a federal court ruling, responded earlier this month to four decades of appeals from World War II oceangoing Merchant Mariners and granted them veterans' status.*
>
> *Under the decision, thousands of (men) who fought in World War II— and saw their fellow Merchant sailors die at a higher rate than either Army or Navy forces—are now eligible for full veterans' benefits.*

34

R.D. JONES
Sailing the Pacific

World War II Navy veteran R.D. Jones says that he "learned a lot in the Navy." Joining in 1942 (he didn't want to wait to be drafted by the Army), Jones went through training in San Diego where he stayed for about three months. He was assigned to the USS *Matsonia* (ID-1589), formerly the cruise liner SS *Matsonia*, which was pressed into service by the Army as a troop carrier during World War II under the name USAT *Etolin*. The ship had also transported troops during World War I.

R.D. Jones was born near Union, Texas, to Riley David, a farmer, and Thelma Jones. R.D. was the oldest of three boys, all of whom served in the military during World War II. One brother served in the cavalry, and R.D. and his other brother served in the Navy. R.D. graduated from high school in Brownfield, Texas, in 1940, where he played football, and he enjoyed studying agriculture. He attended Texas Tech for two years before joining the Navy.

The *Matsonia* shipped out for New Guinea, and R.D. recalls that "the ship spotted a possible submarine and fired at a kamikaze that had dropped a bomb." Dry-docked in New Guinea, R.D. helped direct the boom and loading of the USS *Regal* with food to take to other ships. He remembers vividly seeing ships being hit by kamikazes. On holidays, his ship "would feed the troops on the island, and they were happy to get a good meal instead of rations." Once, he and "some buddies headed into the jungle and found a swimming hole. I dove in and got into an underground current and swallowed some water, barely getting out alive. I said, 'Friends, let's go back to the ship. I'm never coming back to the jungle!'" The natives would "climb up the trees to get a coconut and would trade it for a pack of cigarettes. I tried to climb up, too, but slid down." After being on the ship for a year, he finally got to go to Sydney, Australia, for a 10-day leave. The people were very friendly, and "they ate a lot of fish and chips and drank beer."

34. R.D. Jones

One of his division officers "thought R.D. could be officer material." He passed the test and was sent back to the States where he attended Texas Christian University. (He had five colleges to choose from.) His "math was not strong enough," so he "left TCU after 90 days and was sent to New Orleans, Louisiana," where he was assigned to the USS *Karnes* (APA-175), a troop and cargo ship. Shipping back out to the Pacific, R.D. remembers just when they passed the equator. The ship sailed in convoy and landed troops at Saipan and other staging areas in the Pacific Ocean. Among other memories, the former sailor recalls some "impromptu boxing matches." He also remembers how sad it was to see his first burial at sea. "One of the soldiers was cleaning his rifle, and it went off and killed another soldier."

Jones spent the rest of his service on the *Karnes*. His memories include running into a friend on one of the islands and another time "delivering a load of beer for the troops on liberty." He still remembers when the ship "encountered a large typhoon and the bow [of the ship] would rise up out of the water and fall back down." The *Karnes* also took troops to Okinawa. R.D. recalled that "two or three heavy cruisers were lined up and the big guns were booming [lobbing shells on the entrenched Japanese]." "I saw Navy planes fly over the ships with bombs underneath, and a kamikaze plane hit one of the ships. A little boat put smoke around the big ships. I also saw a destroyer chase a Japanese torpedo boat. Later, we left Okinawa and headed for the Hawaiian Islands to practice for the invasion of Japan. On the trip over, a coxswain and a radioman fell over the side and drowned." When the war ended in August 1945, "every ship horn went off in the Hawaiian Islands." Married men were allowed to go home; single men were not so lucky. They were shipped out to Sasebo, Japan, as part of the occupation.

R.D. was discharged in 1946. He took a train from San Francisco to Lubbock, then a taxi to Brownfield, where he noted that his "folks were real glad to see him." He began farming west of town. He met his future wife, Delma Jean, at a drugstore. They married in 1947. He was 24; she was 16. They had three boys and one girl. One of his boys, Jerry, was working on a water hole for horses when he fell in and passed away. Delma Jean died at the age of 50 in 1982. R.D. later married Elizabeth Jo Jones in 1983, but he outlived her as well. She died in 2005.

R.D. Jones has lived a full life, but the memories of his years sailing the Pacific are still vivid. When asked what he would like to be remembered for, he said "to be a good example to others."

Special thanks to R.D.'s daughter, Jean Ann Banta, for her help with his story.

35

BOB KISER

*Pipeline, Purdue, Petroleum
and People Like Us*

It was late November 1944. Bob Kiser and his buddies were in their tents at the end of the runway of the 14th Air Force near Yunnanyi, China, when several Japanese bombers flew over. Bob said if they "had dropped their bombs just a few seconds sooner," he "wouldn't be here to tell the story." This was the closest call that Bob would have during the war. As he put it, "wars are funny things."

Bob Kiser was born on May 27, 1924, in Marion, Indiana. His father had fought in France during World War I. Bob enlisted in the Army in December 1942 while attending Purdue University, where he hoped to get a degree in electrical engineering. In May 1943, after one year at school, he was called up to active duty and sent to Camp Wheeler, Georgia, for basic training. He was then sent to the University of Alabama for more engineering and math classes, basically repeating his freshman year in college. Following this, he attended Petroleum Engineering School at Camp Claiborne, Louisiana. After completing his training, his class was assigned to the 1382nd Engineering Petroleum Distribution Company. In August 1944 they were sent to Camp Anza, California, to board the USS *General George M. Randall* (AP-115). He arrived in Bombay, India, two months later.

After a long train ride to northeast India, Bob and his company began constructing a pipeline from Chittagong, India, to Kunming, China. "This was to supply aviation fuel to various locations to transport war materials and for bombing raids against the Japanese." In December 1944 the Japanese had been driven out of northern Burma and the pipeline could then be constructed in that region from China. It was here that pilots would "fly the hump" over the Himalayas, so they could attack Axis powers in Europe. It also became a launch site from which to attack Japanese islands.

35. Bob Kiser

Bob was in China when he heard the Japanese had surrendered and was glad to be going home to Indiana. He was discharged at the rank of T5 in December 1945 and was awarded numerous medals and ribbons, including the Asiatic Pacific Theatre Ribbon with three battle stars, Good Conduct and World War II Victory medals. He went back to finish his degree at Purdue University and graduated in June 1949. Bob says he likes to say he "started college in 1942, took a few years off and finally graduated in 1949!"

Bob met his future wife, Marna, in Marion, Indiana, and they married in April 1953. They had 3 children: Jane, Kurt and Carl. In the meantime, he embarked on a long and rewarding career in petroleum engineering, which took him to Venezuela, Australia, Malaysia, Carlinville, Illinois, and finally Midland, Texas, where he retired after 32 years of service with Exxon. Marna passed away in March 2008 after 54 years of marriage. Bob now resides at Raider Ranch.

An important thing Bob mentioned was that he "didn't make peace with the Japanese until 1984." He said he "always seemed to tear up." But one day over 30 years ago, he was "in the airport in Malaysia and noticed a pretty young Japanese woman with her baby in a stroller, and then her young husband came to join them." He looked at this young family and thought "they are just like us" and the hatred just "fell away."

Bob noted that "our job was not glamorous, yet I'm proud of my service."

36

CLEATUS LEBOW
"He Saved My Life Twice"

You might say that 95-year-old Cleatus Lebow is now living out his third life. He could have easily lost it twice back in August of 1945. He was asleep on his bunk a little after midnight on July 30 when he heard the first torpedo hit the USS *Indianapolis*. According to Lebow, "It had a totally different sound. I knew it was a torpedo. It hit forward on the opposite side of the ship that I was on. Then another one hit just after the first, a little farther back." Cleatus couldn't have known it at that instant, but he had only twelve minutes to live or die. When he found out that the ship sank in twelve minutes, he said, "I thought more time had gone by." Only fate had Cleatus on the opposite side of the two torpedo strikes. He recalled, "I had passed my written test for FC 2C [Fire Control 2nd Class] two weeks earlier, but one of the CPOs [Chief Petty Officers] was reluctant to give me the test on practical factors. Our division officer was sure I could perform the work. He gave me the test that afternoon and I passed. He then asked me to move from my quarters in the after-part of the ship up forward near the sick bay and powder magazine for the two forward 8-inch gun turrets."

How did a boy from Abernathy, Texas, end up on a sinking ship half a world away? One of 11 children, Cleatus Archie Lebow was born to Samuel Houston and Elizabeth Lebow near Happy, Texas, on February 8, 1924. Later, the family moved to Abernathy. Farm life was hard during the Dust Bowl as it was for many farmers around the country. Cleatus recalled that, in spite of all the hard work, "all in all, it was a happy childhood." He played baseball and a little football at Abernathy High School and graduated in 1941. He married Norma Crow on December 12, 1941, just five days after the Japanese attacked Pearl Harbor. "I was inducted into the U.S. Navy in Lubbock, Texas, on February 12, 1943. I thought it would be safer in the Navy." He would find out otherwise. "The seven men inducted from Lubbock were sent to boot camp in San

36. Cleatus Lebow

Diego, California. After boot camp, I spent several months in general detail at the destroyer base there. In December, I got sailing orders for Pearl Harbor. We left San Diego on a minesweeper. It took three days to make the trip to San Francisco and I was sick the whole time. I was never seasick again after that. I spent 30 days on Goat Island as a shore patrolman."

Cleatus headed for Pearl Harbor. "I left Goat Island on an LST [Landing Ship, Tank] and made it to Pearl Harbor ten days

Cleatus Lebow, U.S. Navy, World War II.

later. After three days, I was called to go on the USS *Indianapolis*. I recall thinking, 'What a sleek good looking ship.' We set sail for the adventure of this ole country boy's lifetime." The *Indianapolis* sailed to the Gilbert Islands, the Marshalls, the Asiatic-Pacific raids at Palau and Yap, then on to the Marianas where Saipan was captured. Lebow would receive 8 battle stars on his Asiatic-Pacific ribbon. Lebow recalled, "As a range-finder operator, I had a ringside seat to all of the landings. The toughest and bloodiest was Iwo Jima. ... I could not have been prouder than I was on the morning of February 23, 1945 when I watched them raise the American flag on Mt. Suribachi. We went back to continue our bombardment of Okinawa for the upcoming landing. On the morning of March 31, 1945, we were hit by a kamikaze. After getting patched up a bit, we headed back to Vallejo, California, for dry dock and major repairs.

"On June 1st, I was home on leave playing touch football with my brothers and sisters. I went into the house to get a drink of water. My mother followed me in from the porch and asked, 'Cletus, what's wrong.' I said, 'Oh, nothing.' She knew something was bothering me. I told her I was really dreading returning to the ship because I felt like something awful was going to happen. She said, 'I wish I could go with you but you know I can't, but we know who can.' I answered, 'Yes, Mama, Jesus can go with me.' I returned to the ship."

The *Indianapolis* would sail from San Francisco Bay to Pearl Harbor in a speed record of 74½ hours traveling at an average speed of 33 MPH, a record that still stands. Unbeknownst to Cleatus and crew, the *Indianapolis* would be carrying the atomic bomb to Tinian Island. Cleatus said, "We then went to Guam and left there for the Philippines."

"July 30, 1945, was much like any other Sunday in the war zone. Captain [Charles] McVay had requested an escort ship but was told there was no enemy subs [along our route] so we were not to worry." Cleatus and the crew of 1,197 men had plenty to worry about. The ship was hit by two torpedoes from the Japanese submarine I-58.

Cleatus continued, "Since we were not on the side of the ship that was hit, I had time to go back and slip on my shoes, shirt, pants and inflatable life belt before I went up to the main deck to the fire control workshop. There, I started passing out lifejackets and put one on myself. Smitty, Gaither and I went down one deck to help push a lifeboat off. The ship listed hard to starboard again and I told them we'd better get out of there. The ship rolled again as we were going up the ladder and the lifeboat crashed against the bulk head, crushing several men. By then, we knew we had to abandon ship even though the order hadn't been given yet. The three of us climbed over the gunwale and walked down the side of the ship right into the oily water. I never saw either one of them again. By the time I hit the water and started swimming, I

Cleatus Lebow wearing USS *Indianapolis* cap.

36. Cleatus Lebow

was shaking. I remembered Mama saying who would go with me, so I said a little prayer, Lord help me. Immediately a calm feeling of peace came over me. I'm sure this kept me from the urge of drinking the fatal salt water. Many of the men couldn't resist the urge.

"I heard someone holler, 'Over here,' so I swam towards a group that had four life rafts tied together with some guys hanging on the side. A cargo net came floating by and we attached it to the rafts and were able to hang on that way. We didn't have anything to eat or drink. The sharks came, the hot sun by day and the cold wind at night. We would recite the Lord's Prayer together morning and night. My hallucinations came in the twilight of the day we were found [after nearly 5 days in the water].

"I swam away from the group to some survival gear that was dropped from planes that morning. I did this two times and a friend, Clarence Hershberger from Indiana, swam out and pulled me back both times. He asked, 'What are you doing?' I said, 'Can't you see those crates of airplane parts out there? We can put one together and fly home.' He saved my life twice. Finally, the first positive sign of rescue appeared. On a mission in search of enemy subs, pilot Lt. Wilbur Gwinn noticed a long black streak of oil in the water below and dropped to a lower altitude to take a closer look. He noticed small black bumps in the water which became waving arms. He radioed his base back on Palau Island with his position and Lt. Adrian Marks took off with survival gear in his PBY-5A which could land on water, but the men were forbidden to try and land in the choppy ocean."

Upon arriving at the surreal scene, Marks noted men being attacked by sharks and landed his plane in the choppy water. Shutting down his engines, he proceeded to rescue some 56 men, some even strapped on the wings of the plane with parachute cord.

Still waiting in the water with his group, Lebow said, "After resting a little, I became lucid once again and remember a boat from the USS *Bassett* picking us up and taking us aboard their ship. Once onboard, I remember sitting on an overturned bucket while two seamen held me up and scrubbed all the oil off of me and gave me clean clothes." Cleatus told me that months after he got out of the Navy, he received a bill in the mail from them for the replacement clothes. He said, "I was furious. I won't tell you what I wrote back and told them, but let's just say that the Navy still has a bill outstanding! I sat down in the chow hall on the *Bassett* and drank a lot of orange juice and milk." Cleatus and other survivors were sent to Guam where they spent 30 days at a rest camp eating, drinking and resting. He said, "I never knew the Navy had chow that good anywhere!" Cleatus recalled, "While recovering, I received a letter from home. My mom said she was asleep in bed and thought she heard me calling her. She went out to the front porch to look. She repeated this once more and Dad asked her what she was doing and she said, 'I heard Cleatus calling me.' I looked at the date she wrote the letter. It was the date that the *Indianapolis* sank. I couldn't believe it!" It certainly seems that a mother's intuition for her family transcends time and space.

The war was over for Cleatus. "We shipped to San Diego on the USS *Hollandia*. I went home for a 30-day survival leave and then back to California where I was honorably discharged on November 11, 1945. I returned to Abernathy and went to work for the post office but didn't want to sit in a little building and sort mail the rest of my career. I wanted to move around. I went to work for a telephone company that later became GTE and worked there for 35 years and contracted with them for 10 more years. I divorced in 1964 and in 1966 I married Joan Edwards who worked at the phone company in Memphis, Texas." Joan grinned and said, "Cleatus came through town and said, 'Let's have coffee.' We've been having coffee ever since." When asked what he'd like to be remembered for, Cleatus repeated what fellow survivor Jimmy O'Donnell said: "Don't ever give up." Lebow also recalled his mother's words: "Remember who can go with you."

With only 317 survivors out of the crew of 1,197, the sinking was the worst Naval loss in history. The loss of the Indianapolis *was not made public by the Navy until August 15, 1945, two weeks after the sinking. The dropping of the atomic bombs and ultimate surrender of Japan dwarfed the news. Even though over 350 ships had been sunk during World War II, McVay was the only captain to be court-martialed. Unable to bear the loss of so many men and receiving letter after letter from families of lost sailors, McVay committed suicide in November 1968. Many of the survivors thought he was made a scapegoat and in 1999, they lobbied Congress to clear his name. Cleatus delivered strong testimony at a Senate hearing in September 1999 when he said, "Captain McVay was unjustly accused and should never have been court-martialed." In 2000, McVay's name was finally cleared.*

37

George Lewis
Occupied Germany

Rubble and destruction in Germany were everywhere in the fall of 1945, and George Lewis saw it up close. He was a corporal and squad leader with the 3458th Quartermaster Truck Company in charge of about 11 big trucks (part of a convoy) and was "in charge of teaching men how to drive them." His mission was to help repair the infrastructure after all the destruction to Germany during World War II. He remembers an especially arduous 14-day, 140-mile trek from Bamberg to Munich. Most of the railroads had been destroyed and travel was extremely slow in the months after the war.

George Sellers Lewis had attended high school in Broken Bow, Oklahoma, but only made it through 11th grade. In 1944 when he was 18, he met Lee Ester Yates at church. They soon married and their first child, George Lee Lewis, was born on May 26, 1945. Unfortunately, the young father received his draft notice and was inducted into the Army on August 20, 1945. He was sent for basic training to Ft. Leonard Wood, Missouri, and additional training in Cheyenne, Wyoming, and then on to South Carolina where he and his company were shipped out to Germany. Ester and baby George stayed with her mother.

George spent the next several months in Germany with his convoy of trucks hauling gravel to repair roads. After a trip back across the Atlantic, he "rode a troop train all the way from New York to Ft. Sam Houston in San Antonio" where he was discharged. After only one year, his service was over. He returned to his family in Paris, Texas, where he enrolled in a vocational school to be a tailor. George and Lee moved to Lubbock in 1950 where the family continued to grow and thrive. This writer was thoroughly impressed as George, after only a moment to reflect, was able to quickly name his 11 children in order of their birth: George Lee, James David, Mary, Ester, Beverly, Sherry, Winnie, Madeline, Curtis, Debbie and Pam.

George raised his large family, served in his church and worked hard for several companies throughout his career. Among them were Featherlite Block Company, T.G. & Y., the Social Security office, Lubbock Independent School District and Family Promise. When his wife, Ester, died in 1987, he met Rose Higgins from Plainview at a church meeting. They married in 1988 and celebrated 26 anniversaries before Rosie passed away in 2014.

Now 90 years young, George still attends Agape Temple, and he serves as a foster grandparent at the Lubbock State School. His supervisor John McCullough thought George would be a great candidate for the Texas South Plains Honor Flight. The World War II veteran was able to take that trip in 2016. George noted that he was proud to have served his country and was especially proud to go with his fellow veterans to Washington, D.C., to see the memorials and museums built in their honor. His favorite stop was at the Tomb of the Unknown Soldier, and he helped lay a wreath at the Korean War Memorial. He said he "would definitely recommend any veteran to go on this trip if they are able." George Sellers Lewis continues to be a man of service to his church, his community, his country and his fellow man.

38

NATHAN LUGER
The Aleutian Islands

From 1944 to 1945, TSGT Nathan Luger was sent to one of the most remote islands in the world. Attu Island is at the end of the Aleutian Islands chain and is 1,500 air miles southwest of Anchorage, Alaska. It holds the distinction of being the site of the only World War II land battle in North America. The Japanese occupied the island in June 1942 after the Battle of Midway. In May 1943 U.S. troops landed on Attu and eventually recaptured the island after heavy fighting that ended with one of the largest banzai charges of World War II. Out of the 1,000 Japanese troops who began the charge, only 28 remained alive.

Nathan was born in Brooklyn, New York, on May 27, 1919. He joined the Army in May 1938 and was sent to Ft. Dix, New Jersey, for basic training. He then joined the 112th Field Artillery HD in what was to be the Army's last horse-drawn artillery unit. He decided to transfer to the Army Air Corps and would be trained as a Morse code/radio operator and a waist gunner. Based out of Columbia Air Base in South Carolina, his crew would practice bombing targets along Myrtle Beach.

Nathan was assigned to the 11th Air Force, 77th Bomb Squadron on a B-25 Mitchell, which typically consisted of a crew of only 5 or 6 men. They flew numerous missions out of Attu when the harsh weather would permit. He recalled that they "lost lots of planes and crew members due to the bad weather" and that "the weather was so bad that sometimes they could only fly once a month." He would recall that they "dropped bombs on Kuriles, Tirishima and other islands and dropped propaganda leaflets on Kiska." Due to the long distance of the bombing runs, his plane could "only carry 6 bombs instead of the usual 12. They needed to replace the extra bombs to make room for extra fuel."

One day, one of the radio tower guys came to Nathan and asked him if he could take his place on one of the flights. Nathan cleared it with his crew chief and his replacement took off on a mission. It turned out to be a bit more than he bargained for. Nathan said he "had gone on numerous missions by this time without incident." However, when the flight his replacement went on came in and the landing gear wouldn't come down, they had to do a "belly landing." He said "the shook-up radio tower guy never asked to go on a flight again!"

When the Pacific War ended in September 1945, Nathan returned to the States where he joined the reserves to "get [his] 20 years in." He was eventually reassigned to South Plains Army Airfield in Lubbock, Texas, where some B17s were being retired and was "put in charge of the paperwork for the infirmary." He met his wife, Connie, in Lubbock and they were married in the chapel at Reese Air Force Base. Nathan wanted to take his new West Texas bride "back home to Brooklyn." She was very unhappy and homesick in New York. Nathan wisely decided "to keep his new wife happy," so after one year they returned to Lubbock for good. They had two girls and a boy. Nathan retired from the Air Force in May 1958 at the highest enlisted rank, Chief Master Sergeant. He worked for Toledo Scale for a time and then opened his own shop called Luger Scale Service. He retired in 1974 when the I-27 was being built and he was "bought out by the government." After nearly 50 years of marriage, Connie passed away in 1995. While playing dominoes with friends in 1998, Nathan was introduced to Marci Dodd, a widow, whose husband, Don (a 10-year Air Force veteran), had also passed away in 1995. Neither was "in a hurry to get married," but after seeing each other for 7 years, they tied the knot in September 2006.

Toward the end of our visit, Nathan showed me that he was a "card-carrying member of the 'I bombed Japan' club." Looking back on his time during World War II, he simply said he was "just glad when the war was over."

39

C.B. Martin
Life as a Seabee

C.B. Martin learned about the bombing of Pearl Harbor watching a movie with a buddy in downtown Lubbock, Texas, on Sunday, December 7, 1941. As C.B. noted, "Neither one of us had ever heard of Pearl Harbor and we had no idea where it was located. I was very aware of its location before the war was over!"

C.B. was drafted in September 1943 and was interviewed by a Navy Seabee recruiter. When he found out C.B. had construction experience, he offered to make him a Third Class Petty Officer. He decided right then to become a Seabee. The Seabees were formed as part of the Navy in the spring of 1942, by Admiral Ben Moreeall. He came up with the idea of a Construction Battalion that would be called Seabees. Their motto was "We build, we fight." As he noted wryly, "C.B. became a Seabee."

He and a buddy headed to Camp Peary near Williamsburg, Virginia, for boot camp. Here they learned the joy of military training. C.B. began to wonder if he had made a mistake. As he noted, "In the military if one guy fouls up, the whole platoon pays for it." After a two-week leave, he was on his way to Pearl Harbor and sailed past the ships that had been sunk on December 7, 1941, that he had heard about in that movie theater in Lubbock over two years prior. As C.B. said, "What a sight for a country boy."

After a three-month stay in Hawaii, C.B. shipped out to "parts unknown" in the Pacific on the USS *Storm King*. The crew of this converted German ship was from the Army and the only Navy personnel on board were Seabees. Their first stop was at an island called Kwayalain. From there they "just meandered around the Pacific trying to dodge submarines." On the morning of July 21, 1944, he witnessed battleships, cruisers and destroyers firing onto the island of Guam. When they finally landed on the beach, he saw a lot of destroyed tanks, trucks, various equipment and dead Japanese soldiers. The natives of Guam were treated very harshly by the Japanese. C.B. said their resentment of them was deep, but that they loved Americans.

Immediately after settling in, the Seabees began their real work. They "built roads, air fields, power plants, radio stations, warehouses and other projects all over the island." The Seabees knew to stay armed even while working. Toward the end of the war, they "built a makeshift prison camp for surrendering Japanese soldiers." C.B. said that "the Seabees were not noted for discipline." They were building a camp for incoming Marines when a Marine lieutenant came over to talk to the Seabee in charge and asked, "What do you have to do to rate a salute around here?" to which the Seabee answered, "I'll be damned if I know," turned around and walked off.

C.B. finally left Guam in the fall of 1945 and married Conny McDonald on December 21, 1945. After the war, C.B. and his brother Byron joined their dad Claude's construction business in Lubbock, Texas. Claude Martin and Sons built numerous structures around the South Plains, including fire stations, schools, banks and office buildings as well as private homes. C.B. and his wife enjoyed traveling the world. C.B. enjoyed taking photos while Conny painted. C.B. became a watercolor artist later himself. He was a member of the Geriatric Art Society, aka the GAS Group. As to his time in the service, he would say later in life, "I am proud I was able to serve the good ole USA during World War II."

40

HERSCHEL MARTIN
One Man, Three Branches of Service

Herschel Martin received his "greetings from the U.S. Government" in March of 1946. Drafted into the Army, he completed eight weeks of basic training at Ft. Sam Houston in San Antonio, Texas, a training post during World War II. After basic training, Herschel's outfit was sent to a "Repo Depot" (replacement troops) in Baltimore, Maryland. He said it was "crowded with GIs waiting to go overseas." Sailing out of Ft. Dix, New Jersey, Herschel thought they were headed to Europe. "The Army never told us where we were going." To their surprise, they wound up going through the Panama Canal, then on to California. The outfit then headed for the South Pacific on a converted supply ship. After a stop at sea for repairs from a storm two days out of Hawaii, they were bound for the Philippines as part of the Army of Occupation.

Herschel Martin was born near Lorenzo, Texas, on December 31, 1927. He was one of ten children, five girls and five boys, born to Ira and Selena Dixon Martin. After graduating from Lubbock High in 1945 at age 17, he had joined the Merchant Marine. The U.S. Merchant Marine provided the greatest sealift in history for fighting forces around the world during World War II. Herschel spent time working on a tanker that moved between San Pedro, California, and Seattle, Washington. A union strike in Seattle grounded the ship he was on, and he left the Merchant Marine. He took a train back to Lubbock. As soon as he got home, his draft notice was waiting for him. Herschel became a soldier in the U.S. Army.

After his unit arrived in the Philippines, Martin was assigned to the motor pool. He noted that "a POW camp joined us there, and I was in charge of five prisoners. I could not understand them, and they couldn't understand me. We each had a translation book, so we could communicate." When he told one of the prisoners that he was from Lubbock, Texas, the young man shouted, "Cowboy!" He added that the prisoners were treated well by most of the men. While "some of the men that had seen combat or lost loved ones were rough on the prisoners, I treated them like human beings." Herschel left the Philippines in March 1947 and shipped back to the States, where he was discharged. He met Earlene Bloodworth while attending Calvary Baptist Church, and they married on September 19, 1947. The couple had three sons and one daughter.

Since Herschel signed up for the U.S. Air Force Reserve (to get out two weeks early in 1947), he was called up for Korean War service in 1950 and sent to Reese Air Force Base, which had been re-activated in 1949. He was active at several duty stations until 1973 when he "retired from the whole military." He had served in three different branches of service. After leaving the service, Herschel returned to the U.S. Post Office where he had been working before being recalled. A friend later got him on as a policeman for the City of Lubbock; Herschel jokingly said, "I decided he wasn't my friend after all." He retired from the police force in 1988 after 15 years of service.

Herschel was honored to go on the 2013 South Plains Honor Flight not just to see the memorials and museums, but to "visit with my fellow veterans." Herschel has given a lifetime of service—in three different branches of the military, and in law enforcement; that's the definition of a hero.

41

JOHN MCDONOUGH
The Tall Texan

John McDonough, now 95 years old, still stands tall. In 1943, he was 19 years old and stood 6'2". In 2018, that doesn't sound particularly tall, but the average male soldier during World War II stood around 5'6" to 5'8", according to various sources. John was born to John and Minnie McDonough on December 16, 1923, near Plainview, Texas. He had two brothers and three sisters. He graduated from Petersburg High School in 1942, where he played basketball and preferred math classes. Both of his brothers served in the military; one served during the Korean War era and one during the Vietnam era. John also attended Lippert's Business School until he was drafted into the Army on February 19, 1943.

Basic training for John was at Camp Hulen, Texas. He was assigned to the newly created Headquarters Battery 554th Anti-Aircraft Artillery Battalion. Next, he was sent to Tennessee Maneuvers for combat training. In Ft. Jackson, South Carolina, his unit learned to fire on targets. His unit received overseas orders and was sent to Camp Kilmer, New Jersey, where they boarded the RMS *Queen Mary* (converted to a troop ship) and sailed for Glasgow, Scotland, on March 1, 1944. "The *Queen Mary* changed course every seven minutes [to avoid German submarines]," John pointed out. His outfit was attached to the 29th Infantry Division. Sent to Leek, England, for a time, the unit boarded a small ship for the trip to Normandy, France, on June 8, 1944. "After sitting on the water for five days due to rough seas, we finally landed at Port-en-Bessin-Huppain in lower Normandy around June 12, 1944." This was only six days after the Allies landed. "The front was only four to five miles away. We could hear the gunfire. The bodies of Americans and Germans were lined up like cord wood along the hedgerows. We received a lot of AP [armor-piercing] bombs and strafing."

"The first French town we came to [St. Lo] was completely destroyed," he noted. "We [our unit] were the support for the front-line troops. We had a twin-mounted Bofers 40mm gun on a four-wheel trailer." The rapid-firing gun could operate up to 120 rounds per minute in bursts. "We had a commander who wanted us to see Paris, France, and I had a one-day pass; I just happened to be there the day it was liberated [August 25, 1944]." The 29th Infantry moved on up through France, liberating small towns as they went. John noted that he was "in Heerlen, Holland, for Christmas and was there when the Battle of the Bulge began. We were close to the British units and were part of seven divisions. All of them pulled out except our division. We were the only ones left to hold the front line." The 29th was in Holland from December to February.

When asked about the scariest time in combat, John shared, "I was headed back to HQ to pick up the mail [John was in charge of the mail for 850 men] with another soldier in a 6x6 truck when we were strafed by a German airplane while crossing the Rhine on a pontoon bridge. All you can hope for is that the pilot was a bad shot!... We chased the Germans all the way to the Elbe River, which was only 22 miles from Berlin. We were ordered to stop there, so the Russians could take Berlin." Once more a witness to history, John happened to be on a three-day pass in Brussels, Belgium, on V-E (Victory in Europe) Day when Germany surrendered. John's unit remained in Germany as part of the occupation force. They shipped out in December 1945 from Bremerhaven, Germany, and headed back to New Jersey. John was discharged on January 22, 1946, at Ft. Sam Houston, Texas. He received the American Theater Campaign, EAME Theater Campaign with four bronze stars, the Good Conduct Medal, the Victory Ribbon and three Overseas Service Bars.

After heading back to Plainview, John became a building contractor. He met his future wife, Barbara Mickey, at church. They were married on August 8, 1948. They had five children, 12 grandchildren and 18 great-grandchildren. John said that Barbara, who passed away on March 7, 2017, was "the center of [his] life." He misses her every day.

John's contribution to the war effort had more to do with his inner character than his height. He is an example of the kind of soldier who is held in such high esteem by liberated Europeans to this day. The tall Texan got to witness history being made, and he and others like him are the reason American history books document an Allied victory in World War II.

42

GENE MCLENDON
A Good Citizen

Gene McLendon worked at the newly opened Lamesa Army Airfield in the summer of 1942. The field was used as a glider training facility and young McLendon got to ride in one of the tow planes and said, "I got a desire to fly." Dolphus Eugene McLendon was born on November 18, 1923, to Oscar Folkes (O.F.) and Mamie Light McLendon at home on Skinout Mountain in Jones County, Texas. "My father was an itinerant farmer and we moved around a lot. We moved to a farm 8 miles south of O'Donnell [Texas] when I was only 4 years old. I went to Hancock School until I was in the 10th grade. I went to Lamesa High School and graduated there in 1941. I played football, basketball and baseball. My favorite subjects were history and Latin (I wanted to be a lawyer)."

Gene attended Texas Tech in 1941 and joined the Army Air Corps reserves on November 11, 1942, which was supposed to give him a 3-year deferment. Gene noted wryly, "That 3-year deferment only lasted 3 months! I was drafted on February 15, 1943." McLendon's basic training took place at Sheppard Airfield in Wichita Falls, Texas. Next up was the University of Tennessee in Knoxville for special training. Here he would receive 10 hours of flight training. Then he was sent to Nashville to the Classification Center. Here he was grounded from flying. He said, "I was never sure why, but I think I had poor depth perception. I tended to bounce the plane when I came in for a landing, so that might have got me grounded."

Transferred to Jefferson Barracks in St. Louis, Missouri, Gene "developed a severe heat rash from head to toe" and was sent to Amarillo Army Air Field to a B-17 bomber mechanical school, then to Chanute Airfield for electrical specialist training. He was then sent to the replacement depot at Kelly Airfield in San Antonio, Texas. McLendon was finally assigned to the 69th Depot Repair Squadron, 301st Air Depot Group, 14th Air Force. On February 16, 1945, the 69th squadron left Kelly Field headed for Camp Anza, Riverside, California. They prepared to go overseas; however, the exact location was unknown. Their ship set sail and they arrived in Melbourne, Australia, crossing the equator twice. They arrived in Bombay, India, and then endured a 7-day train ride to Camp Kamcharapara, Calcutta. They were divided into three convoys of approximately 75 vehicles that were 6 by 6, 2½-ton Army trucks to prepare for the journey into Kunming, China. The roads were often mountainous and treacherous. The 1,800-mile journey took them around 30 days. For the next three months they focused on the mission of driving the Japanese out of China. They essentially helped open the Burma Road.

Gene noted, "The closest I came to combat is when Chiang Kai-shek, the leader of the Republic of China, was heading to our area. He was a social conservative but also fought with the Communist Party for control of China. There was a fracture group near our post that didn't like him and Kai-shek came over with part of his Army and attacked them. I'm sure he had their leader hung. Our commander told us to stay out of their way. It was over in just 2 or 3 days." Gene recalled, "We had pickled [put heavy-duty grease in the engines] some P-51 Mustangs and were ordered to degrease them and our government had us send them to the communists. That really made me mad."

Gene left China in March 1946 and returned to the United States in April. He took a train from Seattle to Ft. Bliss in El Paso, Texas, and was discharged there on April 14, 1946. Gene's 3-year "deferment" turned into a 3-year stint in the Army Air Corps. Back in West Texas, Gene returned to Texas Tech and obtained a degree in accounting. He went to work for Standard Oil in Tulsa, Oklahoma, and then returned to Tech to work toward a graduate degree. He went to work for the accounting firm of Arthur Andersen in Houston and Glasscock Drilling in Corpus Christi. He was transferred to Mesa Drilling in Denver where he met and married Ann Justice. They had a son and a daughter.

Gene and Ann would divorce and Gene eventually moved back to Lamesa. Here he would meet and marry Lattie Ellen Light who had 5 children (2 were already married). The newlyweds would move to El Paso for several years where Gene worked in accounting. The couple would eventually move back to Lamesa where Gene opened his own accounting office and worked at that for many years. Sadly, Lattie passed away November 28, 2017. Gene has a large extended family with 6 grandchildren, 14 great-grandchildren, and 3 great-great-grandchildren. Reflecting on his long life, Gene said he'd like to be remembered as "a good citizen with a desire for knowledge."

43

TEDDY MCMILLAN
A Hero and a Good Man

World War II veteran Teddy McMillan (now 91 years old) was the last of 17 children born to A.A. and Mary Alice McMillan, who lived near Hermleigh, Texas. His father was a farmer/rancher, and Teddy spent his early childhood helping around the farm. He graduated from Hermleigh High School in May 1943 where he played football and softball. He remembered that his favorite subjects were music and history. Music became a lifelong passion, and Teddy himself became a part of history during his service in the Pacific in World War II.

Patriotism was almost universal during the 1940s, and Teddy and a buddy wanted to do their part, so they enlisted in the Marines in May 1944. They were sent to Parris Island, South Carolina, for eight weeks of basic training and eight weeks of field training at Camp Lejeune, North Carolina. Teddy recalled that "the training was tough. You had to do double time [run] all the time, and they would run your butt off. We were very well trained." After basic training, he was assigned to the 2nd Battalion. The 5th Marine Regiment is the most highly decorated unit in the Marine Corps. "After a train ride from North Carolina to California, we boarded the USS *Ernst* headed for the Pacific."

Since the unit was rushed into combat, they had to "endure a round of nine different immunizations on one of the Russell Islands, and everyone got sick." The Russells were only 50 miles from Guadalcanal. Teddy's unit "was put on a Higgins boat and seemed to go up and down the islands for a long time. Finally, we made a practice landing on Guadalcanal, which had already been secured." Then it was on to Cape Gloucester, Peleliu and finally Okinawa. The Marines "landed on Yellow Beach on Easter Sunday, April 1, 1945." The invasion of Okinawa began with a massive seven-day bombardment of the landing beaches where stiff resistance was expected. However, the Japanese had pulled back to defensive positions further inland.

Teddy's assignment was as "a front man in communications—we had a Jeep with a radio and an antenna—sometimes it worked and sometimes it didn't." He also relayed information via walkie-talkies. Being a "front man" meant you were out front and probing for the enemy—a very dangerous assignment. Teddy noted that "the Japanese were very sneaky, especially at night. The scariest time was pulling guard duty at night." He lost several buddies on Okinawa, which turned out to be the deadliest battle of the Pacific island campaign with almost 50,000 casualties and over 12,000 dead. Besides a "few scrapes and bruises," Teddy made it through unscathed. He said, "We didn't take any prisoners—the Japanese would fight to the death. The locals [on the island] were glad to see them [the Japanese] go." The bloody battle for Okinawa lasted 82 days. His unit was on its way to Hiroshima, Japan, when the atomic bomb was dropped. "We stayed in combat until August of 1945; then we were sent to Tinsing, China, to fight."

After the war ended, the young soldier returned to San Diego, where he was discharged from the Marines in August 1946. He was able to visit one of his brothers in Los Angeles before a long bus ride to Amarillo and then Snyder. His parents came to pick him up, and as he recalled, "We were sure glad to see each other—Mom cried a lot." He picked up where he left off with his music career and was in a group called the Ted Jay Combo. They played all over West Texas, even though "some of the places were pretty rough." Later on, he played with the Caldwell Band in Lubbock. He "worked at Snyder Laundry for over 25 years and got to know everyone in Snyder. In those days, you would deliver their clothes right to their house." He met and married Virginia Taylor in 1947. They had three boys and one girl. Later in life, his Virginia now gone, he met a lady named Shirley Snyder at the local Dairy Queen. They married in May 1982.

The World War II hero is modest about his military exploits and humble about being called a hero. "I had my good points and my bad points, but I always tried to be a good man."

44

FRANK MILLER

From a Quartermaster to a Headmaster

In May 1945, Frank Miller graduated from Marathon High School in Texas. His favorite subjects were math and industrial arts (shop). The love of these two subjects would serve him well in later life. While the war was coming to a close in Europe, it still raged on in the Pacific. Barely 18 years old, Frank received his "greetings" from the U.S. government and was drafted into the Army. He was born to Givens and Jewel Miller on April 11, 1927, at home outside of Sierra Blanco (White Mountain), Texas. His father worked for the Southern Pacific railroad. His mother ran the household. He had 2 brothers and 1 sister. His two brothers would also go into the Army. The oldest survived the Battle of the Bulge and the youngest was in the Korean War.

Frank was sent for basic training to Camp Joseph T. Robinson near Little Rock, Arkansas. The camp was built in 1917. Toward the end of his intensive training as an infantry rifleman (in preparation for the invasion of Japan), he recalls a "sergeant came through the barracks saying 'The war's over! The war's over!' We weren't sure what to think." With the war over, the government wasn't exactly sure what to do with all of the soldiers. The United States was now an Army of Occupation in Europe and in the Far East. After months of "marching and killing time," Frank went home for Christmas in December of 1945. In January he reported to Camp Picket in Blackstone, Virginia, and waited for further orders. After more marching, he finally received his orders. He would be going to France.

He was loaded on a bus with other soldiers and sent to New York City where they boarded a ship that would take them to Le Havre, France. "There were a lot of bombed-out ships still in the harbor." When he told his older brother about it, he said, "Don't tell me about Le Havre.

When I landed there we had to climb down a cargo net on the side of a big ship bouncing up and down. You got to walk off the ship!" Frank noted that due to a physical impairment, his brother was in charge of transportation and guarding German prisoners. Frank continued, "We were put on 40 and 8 boxcars and traveled for days due to so many tore-up railroad tracks." The French railroad was a more narrow gauge than in the States, so the box cars were smaller and they could only hold 40 men or 8 horses. During World War II, they were used to transport troops to and from the front.

The train stopped in Namur, Belgium, for a time, then headed to Paris. Frank was assigned to the Quartermaster Q177 unit. The Quartermaster Corps was established on June 16, 1775, just two days after the U.S. Congress authorized the Continental Army. The need for logistical support was critical to the new Army. During World War II, the Quartermaster Corps operated on a massive scale around the world. They provided over 70,000 different supply items and more than 24 million meals each day. They had also recovered and buried over 250,000 soldiers in temporary cemeteries around the globe. Frank's job in Europe was to pick up mail in Paris and send money orders. Unable to speak French, he had a French driver who drove an Army jeep on their trips into Paris.

Frank recalled a furlough to Switzerland and Italy. He "saw the rope where Mussolini was hung by his own people." He stayed in Academia della Farnesina (Mussolini's school for fascist youth), which had been converted into a hotel and swam in the former dictator's pool. After nearly a year in France and his service over, Miller paid $75 to fly home. He was "told to get rid of everything and report to Orly Field to catch a flight." However, an officer could bump an enlisted man off the list, and days became weeks. After six weeks of waiting, he and a buddy took a train to Bremerhaven, Germany, and boarded the USS *General R.L. Howze* (AP-134), headed for the States. The trip took 11 days and docked in New York City. Miller was discharged in Ft. Dix, New Jersey. He flew to El Paso on a cargo plane and "sat on the floor all the way to El Paso." He took a train to Marathon and his dad picked him up. His dad said, "Let's go home" and Frank said, "No, let's go buy me some clothes. I've been wearing the same smelly clothes for several weeks!"

After attending the University of Texas for a year, Frank wanted to move closer to home to economize and enrolled at Sul Ross State University. He graduated in 1950 with a major in industrial arts and a minor in math. He met Carol Westbrook while in college and they married in January 1950. They had one son, George. Frank got a job teaching math in Bronte, Texas, and Carol also taught there. On his second summer break, he and Carol took a trip to Carlsbad, New Mexico. On the way home, he told her, "Let's stop and visit our old friends Bob and Joann Bell in Snyder, [Texas]." They had been in each other's weddings while students at Sul Ross State. While visiting in Snyder, Bob told Frank that he should get a teaching job in Snyder (which was a much wealthier school district) and to call the superintendent. Back in Bronte, Frank called the superintendent but living outside of town, he was on a nine-party line so by the time he got back home everyone asked him if he was moving to Snyder! Frank and Carol did move to Snyder. He taught shop for a few years and Carol also taught. Frank was "demoted to be a principal at an elementary school" where he stayed for 22 years, finally retiring after 36 years of teaching and principalship.

Looking back on his long life, Frank said he would like to be remembered for his "teaching career and helping the kids get through life." That seems to have been accomplished, as he noted that "several of my kids (now adults) come up and say how they remember me and that makes me feel good."

45

HORACE MORGAN
From the Alcan to the Battle of the Bulge

He was born in Winters, Texas, in 1921, raised on a farm in Amherst, Texas, and a dangerous location in Europe was the last place Horace Morgan expected to find himself. PFC Morgan and his buddies heard Germans coming down the road. They hit the ditch, played dead and prayed they would not be seen. Morgan noted, "You didn't really know when it was safe to raise your head up." The German patrol finally did pass by, and the weary GIs moved on to one more town—one more to be taken in the push for victory in Europe. Horace was part of the 35th Engineer Combat Battalion. His company had been "moving all around Europe."

Horace left school in Amherst, Texas, "around the 10th grade" as he was needed to work on the farm. He was the eighth of ten children. He was drafted into the Army on August 10, 1942, in Lubbock and sent to Ft. Sill, Oklahoma, for basic training. Assigned to the 35th Engineer Combat Battalion, he was shipped to British Columbia to help build the Alaska-Canadian (Alcan) Highway. The secret project started in March 1942. The objective was to build a road to provide an overland route to American air bases in Canada and Alaska. It was thought at the time that the Japanese would try to invade the U.S. mainland through Alaska. The 400-mile road (which included 20 bridges) was built over rugged terrain in 18 months. Seven different engineer battalions worked to complete the road.

The 35th returned to the States in September 1943 and reorganized at Camp White, Oregon. The battalion was moved to Camp Shanks, New York, where they helped build and improve the camp's facilities while preparing for entry into the European Theater. They shipped out on July 2, 1944, for the trip across the Atlantic Ocean. Horace recalled that "all the guys were sick. One of the guys would stick his head out the porthole every so often to throw up. I never got sick, but there were a lot of sick guys." Once in Europe, the 35th was sent to northern France, where they helped capture the port city of Brest as well as thousands of enemy soldiers. Heading east, they cleared mines and repaired roads and bridges.

On September 28, the 35th crossed into Belgium. Horace remembered, "I was driving a truck all over. I saw casualties piled up, and I would notify our guys to go out and pick them up." During this time, he also helped to capture and guard German prisoners. He recalled that "one of the men got hit [by gunfire] and the bullet just went right across his stomach; it didn't even seem to hurt him." An M-1 sharpshooter, Morgan said he had target practice so much that he "got pretty good." On December 15, 1944, the Battle of the Bulge began, and the 35th was called up to help defend Bastogne from the German forces only nine miles away. Along with his good buddies, Lee Regenauer and Hank Ridgway, Morgan helped set up a .50 caliber machine-gun position and mines on the road while they rotated guard shifts. The 35th had spent three hard days defending the town. The 101st Airborne finally arrived and helped hold the town, which was a major turning point of the battle.

After a long hard winter and spring, the war was finally over, and Horace found himself "in Italy waiting for enough points to be sent home." He was "scheduled to go to Japan, but the war ended there, too." He finally arrived at Ft. Dix, New Jersey, and was discharged on November 17, 1945. He took a train to Lubbock and thoughtfully remembers that the "family just sat and looked at him. One of the brothers left at home had constantly prayed for our safe return." All three brothers made it home safely. Horace's sister, Velma, helped build P-51 Mustangs in Dallas during the war as a "Rosie the Riveter." Everyone in the family pitched in during World War II.

Back home and farming, Horace was introduced to Ellen Corley by a mutual friend. He simply said, "I liked her, and she liked me." They married in January 1946. They had two girls and two boys. Ellen passed away June 11, 2018, after 72 years of marriage.

Horace Morgan is a wonderful example of what we imagine when we try and think of the young soldiers America sent to war to save the world 75 years ago. They were united in their mission and brave and tenacious in the execution of it. The U.S. Army Corps of Engineers' motto is "Essayons"—Let us try. They tried; they succeeded; they secured victory for the Allies and for freedom. As he looks back to his service, the 97 year old understates, "When they said go, we went." Thank you, to you and all your brothers in arms, for "going."

46

FRANK ODOM
On the Front Lines in Europe

"You never get used to combat." Frank Odom, age 92, of Lubbock, Texas, spoke these words nearly 73 years after his time in the Army in Europe had ended. They could have been spoken by any one of the thousands of American combat soldiers during World War II. While over 16 million American men and women served during World War II, it is difficult to get an exact number on those engaged in actual combat. What is known is that, by April 30, 1945, over two million American soldiers had served in the European Theater. While the Americans were some of the best-trained soldiers in the world, nothing could have prepared them for actual combat. According to the veterans themselves, you simply had to witness it and endure it the best you could.

Frank Odom was born January 3, 1926, to John and Florence. His dad was a farmer and did odd jobs. He had two brothers who also served in the military. Frank grew up in Wickes, Arkansas, and went to a one-room school—eight grades in one room. He quit for a couple of years to help out his dad. He went back to high school and completed the 11th grade. He was drafted into the Army on March 18, 1944, and sent to Camp Fannin near Tyler, Texas, for 17 weeks of basic/infantry training. Next, he was assigned to Ft. Bragg, North Carolina, and the 100th Infantry Division, which was sending replacement troops into combat.

There were many rumors as to where the 100th was going to be sent—some said the Pacific, some said Norway. Neither destination was accurate. In August 1944, the word came down that they were to be sent to the European Theater. They boarded a train and headed for Camp Kilmer in New Jersey. After a 12-hour leave and a trip into New York City on a sight-seeing tour, on October 6, 1944, Frank and his unit boarded the troop ship USAT *George Washington* and set sail for Marseilles, France—and combat. The Germans had sunk numerous ships in the harbor, so the men had to climb down cargo nets to board smaller boats to get to shore. There were so many men staged there, they "had to sleep on the ground in pup tents for about a week." His unit finally headed out through northern France with the 7th Army. The final destination was Baccarat, France, to relieve the 45th Infantry. Odom noted, "We went into combat on 11–11–44 [ironically, the 26th anniversary of Armistice Day]."

The 100th pushed on through northeastern France and liberated numerous French towns, fighting all the way. As winter was coming on, Frank added. "We advanced quite a bit, but when we would get hit by the German 88s, you had to dig your foxhole a little bit deeper. You had to use an axe on the top layer and then your shovel." Once the Battle of the Bulge began, the 7th Army was ordered to set up a defensive position south of Bitche, France. German counterattacks were repulsed during early January 1945, and on March 16, 1945, Bitche fell to the 100th. The mayor of Bitche made them honorary citizens, and the men were thereafter called "the Sons of Bitche." The division crossed the Rhine River on March 24. Recalling the fighting from town to town, Odom noted, "After a little shooting, we took a lot of prisoners. Once we got to stay in a cellar and had a German prisoner with us." Frank suffered from trench foot (a medical condition caused by prolonged exposure of the feet to damp, unsanitary and cold conditions) and was sent to the 21st General Hospital in Mirecourt, France. There were 45,000 cases of trench foot reported during the Western Europe Campaign during World War II. Frank left France four days after the war was over in May 1945. After returning to the States, he was sent to Brooke Army Hospital at Ft. Sam Houston, Texas, for further recovery, where he was discharged in August 1945.

Frank Odom, U.S. Army, World War II.

Frank headed home to Wickes and went back to high school to complete his studies. On his first day of school, he went to see his

Frank Odom, May 1, 2018.

superintendent, who "reached in his desk drawer and handed me my diploma and said he wanted the best for me." With the help of the government, he went to the University of Arkansas and received a B.S. in education with a math major, graduating in May 1949. He taught math in Dierks and Winthrop, Arkansas, then Gruver and Miami, Texas, where he was also the superintendent. He met his future wife, Janice Turner, in Miami when he "hired her as a teacher." They married in 1958 and had two boys and one girl. They moved to Wellman, Texas, in 1959, where Frank was the principal and superintendent and Janice continued teaching. Both retired from there.

Frank Odom said, "I'm not much of a hero. I just want to be remembered for having the opportunity to serve my country." Odom was awarded the Combat Infantry Badge, Good Conduct, American Campaign, National Defense and World War II Victory Medals. In addition, he was finally awarded the Bronze Star in 2001 for his service in Europe from October 1944 to May 1945. Clearly, his wartime record and the government would disagree about his hero status!

47

Vernon Odom
*Helping Those Who
Can't Help Themselves*

Vernon Lewis Odom, now 94 years old, can look back on a long life devoted to service—not only to his country, but to others in need. His life journey began on October 15, 1924, in Breckenridge, Texas. Born to Henry and Murlin Odom, he was the oldest of three boys. His father moved the family to Wickett, Texas, a small town close to Monahans, where he worked at the Cabot Carbon Black plant. Vernon graduated from Monahans High School in 1941 where he played football. He attended Texas Tech for two years. The year was 1943 and the United States was fighting a war on both sides of the world. Vernon joined the Army Air Corps in December 1943 because he wanted to fly. He was sent to Ft. Sill, Oklahoma, with other recruits to "get our uniforms and shots." Odom noted, "We didn't get much basic training. They needed men so they were pushing us through. They said I could be a tail gunner on a B-17, but was turned down because my vision was not 20/20."

Odom was sent to Sheppard Field in Wichita Falls, Texas, then Scott Field in Belleville, Illinois, and finally Truax Airfield near Madison, Wisconsin. Truax was a major field during World War II for training radio operators. It was here that Odom learned International Morse code. He would remain there for four months. After training, he was sent to Smyrna Airfield in Tennessee. "We marched a little bit here while we were waiting for our orders," said Vernon. The next stop was at Angel Island in the middle of San Francisco Bay. Odom was one of 300,000 soldiers who would be shipped from the island to the Pacific.

"We boarded a troop transport that held about 10,000 men. We had a destroyer that escorted us out of the bay area, but they soon dropped off and the captain of the ship said, 'Boys, we're on our own now.' We were on the water for several days when the captain finally told us that our destination was Australia. After 14 days, we arrived in Sydney. We stayed there for a few days and then were sent to a replacement camp in Brisbane." In October 1943, Vernon was assigned to the 68th AACS (Army Airwaves Communication System) at Amberley Field in southeast Queensland. "There were 7 of us there: 3 radar operators, 1 radio repairman, 2 weathermen and 1 airplane mechanic. Not many planes landed there."

Vernon continued: "I boarded a ship headed for New Guinea. It was critical to capture the airstrips. Later, I was on a ship at the tail end of a large convoy of ships headed for Lingayen Gulf in the Philippines in late 1944 and early 1945. The convoy was attacked by kamikaze planes. I helped pass ammunition from the lower deck to the upper deck for the twin 40mm guns. I had malaria in June 1945 and spent time in the hospital. The war was over in August 1945 after we dropped the bombs on Japan. I had a chance to go to Japan but I wanted to go home. I landed in Washington State and took a train to El Paso [Texas] where I was discharged, then went on to Kermit [Texas] where my folks were living.

"I went back to Texas Tech and was at a skating party when I met Norma Grace Reid. She was a senior home economics major and a good, godly woman. I went home for Christmas and all I could think of was her. When I got back to Lubbock, we stayed together from then on. We were engaged but didn't let anyone know. We got married in August 1948. I let her use my car to go teach at Ralls while I went off to Oklahoma Baptist University to finish my degree."

Odom was a star pitcher for the OBU softball team and even threw a no-hitter. He graduated in May 1950 with a degree in education. He taught math at O.L. Slaton Junior High School in Lubbock for 5 years and then was a counselor at Lubbock High for almost 5 years. He went to work for the American College Testing (ACT) program and was assigned the whole state of Texas. After 13 years, he was promoted to cover all Southwestern states. He and "Gracie" now had 3 boys and he hated to leave her alone with them, but she supported him. Frank would go on to get both a master's degree in 1953 and his PhD in 1964 at Texas Tech.

Gracie opened the Good News Book Store in Lubbock. The business kept growing and she needed Vernon's help, so he eventually quit his job and helped her at the bookstore. They sold the store in 1980, bought a truck and a trailer and toured the United States. One day they realized that "we weren't helping anybody so we took mission trips to Africa, India and a couple of trips to Mexico. We built and opened a clinic for poor people in Chiapas. We contacted a doctor at Tulane University and he went down and did several operations for us and recruited other doctors to come and help," Odom said. Hundreds of people were helped over 25 years, thanks to Frank and Gracie. Frank and his family built a retirement home in Tres Ritos, New Mexico. The couple moved to Carillon in Lubbock in May 2013. Both were sick at the time and Gracie now has Alzheimer's. Vernon visits her every day.

Asked what he'd like to be remembered for, Vernon said, "My work in Mexico. If we had missed out on that, it would have been a tragedy. There's nothing in life better than helping those who can't help themselves." That's a life lesson for all of us.

48

WAYNE OWEN
Smart and Lucky

Many survivors of war talk about how lucky they were to survive. Here is one such story. During his training during World War II, Wayne Owen's fellow soldiers gave him the nickname "Lucky." While he often "slept through the numerous classes, he still made better grades than the other men." While serving in New Guinea, the tent next to Wayne was destroyed by shrapnel from an overhead dogfight between U.S. and Japanese fighters. He was lucky once more. While in Tacloban in the Philippines, a typhoon hit and the only things left standing were the mess hall and, you guessed it, "Lucky's tent." Like many serving in the Pacific Theater, he contracted malaria and spent a month in the hospital where he "had to endure 33 shots of penicillin. It took another 4–5 months to recover" before he could rejoin his unit, which had moved to another island during his convalescence. While onboard a ship in Manila Bay in April of 1945, a transport ship only four from Wayne's was struck by a kamikaze attack. "Lucky" escaped harm once again.

Wayne Owen was born September 13, 1923, in Lamkin, Texas, in Comanche County. He was one of eight children. His dad, Ben Owen, was a veteran of World War I. Wayne graduated from high school at age 16. After "working at a few jobs," Wayne enlisted in the Army Reserve. Three of his brothers also joined up and served during World War II. Wayne spent a year at Texas Tech taking courses in math and calculus, which would come in handy during his training in the service. He was called up for duty in September 1943 and reported to Camp Wolters in Mineral Wells, Texas. His basic training was in Miami Beach, Florida, where they were "put up in hotel rooms that cost $100 per night." That was a large sum back in 1943. He was assigned to the 5th Air Force, 43rd Bomb Group, 64th Squadron, and spent the next year in training for "electronics and radar repair." The training sessions were always under top security.

48. Wayne Owen

Wayne's squad was sent to Utah and then on to Camp Stoneman, California, where they boarded a Navy ship carrying 1,300 troops. The camp was known as the "jumping-off point" and would send more than one million soldiers bound for the Pacific Theater and (years later) to Korea. The Navy would do zigzag maneuvers to avoid Japanese sub-Marines, but they eventually landed in Lal, New Guinea, where they soon began what came to be known as "island hopping." His squad was moved from island to island to repair malfunctioning radar units off of B-24s. On the island of Owi in the Dutch East Indies, the men could "see dogfights over the ocean" and they were constantly being bombed and strafed by Japanese planes. Wayne said he "endured many sleepless nights and saw 45 American planes destroyed."

While stationed on Nab Zab, New Guinea, Wayne's unit learned of the death of President Roosevelt and "wondered if Vice President Truman was up to the task." Wayne noted that he "saw General MacArthur outside the post office in Manila in April 1945." Wayne's last "hop" was to Le Shima near Okinawa where a statue had been erected for war correspondent Ernie Pyle who died on Le Shima. They soon heard that an atomic bomb had been dropped on Hiroshima and the Japanese had surrendered. After two months in Tokyo, Wayne, now a Sergeant, was discharged at Ft. Sam Houston in San Antonio. Wayne married in 1946. He was recalled to service during the Korean War and served from 1951 to 1952. He landed at Inchon and never spent more than 30 days in one place at a time, due to Chinese Intervention.

He and his wife had 2 boys and 2 girls, but divorced in 1960. He married Lois in November 1960. She had one child by a previous marriage. They raised the children, but had none together. They have been happily married for 55 years. Wayne owned a Shamrock filling station in New Deal, Texas, for many, many years.

49

R.L. OWENS

"Red Arrow Division—First In, Last Out"

Pfc. R.L. Owens was in water up to his neck in a jungle in New Guinea and the Japanese were laying down heavy fire on his company. It was December 18, 1942. He was fortunate enough to have a log to protect him from enemy fire, but shrapnel caught him in the nose and he "bled a lot, but continued to help out his men." He spent several weeks in a field hospital due to his injury and malaria on Goodenough Island, where Army hospitals had been set up to treat the casualties. He said the running joke was that Goodenough Island was "good enough for you, but not for me." After recovering, he was returned to the front lines where he fought for two more years.

R.L. Owens was born in Comanche, Texas, on April 27, 1920. His dad was an oilfield worker. He had two sisters and a half-brother. He registered for the draft one month after Pearl Harbor and was inducted into the Army on January 8, 1942. After 13 weeks of basic training in Camp Roberts, California, he was assigned to the 32nd Infantry Division, 128th Infantry, Co. G, and shipped out of Ft. Ord, California, on the USAT *Monterey* and reached Port Adelaide, Australia, in May 1942. In July 1942, they were moved 900 miles to Camp Tamborine near Brisbane. In September R.L. was flown with his company to New Guinea (the second largest island in the world next to Greenland) to begin his long stint in combat. He was trained as a rifleman, bazooka launcher and sniper.

R.L. said, "You had to get used to jungle noises and my company had to have guards all night." Many of the men became so frightened that they "couldn't take it anymore and started shooting." He was nearly shot by one of his own men. One night he and two others were picked for "forward guard duty" and got pinned down by enemy fire. He noted that "the Japanese would try to kill anyone trying to aid or retrieve a wounded man on the field of battle." That night they had to "lie very

49. R.L. Owens

R.L. Owens medals display.

still in the bushes" and they "could hear the Japanese soldiers talking." They realized their company had pulled out and had no idea which way to go to find them. They found a communications wire and followed it back and "wound up right where their company was camped." R.L. said, "My Captain was so happy to see us he came up and hugged us and said, 'I thought you guys were goners!'" R.L. said he "had a lot of buddies wounded" and that he "fired a lot of rounds but wasn't sure how many enemy he hit." R.L. also had to guard a Japanese prisoner one night and stopped him from escaping.

All of the 9,825 men from the 32nd Infantry were casualties of the New Guinea campaign due to either combat or illness. R.L. was awarded the Bronze Star, the Purple Heart, the Presidential Unit Citation and numerous other awards.

He also had a stint as a Palace Guard for General Douglas McArthur. Although still a PFC (all promotions had been frozen), he "had earned enough overseas points to go home." He arrived in McLean, Texas, in July 1944 and was eventually discharged in October 1946. He made his way to Plainview, Texas, where he met his future wife, Oleta, at the 1st Assembly of God. He was 25 and she was only 15 when they married. They were blessed with 2 boys and 2 girls. He worked at Safeway

R.L. Owens, March 20, 2016.

Stores for 30 years, and at 52 years old he went back to preaching. He said he "had done a little preaching before the war." He started in Lorenzo and preached in many small towns in West Texas before finally retiring. Oleta passed away in October 2003.

R.L. was featured in the book *Almost a Family* by Pulitzer Prize–winning author John Darnton in 2011. John was only 11 months old when his father, Barney, a war correspondent for the *New York Times*, was killed in World War II. His dad was on the same ship on which R.L. was stationed and was one of the last to see Barney alive.

50

BILL PASEWARK
Spreading Freedom's Message

Seventy years after the battle of Iwo Jima, Marine Sgt. Bill Pasewark continues to urgently enlighten the public about the cost of freedom. His daughter, Su Hess, assists him during his presentations using memorabilia and a PowerPoint presentation to bring the history of our nation's fight for freedom to the forefront of our current consciousness.

Bill was born in Mt. Vernon, New York, and entered the service in 1943 in New York City. He wanted to go into the Army Air Corps but through a twist of fate (or an unscrupulous Marine recruiter!) he wound up in the Marine Corps. After basic training at Parris Island he headed for combat training in Hawaii. Next came a landing on Iwo Jima after the beachhead had been established.

"During the first days of the battle, I watched as the wounded were being brought back to the ships. A lot of them were veterans of other battles and they said, 'This is not going well.' I began to wonder if I would survive Iwo Jima. The way I saw it there were a couple of problems with the island. The dark volcanic ash was always shifting. It was tough to dig a foxhole. We had trained on hard sand. I had a bad feeling about this island. It was very dark and foreboding. The Japanese were more in the island than on the island due to an elaborate 16-mile tunnel network, which housed 22,000 enemy soldiers." Bill's replacement unit came under heavy mortar fire on the beach and the fire kept coming closer. Not everyone made it to the water for safety. They had no time to help the wounded and that haunts him to this day. He and two others survived unscathed, which totally amazed them.

"The Marines have a tradition of not leaving anyone behind so as the battle was winding down, we were sent to retrieve the dead. We would go up into the hills, and put the dead Marines onto trucks and take them back down to the beach. I was around 20 at the time and had only seen a dead person at a funeral home." While retrieving dead Marines, he came across a young Marine whose lips were pursed and seemed to say, "Keep moving forward." Bill said that "this was the first time in history that Marine Corps casualties outnumbered enemy casualties." Approximately 26,000 Marines and 22,000 Japanese were battle casualties, either dead or wounded. At the end of the battle, a little over 1,000 Japanese survived. Bill recalled being back on ship after delivering the dead to be buried on the beach in a mass grave. "I remember being called topside the next morning to observe a burial at sea. The sea was clear blue and the sound of taps playing. I couldn't hold in my emotions. With tears in my eyes, I bowed my head and saw drops of tears from the rest of the honor guard. Those things stay with you forever." How vicious was the fighting on Iwo Jima? According to the National World War II Museum, 27 Medals of Honor were awarded for action—more than any other battle in U.S. history.

After Iwo Jima he spent the end of his service in Guam and was discharged in 1946. Upon returning to the Bronx, New York, he sought out the wife of a dead buddy who had lived in Brooklyn. Emotionally unable to go, she sent her father-in-law and they met in a restaurant in Manhattan where Bill told him about the fate of the man's son. Bill also said that the war was just as tough on those at home if not tougher than the ones fighting the war. "My parents and relatives would read the headlines and they knew that it was going to be tough on Iwo Jima. The families suffered a lot back home and you never see that mentioned."

While attending Michigan State he met his wife, Jean, at the Student Union Building. After meeting him she told her roommates, "He's nice

Bill Pasewark, U.S. Marines, World War II.

but he needs a lot of help." They married in the fall of 1956. They were blessed with six children, including a son, Scott, who went into the Navy. He and Jean have celebrated 59 anniversaries together. Bill taught in the Texas Tech College of Business from 1956 to 1982. He has authored numerous computer and business textbooks.

From 1945 to 1995 (approximately 50 years) he only talked about the war a handful of times. Not self-aggrandizing their accomplishments, he, like most, rolled up their sleeves, went to work, and raised families.

Bill and Marion Pasewark.

While Tom Brokaw called this group "the Greatest Generation," Bill feels like "the greatest generation began with the founding fathers in 1776" and his "parents who survived the Great Depression."

One of his recent presentations was to a group of seniors at Carillon on the 4th of July. He is both passionate and emphatic as he teaches about the history of the country, the origin of the flag, and his warnings of perpetual evil that must be fought in the world. Bill's philosophy of faith can be summed up in two of his favorite hymns, "My Country 'Tis of Thee" and "This Is My Father's World." A longtime member of the Lion's Club, he celebrates the mission that the club stands for (Liberty, Intelligence, Our Nation's Safety) and the education of children worldwide about their message of peace.

Bill was fortunate enough to return to Iwo Jima for the last time with a group of veterans in March of 2015, fully funded by the Dallas Metroplex Military Foundation. He noted that out of 317 people on the trip, only 12 were Marines. Looking out from the top of Mt. Suribachi he could remember exactly where he was on that beach during his first trip some 70 years ago and think back on all the young lives that were lost there and how fortunate he had been to come out unscathed.

51

MARVIN PLATTEN
An Artful Journey

Marvin Platten from St. Paul, Minnesota, was 17 years old in 1944 and "wanted to get in the war somehow." He saw a recruitment ad in the paper that read, "Join the Navy and serve on your city's namesake, the USS *St. Paul*." Marvin's folks signed the papers and he joined the Navy on December 27, 1944. He would take his basic training at the Great Lakes Naval Training Station. As he noted, "Boot camp was challenging, yes, demanding, yes, enjoyable, no!" The second to last week of boot camp, he fell ill and was diagnosed with pneumonia with a 104°+ temperature. Marvin wistfully noted that he "never did see the USS *St. Paul*." He would take signalmen's training at Camp Sampson in New York State and ships' training at the Naval station in Newport, Rhode Island. After a train ride to Baltimore, he would be assigned to the USS *Allagash* (AO-97) that was a Cimarron class oiler for use in World War II. The *Allagash* was put out to sea from Norfolk bound for the West Indies and spent the next 10 weeks carrying oil fuel between ports and the "distinct feeling that we were still at war."

Once every five months the *Allagash* would have to go into a dry dock to be "degaussed" (a process that demagnetized the ship). At the start of World War II, the Germans developed a new magnetic trigger for mines—based on the mine's sensitivity to the magnetic field of a ship passing nearby. The design of such mines fortuitously fell into British hands, allowing them to develop countermeasures for such mines that eventually would be known as degaussing. The purpose of degaussing is to counteract the ship's magnetic field and establish a condition such that the magnetic field near the ship is, or as nearly as, just the same as if the ship were not there. This in turn reduces the possibility of detonation of these magnetic-sensitive ordnances or devices. Modern warships have built-in degaussing systems but for the *Allagash* at that time a different process had to be used. Thick bands of electrical wire, aligned with the main deck, were fastened around the length of the vessel. The wire was energized with an electric current that neutralized the ship's magnetism. However, degaussing at this time had to be repeated periodically before built-in degaussing systems could be developed since we were operating in the Atlantic Ocean where there were a number of German mines still in the ocean that had to be degaussed. The process took about 12 hours to complete, which necessitated the crew to depart the ship.

Underway replenishment was first perfected by the U.S. Navy in the late 1920s and 1930s, the technique was used extensively during World War II, and gave ships increased range and striking ability without the need to put into port for fuel and supplies. Actually, World War II's end of hostilities didn't "officially" end until December 30, 1945, so technically the *Allagash* was still at war. Platten found that fueling at sea was exhausting and dangerous. Exhausting because winches operating the booms to cradle the heavy hoses full of fuel to be secured to the intake valves demanded constant monitoring. A winch is a stationary motor-driven machine used for hoisting or hauling, having a drum, around which is wound a cable attached to the load being moved, the load being the flexible hoses though which the fast-flowing fuel is pumped. The hoses bump and rock to the extent that hand-held ropes attached to the bucking pipes must constantly guide them. Dangerous, because the fueling at sea is done while the ships are under way at 5 knots and only about 30 feet apart, creating heavy seas between the ships. The oilier usually fuels two ships at one time: one on the port and one on the starboard sides. Platten was also assigned a gun watch on the fantail sometimes during refueling where the 5"/38 deck gun was mounted, on which "was good duty, indeed."

One of his most memorable voyages was on "Operation Frostbite" with the new carrier USS *Midway* (CVA-41), which "included an effort to test the fueling at sea technique in extreme frigid conditions." The destination was about 200 miles north of the Arctic Circle between Greenland and Baffin Island. But the continually forming heavy ice, due to the heavy ice and seawater spray, inhibited the fueling process severely, not to mention the terrible effect it had on the seamen trying to operate the equipment. This dismal condition was especially noted when the *Allagash* crew was attempting to fuel the destroyers. It proved to be impossible for the receptors to receive and latch onto fueling hoses. They would try to chip away the ice that had encased to receptors but were unable to secure footholds to do so. Several of them had fallen into the sea but all were fortunately rescued. The solution to the problem appeared either to not attempt fueling at sea operations under these conditions or to radically change the procedures. Of course, this became a mute point later with nuclear power. Later, another dangerous situation developed.

The *Allagash* was involved in a major collision. Platten recalled, "While fueling at sea in the Caribbean Sea, southeast of Guantanamo Bay, a destroyer was secured from fueling on the starboard side and left the area while we were beginning to secure the fueling of the USS *Tarawa* [CV-40], an Essex-class carrier that had seen extensive action in the South Pacific. Without warning and for whatever reason, the skipper started to veer the *Allagash* away from the *Tarawa* but then stopped the engines that caused our ship to collide with the carrier setting off its smoke bombs that were carried under the edge of its flight deck and at the same time setting us afire. Humor intermingled with the potential tragedy. *Tarawa* sailors on their flight deck were waving at us and shouting 'hit us again.' Things changed rapidly when a huge plume of smoke pillared up from below from the exploding smoke bombs. Two *Allagash* shipmates suddenly abandoned ship by jumping off the fantail. A seagoing tug picked them up later. During the interrogation they shouted that they 'didn't want to be blown to bits as they saw other sailors do so when their tanker was exploded in the South Pacific.' World War II ships were notoriously flammable, especially oil tankers carrying thousands of tons of fuel oil and high-octane gasoline. Added to this was ammunition for the ship's guns, which was stored primarily in the ship's magazines. In contrast to today's Navy ships, oil-based paints were used extensively. The ship's wiring was filled with insulation that could ignite at high temperatures. And there were many more flammable materials aboard—paper, reports, manuals, cotton bedding below in crews' quarters as well as innumerable other objects and material that were instantaneously ignitable." Platten was at the 5"/38 deck gun when they struck the *Tarawa* and a bunch of guys were waving at him to leave that deck gun and climb up on the main aft deck and hollered for him to help them carry CO_2 fire tubing and canisters and a CO_2 hose down two ladders inside the dark of the ship as they were holding one hand on the guy's shirt collar. They were hampered by the darkness and down a deck to where the fire was a growing mass of flame. Then two guys carried the canisters and another CO_2 line to where they could smother the fire. The fire was indeed smothered.

"It was a tribute to our training that we were able to get the fire out eventually!" Platten reported. That mock-up course they had during ships' training, designed to simulate shipboard situations that they encountered in an emergency, paid off. That training included going into an inferno of fire in the mock-up of a ship's superstructure and putting the fire out with carbon dioxide (CO_2) and water, creating a spray of "snow" that was very effective in distinguishing gasoline fire. For a terrible moment the thought came to Platten that he'd never see his sister and his folks ever again! He feared that he would join two cousins that had perished a few months earlier. Jim Graba was a B-17 pilot after 25 missions to Germany and was killed on his 26th flight, and Chuck Platten was killed with a buddy while fighting with the 10th Mountain Division in northern Italy. Those of Platten's group that actually put the fire below decks out completely (and there weren't many) put their arms around each other's shoulders and cheered as if they had scored a touchdown. They spent the next day throwing the extensive piles of wreckage, including a 3-inch gun mount overboard from the port side. They were puzzled by how much wreckage there was. After more months carrying fuel between ports on the U.S. Gulf Coast to bases in the West Indies, Platten was honorably discharged on July 14, 1946.

Marvin and his sister Beverly were always close, and he said his "little baby sister for some reason called him 'Buzz' and also called the shots and we'd get into some mischief." During his early school days, Marvin discovered that he "had something—I could draw!" He "became pretty good at drawing things like cars, airplanes and trains." Thus would begin a long and fruitful career as both an accomplished artist and an art teacher. Marvin had one problem: he stuttered and had to work hard to remain calm and get his words out. While listening to Jack Benny on the radio, he learned to pause before he spoke and that helped him with difficult words. He recalled hearing the great horse race between Sea Biscuit and War Admiral on the radio in 1938. He noted that "the family lived in dilapidated upstairs apartments during the Depression and money was short." Marvin was heading to learn a trade in carpentry but got off a streetcar in front of the University of Minnesota so he thought "why not!" He changed his degree from architecture to art with a math minor in the spring of 1949. He would meet his future wife, Marion Middlestaedt, "virtually over an easel in Jones Hall." "She is the joy of my heart" Platten reported. They would marry on September 8, 1951. Marvin's first teaching job would be at Detroit Lakes, Minnesota, and then Minneapolis. He would get his master's degree in 1956. He, his wife and now 4 children would "take some major driving trips starting in 1962" all across the United States. Marvin would teach at Central High and Metropolitan Junior College.

Marvin began to think about teaching overseas and in the fall of 1966, he and the family packed up and moved to Ramey AFB in Puerto Rico. Here, he would not only teach art, but sell some of his own artwork. Here he would meet President Lyndon B. Johnson on one of his visits to the base. During the tumultuous year of 1968, Marvin would move the family to Japan where he would teach art at an elementary school just north of Yokota Air Base. Later he would become the art director for all Department of Defense facilities in Japan and travel all over the country visiting the various facilities and art departments.

After three years in Japan Marvin decided that maybe it was time to think about going back to the States. He wanted to teach at a university but did not have his doctorate so he didn't think he had a chance. He learned about an opening at a place called Texas Tech University in Lubbock, Texas, so he applied. After a lengthy correspondence with Dr. Lee, the dean of the College of Education, Marvin was offered a one-year appointment. Dr. Lee wrote, "I took the liberty of exploring your candidacy with Dr. Hastie, your professor at the University of Minnesota, and you will be pleased to know that he commends you to us most warmly and asks me to urge you to get the hell back to the United States as soon as you can!" It became a family joke for many years. Surprisingly, he would accept the job sight unseen after he was offered the position of a lecturer. When he called his wife upon arrival, she asked, "Are there any trees?" Buzz would "finally get his PhD at age 49 in the spring of 1977." He said that he was "brought back to earth when his 9-year-old niece exclaimed to his sister, 'He must be a very slow learner!'" The one-year term in 1971 turned into 22 years as he retired from full-time teaching in 1993. He continued teaching a graduate class for four more years. After 41 years of teaching, Dr. Platten noted that he "missed teaching dearly and the joy I was deriving from my interaction with students."

52

LEON POPE

From POWs to Paradise

For Leon Pope of Lubbock, Texas, service during World War II and Korea were two totally different experiences. During World War II, Pope was sent to the Pacific Theater. During the Korean War, he was sent to Hawaii. As a 2nd class electrician in the Navy, Leon's skills were needed during both wars. In World War II, he was taking care of prisoners. In the Korean War, he was taking care of a radio station's equipment. As Leon stated, "In the service, you go where they tell you to go." Anyone who has served in the armed forces knows this all too well. It's always an adventure. You can be sent anywhere in the United States or anywhere in the world "at the convenience of the government."

Thomas Leon Pope was born on September 21, 1926, in Cisco, Texas, to Thomas and Elsie Pope. He had one sister. His father worked for Southwestern Bell Telephone Company in Ft. Worth. When he was around 10 years old, his family moved to the county near Euless, Texas. The Lee R. Smith family had become close friends of theirs in Ft. Worth and had moved to Hurst nearby the year before. The adults regularly played 42 (dominoes) on Friday nights while the kids played outside games. Leon played basketball at Euless High School where he graduated in 1943 in a class of 6. He tried to enlist in the Navy but wasn't old enough, so he attended Texas Wesleyan College for a year, thanks to his father's support, then joined the Navy.

His basic training was at San Diego Naval Training Station and he continued his training at radio school for approximately 20 weeks. He was shipped out on the USS *H.W. General Butner* (AP-113) attack transport troopship on February 17, 1944, headed for the Pacific Theater. After dropping off troops at various islands in the Pacific, Leon and others were "dropped off at Luzon, Philippines." He recalled, "I had been training with the Marines aboard ship and my first responsibility on shore was sniper patrol duty. They told us that we need to be quiet and alert while looking for snipers, but we were loud and joking. I was scared once when I heard a noise and shot in the trees. Fortunately, there was no sniper.

"I was assigned to the USS LST-569 [Landing Ship, Tank]. The maximum speed was only 16 knots. We were assigned to go pick up Japanese prisoners in Vietnam who refused to surrender to anyone but U.S. forces. We went up the river with two other LSTs. Our skipper was the task force unit commander. We heard that there was a whole company of Japanese up in the mountains. I went along as the only enlisted man with a small group of officers and an interpreter in rickshaws up the mountain. When we reached the top of the mountain and looked over, there were many, many Japanese troops milling around. They had all types of guns, tanks and ammunition. What looked like the top man of the group led a surrender party up the hill to meet us. They marched in perfect military formation. They bowed to us and started offering up guns and weapons. I got a Japanese rifle, a pin off a hat, a Samurai sword and a wristwatch. I said I can't take these but the skipper said to take them. It was a matter of honor for the Japanese."

Leon continues: "Since I was the radioman, I contacted the other LSTs waiting at the river. I gave them a secret code word that we had the Japanese prisoners. We formed up hundreds of them and marched them to the LSTs. They were as thick as fleas. We took them to Korea and unloaded them. We loaded up another group of Japanese prisoners and took them to Sasebo, Japan, where we had a big POW camp. Troop trucks picked them up. We headed back south. I got on another ship, the USS LSM-349 [Landing Ship Medium]. We took ammunition and all kinds of supplies to Shanghai, China. I spent a lot of time with the skipper on the conning tower. I was a radioman and signalman. I enjoyed my time on that little ship. It was going to be decommissioned. The skipper asked me what I like about the Navy. I told him the vibration of the ship, the ride, the sea breeze, et cetera. About this time, a seagull flew over and pooped right in the skipper's pocket. I told him I even like that! He tried to get me to stay in the Navy but I told him that I was ready to go home.

"I was discharged at Norman, Oklahoma, on August 15, 1946. I hitchhiked to Ft. Worth and got on a bus to Euless, Texas. The bus driver let me off at the Smiths' house and I visited with Ann and her family. I told them I had been discharged and they drove me to my folks' house about a mile away." During the time Leon had been away, Ann's grandpa told a bunch of young people standing around church one Sunday night, that she had said when she was about eight years old that she was going to marry Leon. Ann was very embarrassed and was thankful that Leon wasn't there.

52. Leon Pope

Leon worked at Montgomery Ward for a while and then got a job with Southwestern Bell Telephone Company. He worked in Pecos, Texas, for a short time and was loaned to the phone company in Odessa, Texas. After a year there, the move was made permanent. During this time, Leon and Ann had begun their courtship and were married June 12, 1948, and made their home in Odessa. Leon was contacted by a man with the government about opening a Navy radio station on one of the school campuses. He could arrange for all the equipment and wanted to know if Leon could teach wiring and code. In order to open the radio station, Leon had to be in the Navy Reserve. The man got all the equipment and Leon installed it and started teaching classes. However, Leon was recalled to active duty during the Korean War. He reported to Dallas on September 12, 1950, and was sent to the Wahiawa Naval radio station about 20 miles from Honolulu, Hawaii. The station was built during World War II and saw increased activity during the Korean and Vietnam wars. Ann and their son, Tommy, nearly 2 years old, joined him in April 1951 and they lived in Honolulu. Leon had duty on base (he was the manager of the electric shop) every fourth night. Otherwise, he was able to spend his nights with the family. "Our second son was born there in January 1952 at Tripler Army Hospital. I was discharged (again) on April 24th, 1952, in San Francisco," Leon explained.

The Pope family returned to Abernathy, Texas, where Ann's parents had bought a grocery store. Leon went to work at Thompson Implement Co. in Abernathy while waiting for a job at the Arlington, Texas, post office. The family moved to Arlington in the fall of 1953 where their daughter, Trisha, was born in 1954. Leon worked in the post office until he received a call from the chief postal inspector in Washington that he had passed the exam for the Postal Inspection Service and was sworn in as a postal inspector in the fall of 1964. He was assigned to the San Francisco Division, which covers northern California and northern Nevada. They lived in California for 33 years and came to Lubbock, Texas, in 1997.

Even though they enjoyed their years in California, they are thankful they decided to retire in Lubbock. They say they have the best neighbors anyone could ask for and they feel a warm welcome to be back in West Texas.

Special thanks to Anna Pope for her hard work in helping me get this story in the proper chronological order.

53

JAMES RICH
A "Rich Life"—Flirting with Death

By his own reckoning, World War II veteran James "Troy" Rich "nearly died 15 times—more lives than a cat." He "was always a bit of a daredevil," but not all of his close encounters with death were due to his risk-taking. He was born on November 8, 1926, near McAdoo, Texas, to Ezra and Ada Rich. His father, a farmer, was a veteran of World War I, who, among other responsibilities, shoed horses for the Army in Bulgaria. Troy's brother also served during World War II as an airplane mechanic in the Army Air Corps.

Troy graduated from McAdoo High School in 1944 and was drafted into the Army on March 26, 1945. After completing eight weeks of basic training at Camp Wolters near Mineral Wells, Texas, his unit was ordered to ship out for overseas deployment. After undergoing a series of immunizations, Troy "came down with a 107-degree fever and nearly died." The deployment proceeded without the young soldier, and "many men in my unit were either killed or wounded, and I would have been one of them." The official website for Grove, Oklahoma, documented that Troy's unit, the 11th Airborne Division, suffered 2,431 casualties during World War II. America had lost many of her young men, but V-J Day on August 14, 1945, brought welcome relief. Troy said that he "jumped up and down and shouted for joy when he heard the bombs were dropped on Japan." The war was finally over.

Leaving from Oakland, California, Troy and his outfit sailed for Japan. General Douglas MacArthur had picked the 11th Airborne to lead the invasion of Japan, but after the Japanese surrender, he used them instead to lead American forces who would occupy Japan. The adventurous young man was "only making $50 month, but if you could qualify as a paratrooper, you could earn $100." The physical training was quite intense, and Troy remembered that "we had to do double-time [running] all the time. Even if we stopped, we had to walk in place." After five jumps, Troy earned his parachute badge and the much-needed extra $50-per-month pay. On one jump, he landed on top of another paratrooper's canopy and "had to slide off and move away from the other jumper, or they both might have plunged to their death." On another jump, a wind shear hit him about 100 feet from the ground, and even though he tried to correct his landing, he "landed hard on a big mound of dirt and bent [his] tailbone under." Instead of being taken to sick bay, he was just picked up by the other men. "I should have been drawing disability, but the accident was not in my records." He has suffered from a bad back for the rest of his life.

Rich was a jack-of-all-trades. He also drove an M35 2½-ton 6×6 truck as part of the 408th Airborne Quartermaster Company. Part of Troy's job was moving equipment around. Once, a former kamikaze pilot was working with him. He told Troy that he "was forced to do it, and that the pilots were given opium before the flight. If you did not do as ordered, your family would be disgraced and shunned." Fortunately, the war ended, and the young Japanese pilot did not have to fly the suicide mission. Troy also became a qualified glider pilot before his tour in Japan ended in the fall of 1946. After a long train ride from California, he was discharged at Ft. Sam Houston near San Antonio on December 7, 1946. Back home in McAdoo, he used his savings "to buy a Ford coupe and a Ford tractor. I was ready to be a farmer."

Troy met his future wife, Libby, literally by accident. He and a date were heading home from a movie in Spur, Texas, when they "came upon a car that had hit a steer. It was a family of a dad, a mom and a young girl. I could barely squeeze them in my car. The young girl, Libby, sat close beside me, and we got to know each other pretty well." After only three weeks of dating, Troy and Libby married. They raised three daughters and a son. The Riches were married for 62 years before Libby's death in February of 2010.

Even in his later life, Troy continued to be a daredevil. On a trip to the Royal Gorge, he got too close taking a picture and "had to crawl on my hands and knees to keep from falling into the gorge!" Once, a vehicle he had jacked up on blocks slid on top of him and pinned him to the ground. "Fortunately, I was on my back with my arms up and was able to slide myself out from under the tractor, but it tore all the hide off my back."

Now 92 years old, the adventurous Mr. Rich can look back and be thankful he survived so many close calls during his long life. His many brushes with death have only served to enhance his appreciation for life.

54

EUGENE ROBERTS
"Hard to Turn Off the Switch"

Eugene Roberts had seen the worst of war. He spent the last few months of World War II in the Pacific. One of hundreds of young men plucked from American cities and farms, he was sent halfway around the world to help bring an end to the Japanese reign of terror. It was not going to be easy, and many young men would lose their lives. The war in Europe was over; the Pacific war was not. It took three more months of close combat, often hand to hand, from island to island, before the Japanese surrendered. One American soldier put it this way: "You can surround thousands of Germans and they would surrender, but surround one Japanese and he will keep fighting."

Eugene was born July 10, 1924, in Mt. Pleasant, Texas, to Silas and Delia Roberts. Silas was a farmer, and Delia was a homemaker. He had five brothers and two sisters. Two of his brothers served in the Army during World War II. He graduated from Mt. Pleasant High School in 1943.

He traveled to Temple, Texas, in February 1944 to sign up at a recruiting station. After registering upstairs, he was told he had "two weeks to go home and get ... affairs in order." He was told to go downstairs for further instructions. He found the Army, Navy and Marines there signing men up. He said, "Every third man was picked by the Marines, and I was the third man." He was told to "get on the bus outside." He did not have two weeks to get his "affairs in order."

After six weeks of basic training, getting numerous shots and one week of tank training, Eugene was shipped out, headed for the Pacific. After stops in the Marshall Islands, his unit, 2nd Marine Division, 2nd Tank Battalion, was "part of the third wave to land on Saipan." He noted, "On the trip over, you could not see the sun for so many Japanese planes flying overhead [trying to slow down the advancing armada]." Once Saipan was secured, the Marines waited for their next assignment. By

July 1944, Eugene's division landed and occupied the island of Tinian, where they camped next to the runway and where B-29s would eventually leave to deliver the atomic bombs. In March of 1945, they were told that "half of the Marines had been wiped out on a place called Iwo Jima, and we were loaded on ships to be sent there the next morning." But their Marine commander decided not to send them, and their orders were changed to land on Okinawa instead.

As Eugene recalled, "On April 1, 1945, Easter Sunday, we landed on Okinawa, serving as a Floating Reserve, for a final push to Japan." The initial invasion of Okinawa was the largest amphibious assault in the Pacific Theater of World War II. "We conducted seven false landings in one day to confuse the Japanese." Meanwhile, other U.S. forces were able to establish a beachhead on the opposite side of the Island. Eugene was part of a five-man crew on an M4 Sherman Tank. Heavily armed, the tanks were outfitted with 75 mm, 50 mm, and 30 mm guns. "It was extremely hot and not well ventilated inside," said Roberts. The battle, the last of World War II, was extremely costly. There were an estimated 49,000 American casualties, and over 110,000 Japanese lost their lives.

On August 6, 1945, President Truman elected to drop an atomic bomb on Hiroshima, and when the Japanese would still not surrender, another atomic bomb was dropped on Nagasaki on August 9. They finally surrendered on August 14.

Elements of Eugene's division were sent to Nagasaki 25 days after the strike as part of occupied Japan. He recalled, "It was complete destruction—there were dead bodies everywhere." He was stationed in Nagasaki until his honorable discharge in July 1946.

Discharged in San Diego, California, Eugene took a bus back to Mt. Pleasant, Texas. When asked about the difficult transition from the horrors of combat to the civilian world, he said, "It's hard to turn off the switch. In the Marines, you were taught to kill Japanese. They didn't teach you how to handle being a civilian. They just turned you loose. A lot of guys turned to alcohol to cope. We didn't know what PTSD was back in those days."

At that time, no one saw a psychiatrist or sought therapy because of the intense stigma associated with such actions, which would brand you as "crazy" and therefore unemployable. "Act normal, and you'll feel normal" was about all the therapy advice they got.

Eugene met and later married Maggie Ruth Homer in 1946 in Mt. Pleasant, Texas. The union produced two daughters, Linda and Debra. Eventually the couple was blessed with three grandchildren, Brandon, Tonya, and Heather, and four great-grandchildren, Tyler, Kaden, Karter, and Hazel.

Eugene worked at a furniture store and then a grocery store in Mt. Pleasant. He and his family moved to Lubbock, Texas, in 1949 where he "took a job at Coca-Cola on 16th and Texas." Through his 46-year career at Coca-Cola, he progressed through the management ranks, eventually retiring in 1990 as general manager of bottling/vending for West Texas and Eastern New Mexico. He remained on the board of directors until 1996.

Eugene now resides at Raider Ranch in Lubbock. He stays busy in retirement, spending time with the family and enjoying his hobbies of golf, fishing, woodworking, Texas Tech sports, and traveling.

Mr. Roberts can attest to the fact that war is brutal, especially for those who face combat. Those who overcome the atrocities they faced, as well as the ones who continue to struggle, are owed an immeasurable debt of gratitude for their sacrifices.

55

MAX ROBERTSON
Navy Battles Mother Nature

The account of a crippling typhoon is still strong in the memory of 94-year-old Lubbock World War II Navy veteran Max Robertson. He was onboard the USS *Bougainville* (CVE-100) in December 1944 when the enormous typhoon hit in the Philippine Sea. When one thinks of the dangers facing the U.S. Navy in the Pacific during World War II, one imagines ships being sunk by the enemy's ships, submarines or bombers. The typhoon that hit the Pacific fleet on December 18, 1944, came with little warning and significant destruction, damage and death. According to Navy documents on the Warfare History Network website, Task Force 38 was operating about 300 miles east of Luzon in the Philippine Sea on December 17 with 90 ships, including carriers, battleships, cruisers and destroyers. The carriers had just completed three days of heavy raids against Japanese airfields in the Philippines. The storm inflicted the worst damage on the Navy of any storm since 1889. Four destroyers capsized and went down with nearly all hands. A cruiser, five aircraft carriers and three destroyers suffered serious damage; 146 planes on various ships were lost or damaged. Nearly 800 officers and men were lost or killed, with another 80 injured. Max recalled, "The ship would roll over so far that I didn't think it would come back [upright]."

Max Dale Robertson was a Texas boy, born near Union, Texas, on May 6, 1924, to Estel and Esther Robertson. He and his two sisters were raised by his dad, a farmer, and his mother, a housewife. He graduated from Cooper High School in 1940 in Woodrow, Texas, and attended Texas Tech, completing 85 hours of class work toward a degree in petroleum engineering. Feeling like he could be drafted at any time, he and a buddy joined the Navy on May 5, 1943, one day before his 19th birthday. After several weeks of basic training in San Diego, California, Max was assigned to a new ship, the USS *Bougainville* (CVE-100), which was launched on May 16, 1944, by the Kaiser Shipyards in

Vancouver, Washington. After a "shake-down cruise to San Diego," the ship departed San Diego on July 25, 1944, and steamed to Pearl Harbor. The ship was an escort carrier and, according to Max, "carried numerous aircraft, including gull wings, B-24s and P-47s in support of Task Force 58 and 38." As a Fire Controlman 3rd Class, Max manned one of the sixteen Bofers 40 mm swivel guns onboard, with "every fourth round a tracer."

The *Bougainville* rendezvoused at sea with the ships of Task Forces 58 and 38, delivering planes, replacement pilots and aircraft crews and providing vital logistic support to the 3rd and 5th Fleets as they engaged the Japanese at both Iwo Jima and Okinawa. Robertson was part of the U.S. strategy in the Pacific known as "island hopping," where U.S. forces moved from island to island, using each as a base for capturing the next one. At one stop, Max recalled one of his buddies "climbing a coconut tree to get me one." On another island, "The men were told not to even light a cigarette due to a blackout in effect, because Japanese bombers were flying overhead.

"It took us 17 days to sail from Guam back to San Diego [after the war was over]. I was sent back to the destroyer base for training I already had. I was offered a raise in rank but declined and rode the battleship USS *Texas* [BB-35] to San Pedro, California, for discharge." Max took a train to Clovis, New Mexico, and then hitchhiked to Shallowater, Texas, where he "carried his duffel bag all the way to Slide Road [in Lubbock, Texas]." He later met and married Virginia Mote and settled into farming near Lorenzo. They had one son, Max. The elder Robertson "farmed for 15 years and then went to work in the petrochemical business in Jal, New Mexico. I helped put in a 40" gas line to El Paso, worked in Borger and then up and down the Texas coast as a pipefitter for Halliburton and others." After retiring, he moved to Choke Canyon Reservoir in Three Rivers, Texas, where he loved to fish.

Max divorced and then married two more times during his life. He adopted the three children of his second wife, Nannie Mae. Max moved back to Lubbock several years ago to spend time with his elderly mother.

When asked how he'd like to be remembered, he said, "I tried to treat everybody right and expected to be treated right." His accounts of the tragic hurricane at sea are still riveting reminders of the extraneous hazards American soldiers and sailors faced during the years of World War II.

56

EARL ROBINSON
"The Good Lord Had My Hand"

It was a cold winter day in Belgium on January 3, 1945, when Corporal Earl Robinson and his company were ordered to move out. This was the middle of what came to be known as the Battle of the Bulge during World War II. On December 16, 1944, the Germans launched the deadliest and most desperate battle of the war in the west. The blitzkrieg was from the Ardennes in France to Antwerp, Belgium. It was to be the costliest battle ever for the U.S. Army with over 100,000 casualties. This scenario was Corporal Robinson's indoctrination into combat.

Earl Robinson was born at home to rancher James and his wife, Mabel Robinson, on October 9, 1925, in Parsons, New Mexico. Located in Lincoln County, a gold strike in the mid–1880s by R.C. Parsons gave the town its beginning and its name. Earl had two sisters and four brothers. His family later moved to Melrose, New Mexico, where Earl enjoyed playing football, basketball and baseball. When asked his favorite subject in high school, he jokingly said, "Athletics." He "dropped out of high school in May of 1944 at the request of the Curry County draft board," entering the Army in June of 1944. Three of his brothers also served during World War II. When told not all brothers should serve at the same time, he said, "Tell that to the draft!"

Earl completed a "13-week crash course in basic infantry training at Camp Wheeler, Georgia." He was assigned to the 3rd Army's 84th Infantry, the so-called Railsplitters, and "sailed out of New York on the Ile de France, a cruise liner converted to a troop ship" in the fall of 1944, headed to Scotland and then to Southampton, England. They boarded a ship to cross the English Channel to France and were moved near the front lines in Belgium via bus. Moving to the front lines, the men were told to "start digging foxholes." But, as Earl recalled, "the ground was frozen solid, and you couldn't dig a foxhole!" His unit moved forward into a wooded area when "the German 88 cannons opened up, cutting through the trees" in the Ardennes Forest and raining flak down on the troops.

Moving into an open field, Earl saw the body of a German soldier and realized "this was the real thing." He noted that "about this time, [he] was hit." Earl had been hit by shell fragments, one tearing into his leg. He was sent back to France and then to a hospital in England to convalesce. He was returned to the front lines in Belgium in April 1945 and moved with his unit toward Germany. Here he received the Purple Heart for his wounds. After crossing the Wessel River, his unit was "just clearing the way—the Germans were disorganized, and resistance was light unless we ran into the SS [Schutzstaffel], and they kept fighting." During their advance, "his company commander was standing in a doorway directing his men and was hit by a mortar shell and killed." He also recalled that the 2nd Platoon was "trying to outflank some Germans across an open field, and the enemy opened fire on the platoon and killed eight GIs."

When asked why the 84th Infantry stopped at the Elbe River in Germany, Earl said, "We could see the Russians on the other side of the river." This meant that the German Army had been cut in two, and the end of the war was near. He also said that "hundreds of German civilians fled to the American side to get away from the Russians." Moving into Berlin, Earl remembered "total destruction—no building was left standing." He joined the 59th Finance Group as part of occupied (Army of Occupation) Germany, which "worked out of German houses." He left Germany and headed for the United States in May 1946 and was discharged at Ft. Bliss, Texas, in June 1946.

Earl returned to Clovis, New Mexico, and Eastern New Mexico University to study accounting. He met his future wife, Mona Ribble, after being invited to a school party by a friend. After graduating, Earl and Mona were married in September 1949, and he went to work at a CPA firm, while she began working as a librarian at Clovis High School. Earl eventually opened his own accounting firm, which he headed for 41 years. He and Mona had two daughters, two granddaughters and four great-grandchildren.

Remembering his time in combat and looking at the shell fragment that he now has framed, along with his Purple Heart and Nazi war souvenirs, Earl simply said, "The good Lord had my hand."

57

JAMES T. RODEWALD
"Hot Meals and a Place to Sleep"

When asked why he chose the Navy back in 1945, James T. Rodewald of Lubbock simply said, "They had hot meals and a place to sleep." That sounds simple enough. However, Jim's two years in the Navy was anything but simple. Jim was born in "a town that doesn't exist anymore," Obar, New Mexico, to Otto and Monetta Rodewald. His father was a dairy farmer and Jim said he would "milk 27 cows by hand every day." Jim was the firstborn and he had 2 brothers and 2 sisters. Since there was no school in Obar, Jim attended Logan High School where he graduated in 1945. He enjoyed physics and math. He "once monitored a class of juniors as a freshman and was so proficient, he received credit for the class." He enlisted in the Navy on August 4, 1945. As Jim noted, "just two days later, we dropped the bomb on Hiroshima and then Nagasaki, and the war was over."

After basic training in San Diego, California, Jim asked for duty in Jacksonville, Florida, and went there for aviation school. He took 4 hours of classes to determine various ratings that described what jobs were available. He noted that "one fellow from Aerographer School [Meteorologists and Oceanographers] got up and said that the school in Lakehurst, New Jersey, was the best duty. Instead of a large barracks of men, they only had 2 men per room and said it was a nice assignment." Jim decided right then and there, "That's for me!" Jim found out that if you finished in the top 10 of your class in Jacksonville, you could get your choice of assignment. Also, if you finished in the top 10 percent, you would get another stripe. Jim said, "I worked extremely hard to get that and finished number 9 in my class of 112 men." As for his choice of assignment, that didn't happen. Furious, Jim went to the commander to find out what happened. He found out the commander was from Albuquerque and they had a New Mexico connection. The commander said there was no quota for Lakehurst. Jim would have to wait for an opening. He was asked to teach algebra. Only three days later, a slot opened up and Jim was finally on his way to Lakehurst.

Jim's Navy duty took a lot of twists and turns after his time in Lakehurst. Jim volunteered to go to the South Pole in 1946 with Admiral Byrd and was assigned to the USS *Currituck* (AV-7). Upon arrival in San Francisco, he found out they had all the Aerographer's Mates that they needed and he was sent to North Island (San Diego) at a receiving station and stayed there 5 months. While waiting for permanent duty, 3 aircraft carriers came in and Jim loaded 5" shells on the ships. "The shells came in a wire bail and my tender hands got all cut up and I had to go to sick bay." He once again went to his commander and "raised hell." He went with Commander Dorsett who needed a man at a seaplane duty station checking the wind. Jim went with Dorsett about 20 miles offshore to the USS *Iowa* (BB-61). Jim was now part of the U.S. 5th Fleet.

Jim noted that "there were only 13 officers, 21 enlisted men, 14 Filipinos, 6 boat crew and 6 Marines on the admiral's staff." Jim's job was to "do weather observation maps and forecasts and ... hand deliver them to the admiral." He recalled one trip to Johnston Atoll (midway between the Marshall and Hawaiian Islands) where "we shot off our 16" guns. We launched a broadside [all guns firing] and the ship went about 50 feet sideways." Rodewald stayed on the *Iowa* until September 1947 when he transferred to the USS *Sierra* (AD-18). Jim's job was to pick up weather maps in San Diego and take them to the *Sierra*, which was anchored in mid–San Diego Bay. Discharged in October 1947, Jim returned to Logan, New Mexico.

Back in Logan, Jim went to work for the "52/20 work program at the employment service, which meant that you got paid $20 per week for 52 weeks." Thanks to his Navy training, Jim went to work at the National Weather Service in October 1948. He also married Nina Beverly that month. His sister had introduced them earlier when he was at home on leave from the Navy. They had 2 boys and 2 girls. The young family moved to Del Rio, Laredo and Lubbock, Texas, then spent 45 years in Juneau, Alaska. Jim spent 17 years working at the National Weather Service and 5 years working for Alaska Power. After his retirement in 1982, Jim and Beverly wanted to move to California but "the retirement village there was too expensive." Later, they looked into Carillon LifeCare Community in Lubbock and moved there in 2007. Beverly passed away in October 2009, just short of their 61st anniversary.

When asked what he would like to be remembered for, he said, "My kids. They have all done OK. I'm proud of them."

58

ELDIE SCHEFFEL
"The Coldest Winter I Ever Saw"

For 97-year-old Eldie Scheffel, the time he spent on the Aleutian Islands was the coldest he'd ever been before or since. He was part of the Army's 18th Infantry Division sent to rid the island of Kiska being occupied by the Japanese in 1943. The islands, part of the Alaskan territory, were critical to Pacific supply routes for both Japan and the United States. Eldie said he stayed in a "two-man foxhole on a cliff overlooking the bay." Their job was to watch for enemy soldiers still left on the island after the invasion. His unit narrowly averted disaster on the way to the island as their ship was fired on by a Japanese submarine but missed both the front and back of the ship. Eldie would spend over a year on the islands. With temperatures reaching -59 degrees, he noted that you would "turn blue before you could finish taking a shower."

Eldie was drafted into the Army 52 days after the attack on Pearl Harbor on January 28, 1942. He spent 13 weeks in basic training in Ft. Robinson, California, with many of them spent being a calisthenics instructor. He finally asked his sergeant for a transfer, which was denied. He finally went to a colonel who granted him a transfer to Ft. Benning, Georgia, where he would begin infantry training and continued as a calisthenics instructor. Toward the end of his "3 years, 9 months and 4 days" of service, Eldie was once again stationed at Ft. Benning when the news came on April 12, 1945, that President Franklin D. Roosevelt had died at the so-called Little White House in Warm Springs, Georgia. He was selected to be one of the soldiers who escorted the president's body to the train station. Eldie left the service on November 1, 1945. He said that the military "helped him to appreciate life and discipline."

Heartwarmingly, upon first meeting and any time one speaks with Eldie W. Scheffel, the sparkle in his bright blue eyes is evidence of many adventures well lived. He beams as he tells of his first memories of the two-room schoolhouse in Prairie View, Texas, where he fell in "puppy love" with his first crush, Maureen, describing the color of her hair and eyes, and he confesses to a few childhood pranks he took part in (we will refrain from going into detail here, to protect the innocent). When asked what he wanted to be when he grew up, he states, "Not a president. I wanted to go back and buy me a farm." His parents, Gustav William and Wallie Rose Miel, were farmers and he grew up with six siblings, him being number five. Eldie grew up being a farmer. Eldie was born on March 11, 1920, in Austin, Texas. He noted that "dad was a dirt farmer and that the family was dirt poor." During the Depression, most folks were dirt poor. Eldie wanted to continue his education, but by the end of the 8th grade, he was "working from sunup to sundown and had no time to go to school." After the service, he trained as a carpenter and loved working with wood.

Eldie fortified his inner strength over the years as he learned to endure the dreary foxholes during his military service, and to handle the challenges later in life, from losing one of his sons at age 62, and supporting and eventually outliving both of his wives as they faced life-limiting illnesses. He was married to Anne Merle Ratliff for 24 years and to Odessa Marie Houx for 40 years.

His favorite secular song is "The Yellow Rose of Texas" and he likes the gospel song "When the Roll Is Called Up Yonder." He is a huge Miranda Lambert fan and is very verbal about his following her life and career for years. His family has saved her picture to his phone's home screen, and he calls her his "girlfriend, but she don't know it yet."

59

HAROLD SCHULTZE

D-Day Remembered by Former Higgins Boat Driver

In October of 2012, I had the honor of sitting beside one of our World War II veterans on the return trip of our inaugural Texas South Plains Honor Flight. When then 87-year-old Harold Schultze began to tell his story, I knew I should get my notepad out and start writing. Harold was born in Monroe, Louisiana, on September 21, 1925. His family moved to Birmingham, Alabama, where he entered the U.S. Coast Guard in September 1943 when he turned 18 years old. Six weeks of boot-camp training would be at St. Augustine, Florida, followed by maneuver training at Camp Lejeune in North Carolina, as a coxswain (driver) on an LCVP (Landing Craft, Vehicle, Personnel).

The LCVP (the military's term) was often called a "Higgins Boat," named after the designer and builder, Andrew Higgins, in the 1930s. The craft could operate in a mere 18" of water and could easily land its bow ashore and back out to deeper waters. It could travel at a speed of 12 knots (14 MPH). Higgins started selling the boats to the U.S. Coast Guard, which helped him establish a rapport with the American military. The craft could hold a crew of 3 or 4 personnel and up to 36 tightly packed troops or a jeep and 12 troops. The boat was held in such high esteem, that several high-ranking Allied service men credited Mr. Higgins with "winning the war." The former National D-Day Museum, now called the National World War II Museum, was opened in New Orleans on June 6, 2000, in honor of the Higgins Boats.

As Schultze recalled, "We headed for Brooklyn, New York, and boarded the USS *Bayfield* [APA-33], an attack transport ship. We joined a convoy headed for Scotland. We then shipped out for training on the east coast of England and did maneuvers until June 5th when we headed for Normandy and D-Day. We enjoyed our training but everyone was excited to get going." With the *Bayfield* anchored off of Normandy, Harold's crew headed for Utah Beach with a load of troops. Continuing, Harold said, "We didn't really take it too seriously until we started heading for the beach and the big German 88s would go off. German fire was extremely heavy. As the driver, I would try to get to the beach and the bullets were hitting all around you, off the ramp and everywhere. You think, 'A guy can get hurt out here.' It was hard watching those young men drop off into the water. They had over 50-pound backpacks and were trying to hold their rifles over their heads all while being under heavy fire. Often they couldn't get their footing and many of them drowned before even getting to the beach. These were some of the bravest men I have ever seen.

"We were the first landing craft at the beach. We hit a sand bar and the lieutenant told me to 'drop the ramp.' I said, 'No, we don't drop the ramp now.' The lieutenant kept telling me to drop the ramp and I said, 'No, we are in 10–15 feet of water. If we drop the ramp now, you will all drown!' He apologized and didn't ask me again until we could get off the sandbar and move to shallow water." Schultze struggled to describe the scene. "The troops tried to run to shore. Some of them never touched the beach. Before they could even get solid footing, they would be shot." During the first wave, Harold remembered seeing the beach when the ramp dropped. "It was a tangle of barbed wire and cement and all kinds of things to keep you from getting on the beach. You couldn't see any Germans; they were all up on the hill firing down on us." Schultze had to do his duty and ignore the carnage and return time after time to the *Bayfield* to pick up another load of men. The worst part of his job, he noted, was to "remove the dog tags off of the dead soldiers floating in the water. That got to me. You eventually became numb to the sights and had to carry on but you could never forget."

During the attack, Schultze went 72 hours straight without sleep. He could land men on the beach, but since he was the driver, he couldn't get off. He noted that he "got awfully hungry. I was more hungry than sleepy. Who could sleep through all of that noise? The men got off to get some food, but I never got any. A storm came up, preventing us from going back to the ship. It was raining hard the whole time. You couldn't stay dry at all. When I finally got untied from the dock, I went back out to find our ship. I had no idea where the thing was. I just knew it was out in the channel somewhere. I tied up to another landing craft and took it with me until I finally found our ship. When I got close, they dropped other people down to take over. I was wet, hungry and exhausted."

Harold's time in the war was not over. He noted, "We then set sail for Naples, then to Saint-Raphael in Southeast France. On August 15,

1944, there was an air attack. I volunteered to go over the side and lay down a smoke screen. I was hit by a German anti-personnel bomb ['Butterfly']. The shrapnel hit the lower part of my body, breaking my leg and causing other wounds. I knew I was hurt but really didn't feel anything. But a chaplain came by and said, 'I think we ought to say a prayer.' I told him I'd already said one. He said, 'Then we ought to say another.' That's when I realized I was hurt more than I thought." Schultze would receive a Purple Heart for his wounds and be offered the option of being discharged or remaining a ship driver. He opted for the discharge. He was treated for his wounds on the ship. He was shipped back to the states and spent several months in the Marine hospital in Norfolk, Virginia, finally getting discharged in June of 1945.

Harold Schultze greeted by Congressman Randy Neugebauer.

Schultze married Mildred Priestley in Ensley, Alabama, on October 11, 1946, and moved to California and worked in the insurance business for 42 years. He and his family moved to Lubbock, Texas, in 2004. He passed away on December 29, 2018, at the age of 93. I have been privileged to meet and interview many of our area's World War II veterans. We, as a nation, owe them so much for the freedom that we still enjoy today. I know Harold would want everyone to remember that day over 75 years ago when so many of our nation's young men gave up their lives and their futures at Normandy. In honor of Harold Schultze—Coast Guard Higgins Boat driver, only 18 years old on June 6, 1945.

60

CHARLES SEARS
Blinded by the Light

Charles Odell Sears had a secret—one he carried with him for 41 years. Odell, from Brownfield, Texas, entered the U.S. Army in February 1944. He and 27 other men from Brownfield all passed their physicals in Lubbock that month. They were soon headed for Ft. Sill, Oklahoma, and their "introduction" to the Army. Next stop for Odell was in Ft. Lewis, Washington, for three months of training where he was told he was now a member of the 739th Tank Battalion. Then it was on to Ft. Knox, Kentucky, for tank field training. Here is what happened next in Odell's own words.

"We were converted to a top-secret outfit but it was still the 739th. We were all investigated by the FBI and sworn to secrecy. We were not allowed to speak or get in direct contact with anyone outside our outfit. The British had invented a secret tank gadget [CDL, or Coastal Defense Light] that they thought would revolutionize the use of tanks in combat. It was a carbon arc lamp that was placed in a tank's turret and its light was projected through a slot in the front of the turret. An operator would intermittently change the light colors. It was meant to confuse the Germans and allow our infantry to advance between the tanks and launch surprise attacks. Because of the hedgerows in Germany, it was not nearly as effective. By the time we arrived in Germany, the Germans were retreating and as far as I know, we only used it twice.

"We were sent to Camp Bouse in the Arizona desert about 50 miles from Phoenix. We were there from January to April 1944 for infantry and night tank training. This was top secret beginning in 1942 and the story was not released until 1983. The 190,000 men who trained there still remember many of the hardships. Nothing was out there that didn't bite, stick or sting. After three months we went back to Ft. Knox, Kentucky.

"We left New York on the troopship USS *Mitchell* [AP-114] and were on our way to Europe on July 25th, 1944. We landed in Liverpool, England, around noon on August 6. The ship we were on carried 5,000 American troops, its crew and a large cargo of vehicles, guns, suppliers, tanks and equipment. We were in a large convoy of 92 ships."

Odell's outfit left England for Le Havre, France, on November 12, 1944. The 739th made its way through Paris, Vézelay and on to Gulpen, Holland, and went through the Battle of the Bulge area. They encountered heavy resistance on their way from the Germans. One of Odell's good friends, Samuel Walker, was killed by German 88 artillery in Germany as he and two others were getting their mess kits from their tanks. Odell had many other close calls and in one German town his unit captured around 200 enemy soldiers. One of his own men dropped a Belgian pistol, which went off and shot Odell in the leg. After a medic stopped the bleeding, he was taken to a field hospital to recover.

Odell was discharged on November 29, 1945. He says he "got back into battle on December 15, 1945." That's when he and Louise married! However, he went on to say, "She is the love of my life and has been by my side for 68 years." They were blessed with two children, Joe and Susan, and grandchildren. Odell worked in hardware in Brownfield for many years and was a city judge for 11½ years and very active in his community.

61

J.L. SLAUGHTER
A Final Mission

Navy veteran J.L. Slaughter had an opportunity to go on earlier flights but "just didn't feel like he deserved to go." At 95 years old, he was finally convinced by family and friends that he should go on the 2016 Texas South Plains Honor Flight. He was looking forward to the trip but little did he know at the time that it was to be his final mission. The annual flight, which takes place in the fall each year, takes area veterans on a three-day trip to Washington, D.C., at no cost to them to see the memorials and museums built to honor their service to their country. World War II veterans are the priority, followed by Korean, Vietnam and other era veterans.

J.L. "Heavy" Slaughter was born April 1, 1921, to James and Dola Slaughter in Terrell, Texas. When he was in elementary school, his family moved to Kermit, Texas. J.L. came by his nickname "Heavy" honestly due to his large size. Always big for his age, he made the varsity football team in the sixth grade! His coach said he had so many stripes on his sweater (for each year he played) that he "looked like an escaped convict."

After high school graduation in 1939, J.L. considered playing college football. However, the world was going to war in Europe due to Nazi Germany's expansion and he noted "at that time I felt the U.S. would be at war with Germany." He and a group of buddies decided to join the service. J.L. was inducted into the Navy on September 9, 1939. He took his basic training in San Diego, California. He was trained as a WT (Water Tender). His duty on board the ship consisted of taking care of the fire room while under way and to maintain, repair and overhaul the boiler system.

In January of 1940, J.L. was assigned to the heavy cruiser USS *Indianapolis* (CA-35) and set sail for Hawaii where he would be stationed for 17 months. He transferred to the USS *Washington* (BB-56), which was to be a lucky break. The *Indianapolis* would be sunk by two torpedoes from a Japanese submarine on July 30, 1945. The *Indianapolis* had just finished delivering the atomic bomb that would be dropped on Hiroshima to the island of Tinian. They were headed for Leyte when the ship went down. Out of the nearly 1,200 on board, 900 were able to hit the water before the ship sank in 12 minutes, taking over 300 of her crew down with her. Out of 900 men, only 317 survived through 5 days of shark attacks, exposure, hunger, thirst and wounds. This was the greatest loss of life at sea in the Navy's history.

In late April 1942, J.L.'s new ship, the USS *Washington* (BB-56), was designated the flagship of Task Force 99. The ship led the task force in reconnaissance and patrol duties in the North Atlantic. The *Washington* sailed out of the New York Navy Yard for the Pacific Ocean on August 23, 1942, escorted by three destroyers. She would go on to win 13 battle stars and was the only World War II battleship to defeat another (the Japanese battleship *Kirishima*) in direct combat. According to J.L., "The Japanese feared her more than any ship afloat." She also had the distinction of being the only battleship of never losing a single life due to combat during World War II.

During the latter part of the war, J.L. was assigned to the new USS *Alaska* (CB-1). The USS *Alaska* website (http://www.ussalaskacb-1.com/) states, "Between February and July 1945, the Alaska provided anti-aircraft protection for the carriers during raids on Japanese home islands and during the Okinawa campaign. She also fired two shore bombardment missions with her 12" guns." J.L.'s service would finally end on Veterans Day, November 11, 1945. He participated in several sea battles during the war and would win numerous ribbons and medals. J.L. had done his duty and then some.

He married Doris Murphy on December 1, 1945, in Glassboro, New Jersey, and moved to Kermit, Texas. He worked with his dad in the grocery business and then owned and operated a drive-in theater there. He served on the Kermit City Council for 8 years, and as a municipal judge. He also enjoyed raising cutting horses for many years. After the death of his wife, Doris, in 2004, J.L. would move to Levelland, Texas, to be closer to his family. It was there that he met Betty Hacker, a widow from Olton, Texas, who was going to move to Levelland when she met J.L. at a senior citizens' dance there. They would marry (with the family's permission) on November 19, 2005.

J.L. and Betty would go to the dance every Friday night. Domino playing was a "guy thing" and they kept the players exclusively male. When J.L. joined the group, he asked them if they played for money. They responded by saying, "No, just blood." J.L. would fit right in. He

J.L. Slaughter, U.S. Navy (far right) with Navy buddies.

would drive himself to Ropesville, Texas, to play dominoes even though his vision was poor. Betty said "nobody wanted to ride with him." He would never admit he couldn't see to drive and was so proud to still have his driver's license at 95 years old that he was buried with it in his hand.

J.L. was ready to go on the 2016 Texas South Plains Honor Flight and was assigned Barry Sims from Brownfield as his guardian. Though they had never met, they quickly formed a bond. Barry said that "J.L. was honored to lay the first wreath on the Pacific War side of the World War II Memorial in D.C. and became very emotional." He would go on to see some of the Marine Corps Museum near Quantico, Virginia. He called Betty from his hotel room to recount the hero's welcome in Baltimore, Maryland, and Washington, D.C. and the day's emotionally moving events. Later, he told Barry that he was not feeling well and went to bed. When he got up around 6:00 a.m., he was sick and Barry contacted the Honor Flight medical team and they decided to take him to a local hospital. It was clear that he would not be able to travel back to Lubbock with the Honor Flight.

After surgery for an obstructed bowel, J.L. seemed to be doing better and the family flew up to D.C. and spent a few days with him. His son Bruce said he liked to talk about history and what he had seen while on the Honor Flight. A couple of days after they returned home, they received a call that his breathing and blood pressure were irregular and he was put on a ventilator and that the family should come. Bruce and

61. J.L. Slaughter

J.L. Slaughter (in wheelchair) with guardian Barry Sims.

his son Jody were at his side when J.L. passed away on October 5, 2016. His guardian, Barry Sims, noted that "he got his last request to go on the Honor Flight and lay the wreath at the World War II Memorial. He was a real gentleman." The family thought so much of Barry that they asked him to be a pallbearer at J.L.'s funeral.

62

CLIFFORD SOLOMON
"God Bless America"

Clifford J. "Bunk" Solomon is still a spry 96 years old. He says he "forgets a lot of things now," but after we started talking about his life and his time as a soldier during World War II, his recall is quite amazing. Clifford was born at home on August 5, 1923, to Ples and Pearl Solomon near Comanche, Texas. He was the 4th of 11 children born to the couple although one died at birth, which was not uncommon in those days. With a big family to support and the country in the midst of the Depression, Bunk's formal schooling ended at the 7th grade. He said he was "too busy on the farm to play any sports in school—Dad needed my help on the farm." When asked about his unusual nickname, Bunk said his mother's uncle used to call him "Bodunk" and somehow the name became Bunk, which he has gone by ever since. The word "Bodunk" generally means a hick location or town. Bunk was certainly from a small town.

Bunk married Edna Myrle Bingham in Comanche on October 14, 1942. He was only 19 and she was 17. The couple began raising a family. However, Bunk received his draft notice and was inducted into the Army Air Corps on February 22, 1943. Sent to Camp Wolters in Mineral Wells, Texas, to be inducted, he was assigned to the 11th Airborne Division ("Angels") and sent to Camp MacKall in North Carolina for intense basic training. "The place was nothing but sand and pine cones. I was assigned to the 187th Glider Infantry Regiment. I think I saw all of North and South Carolina from a glider during our training. We were always doing double time [running] everywhere. We were very well trained. We were put on a train to Camp Polk in Louisiana for further training. Around this time I came down with what they thought was meningitis and stayed in the hospital for 42 days. The 11th Airborne was shipped out in April to the Pacific. My brother-in-law, Earl Bingham, who went in the service with me, was killed on his first jump. He had written his folks and told them that if he was killed, to not bring his body back to the States but to leave him with his buddies, so he is buried on an island in the Pacific."

With his unit now gone, Bunk was assigned to the 94th Infantry and shipped to Camp McCain near Grenada, Mississippi. The 94th was going through basic training and Bunk joined in. "Their training was easier than ours," he said. "We shipped out of New York Harbor on the RMS *Queen Elizabeth*, a converted troop carrier. It was big enough to take the whole division. We zigzagged all the way to Scotland. We then went to England via troop trucks. We sailed across the English Channel and landed on Utah Beach in September 1944. There was still a pocket of 60,000 Germans there surrounded by Allied forces in the ports of Lorient and St. Nazaire. The Germans had an 88 mm cannon hidden in a church. They would roll that out and fire at the Allies, then roll it back under the cover of the church steeple. At first, the American commander tried taking it out with 105 mm cannon, which wasn't powerful enough. Then he had two 155 mm cannons fire at it and the steeple collapsed, taking out the German 88." The 94th inflicted 2,700 casualties on the enemy and took 566 prisoners before being relieved on New Year's Day, 1945. The 94th moved out across France. During the next five months, Bunk endured several battles, sniper fire and more German 88s. Fighting in the small towns was often street to street. Bunk recalled, "We were taught that jumpoffs [a military term for moving forward into combat] should occur during the morning. That didn't work. We were shooting at Germans across the street and they would shoot at us. You would hear guys cry out that they were hit. A German woman gave away our positions until she was captured and ended that threat. We went through a lot of towns where houses were just blown to bits. Most were left no more than six feet high. Even the chickens had no feathers left on them. The animals lived in the house with the German families, usually on the first floor and the families lived on the upper floors (if they were still standing)."

Bunk's unit headed west and took positions in the Saar-Moselle Triangle, facing the so-called Siegfried Line. Recalling the move, Bunk recalled, "We knocked out some pill boxes. Our unit pulled out, but 22 of us were left out on the point. One of the German tanks rolled up and aimed their 88 mm right at the pill box we were in and we were forced to surrender." Bunk was now a POW (prisoner of war). "Our artillery started firing, making holes about 5 feet deep, so the Germans pulled back about 5 miles and took us with them. They interviewed each one of us. We would only give them name, rank and serial number. Noting my last name, Solomon, the Germans kept asking me if I was Jewish.

Being a young smart-aleck kid, I said, 'No, but I wish I was.' It's a wonder I wasn't shot! I told them my granddad was ¾ German. I don't think they believed me." Remembering his 4 months in captivity, Bunk recalled, "They put us in an old schoolhouse at first. A German sergeant came in one day and said a local farmer needed some help. Me and a boy from Iowa went. It turned out the farmer raised tobacco and had us rolling cigars. The farmer asked where we were from and I told him I was from Texas. He went and got a postcard from the U.S. He said his son was a POW of the Americans in Texas. It was in Brownwood [Texas] close to where I grew up. The farmer had also been a POW of the Americans during World War I. He treated us real nice after that. I even received a letter from him after the war."

In February 1945, Bunk and his buddies along with other prisoners from England, France and Turkey were assembled and ordered to start marching. Bunk continued, "We would march with a few German guards and German Shepherd dogs to keep us in line and moving. We marched day and night." During this time, out of over 257,000 prisoners held by the Germans, approximately 80,000 of them were forced to march west toward Poland, Czechoslovakia and Germany in extreme winter conditions. Many of the survivors called this "The Long March." Many of the POWs believed that Adolf Hitler had issued orders to kill all Allied prisoners. Thankfully, many of the German soldiers ignored this edict. They just kept marching all around Europe. Bunk did note that "if you fell out, they would shoot you. If you tried to help a buddy, they would shoot you. It's a shame what one man can do to another. We did our best to help each other out. We had very few clothes on and sometimes wouldn't eat or drink water for 3 or 4 days. We found shelter wherever we could. You found out you could sleep

C.J. Solomon, U.S. Army World War II.

while walking—I know, I did it. They kept us marching. It seemed like we were walking in circles. They marched through several towns in Germany where people would yell at us, throw things at us and spit on us. We eventually wound up in a little town close to Austria (as the war was coming to a close) and came to a halt and the guards turned us loose and told us which direction to go. A German officer and sergeant had slipped behind American lines and told them where to find us." Recalling the happy day that the men were liberated, Buck said, "A big green tank with a large white star rolled up (to liberate us). I could have kissed that tank. My first thought was God bless America! There were only 10 of us left out of the 22 who were captured in my outfit.

"We had a few days not doing anything. A buddy and I found a German motorcycle with a sidecar and rode it all over the place for 2 days and then left it in a bar ditch." The men were cleaned up (many had lice and were still wearing the same clothes that they had been captured in months earlier) and put on a boat headed for the United States. Back in the States, Bunk said, "They told a group of us that if we cooperated, they would have us back in El Paso, Texas, within 72 hours by train. Once in El Paso, a guy picked us up in a car and drove four of us to Abilene. I had a 30-day leave and went home. I didn't have enough

C.J. Solomon, February 21, 2019.

points to be discharged, so I reported to Ft. Sam Houston. They told me I could either go to Japan or join the Army Air Corps. I was back where I started out [in the Air Corps]. I was sent to Randolph Field where I drove for a Colonel Gunn. I found out there was a lot of difference in Air Corps and Infantry officers. Colonel Gunn was very nice to me."

With tears in his eyes, Bunk sadly recalled that he and his wife, Myrle, lost a baby girl during the war. "She passed away from whooping cough while I was overseas." The couple had 1 son and 2 daughters and was married for 61 years before Myrle's death in October 2003.

Discharged in December 1946, Bunk and his brother opened up an auto repair shop. He went to work for Clemmons Ford in Comanche until 1951, then moved to Abilene and worked at Haynes Ford until 1951. A short stint in the oil patch followed in Snyder, Texas. The Solomon family would move one more time, to Lubbock, Texas, where Bunk went to work for Harmon Tank and retired there in 1988 after 33 years. Soon bored of retirement, he worked for several car dealers in Lubbock delivering and picking up cars all over the country. He said, "In 2009, I drove 99,000 miles and flew 82 times for car dealers." He met a widow, Dorothy Cox Hooten, and they married in October 2004. She had 5 children from her previous marriage. Bunk said he would like to be remembered for "being a good man who loved his family and his country." His final comments echoed the thoughts of many veterans that I have talked to: "I wouldn't give a million bucks for my experiences, but sure wouldn't want any more like 'em!"

63

ELMER TARBOX
Texas Tech All-American

Elmer Tarbox once said that when he made his first bombing run in a B-25, "I had a knot in my belly as big as a sweet potato. My hands shook, my palms were sweaty and I kind of wished I was back in Texas." Despite his fear, Elmer had a successful run and would go on to fly 27 more missions against the Japanese in the China-Burma-India Theater. December 27, 1942, was to be his 28th and last mission. While returning from a run over the Salween River, and flying through a mountain pass only 100 miles from their base, Elmer's plane was strafed by Japanese machine guns. He said, "The one that got me came through the side wall of the ship, just missing the armor plate. It tore through my thighs. It was a terrific wallop. I blacked out and Brownie [his co-pilot] took the ship in." The bullet had struck one of the steel supports on the co-pilot seat and dropped to the floor. Brownie picked it up and later gave it to Elmer who kept it as a war souvenir. When the crew brought their B-25 back to base, they counted 89 bullet holes in it.

Elmer was born on March 7, 1916, in Bishop, Oklahoma, the son of J.E. and Emma May Tarbox. He grew up and attended school in Higgins, Texas, and was the valedictorian of his 1935 class. He entered Texas Tech that year, and even though he had never played football, he played it so well at Tech that he made several all-American teams. He set several national records for passes intercepted, yardage gained from interceptions and touchdown runs with intercepted passes. He still holds the season record for interceptions with 11 (and only played in 11 games!) and is second in school history with 17 in his career. His 1938 team went 10–0 before falling to St. Mary's in the Cotton Bowl 20–13. Elmer scored both of Tech's touchdowns. Coach Pete Cawthon had given him the name "Elmer the Great." After graduating, he was drafted number 18 in the NFL draft by the Cleveland Rams but declined their offer. He also lettered in basketball and track and boxed in the off-season.

Elmer worked for Lubbock Auto Company for two years after graduation. He enlisted in the Army Air Forces as a cadet on June 27, 1940. He received flying instruction at Love, Randolph and Brooks Fields in Texas. Upon graduation from flying school, he was transferred to Tacoma, Washington, as a co-pilot in a bombardment group. In the spring of 1942 he was transferred to an airbase at Columbia, South Carolina. In June of that year, he was sent overseas as a bomber combat pilot in the China-Burma-India Theater. He mentioned that the "Japanese would bomb our base ... and often." He also noted that the Japanese Zero pilots were "gutsy and they could fly." He and his fellow B-25s were strafed many times during their missions and were impressed by the aerial skills of the Japanese pilots.

After being wounded, Elmer was flown to New Delhi where he spent four and one-half months in the hospital recovering. He returned to his base and was put in charge of armament and bomb-site maintenance. He developed a machine gun that could be mounted in the tail section of a B-25. This had heretofore been a weak spot on that craft, and Elmer was credited with saving numerous lives as a result of his invention. He was awarded an Air Medal, a Silver Star, a Purple Heart, a Golden Eagle of China and other medals and ribbons.

Upon being discharged, Elmer was involved in numerous Lubbock businesses. One was Elmer's Weights, which he developed for athletes to use in conditioning. In 1966 he won the first of what would be five terms in the Texas State Legislature. He sponsored numerous bills, including one that funded the building of the Texas Tech Medical School and another that established the Tarbox Parkinson's Disease Institute (one of six such facilities in the world) at Texas Tech in 1972. He was a member of the board of St. John's Methodist Church in Lubbock, a president of the Texas Tech Ex-Students Association, and a member of the Texas Tech Athletic Hall of Fame. Tarbox married Maxine M. Barnett (his college sweetheart) on March 29, 1944, and they had four children. He died in Lubbock on November 2, 1987, of complications of Parkinsonism.

Special thanks to the Bill E. Tarbox family for their contribution to this story.

64

Dominic Tartaglione
Survivor of Three "Wars"

Dominic Tartaglione was drafted in the U.S. Army in New York City in 1941. He took his basic training in New Jersey and was trained in recon to help determine where to put field hospitals close to the front line during combat. He was in the 3rd Army, 108th Evacuation Hospital in Europe under General George Patton. Dom told me that they "came under heavy fire numerous times." He was unable to land on Utah Beach at Normandy on June 6, 1944, because his landing craft was stuck on a sand bar and "didn't hit the beach until June 12." The 108th was involved in five of the major battles during World War II in the European Theater. Dom was very resourceful during his time in the Army and was able to "procure" numerous items that would help make his job easier or faster while scouting out a possible site for a field hospital. This included a German BMW motorcycle, which his buddies painted a star on to look like an American motorcycle! One of his "offbeat" orders was to help his captain to disassemble unexploded hand grenades. They dug a hole 3–4 feet deep, laid flat on the ground, stretched out their arms so their hands were just over the hole and slowly took apart the hand grenades.

Dom got out of the Army in December of 1945, and returned to New York City. His first job was working in auto parts. Dom said he "met his future wife, Josephine, at a teenage dance." He was 18; she was 16. They married in October 1946. They had a son, Dana, and a daughter, Joanne. He took the test to become a policeman in 1949 and retired in 1971. Dom's son, Dana, himself a former Major in the Air Force (he first went through the enlisted ranks and then joined the ROTC during college), told me his dad's time as a policeman was also like being at war—only his dad called it "urban warfare." Dom had many adventures as a policeman in New York City. Whether it was a humorous or a deadly situation, Dom distinguished himself during his career.

He was in the Air Force Reserve during his time as a policeman and made numerous trips to Vietnam to deliver troops and supplies as a Chief Loadmaster on a C141 Starlifter and various other aircraft. He retired at the highest enlisted rank of Chief Master Sergeant in 1981 at 60 years old.

Dom and Josephine moved to Lubbock, Texas, in 1996 to be closer to his family. However, Josephine passed away in April of 2007 and Dom moved to Raider Ranch in 2011. Sadly, Dom was on his way to visit his daughter when he was killed in an auto accident on March 17, 2014. Exiting off of I-20 in Alabama, he struck a tree. Witnesses said it appeared he did everything he could to keep from hitting a woman walking a dog. As Dana said, "That sounds like Dad—always a life of service."

65

Pat Thurman
Twice as Lucky during Two Wars

"I went on the 2nd Honor Flight and my favorite memorial was the majestic Lincoln Memorial," said Pat Thurman, who went on the Texas South Plains Honor Flight in 2013. "I agree with my generation being called the Greatest Generation because we volunteered to serve our country. I thought the Honor Flight was a great experience and would recommend it to any veteran who served in the military."

Pat's dad was an engineer and had his own business, but lost everything during the Depression and moved his family to Lubbock in 1935 so the kids could attend Texas Tech. He worked for the government here as an inspector.

While at basic training at Camp Roberts, California, in 1944, Pat had two experiences that challenged the fibers of his being. One was "when one of the guys took the plug out of the grenade and almost dropped it. He was grabbed by someone who saved us all. Another was when we were in the hills in a training session and a huge snake came out of the bushes and crawled across several of our laps."

Pat was supposed to go to the Battle of the Bulge with his unit, the 751st AAA Battalion, but he caught pneumonia and was held back. He noted that "most of the soldiers from his unit got killed." He was sent to Ft. Eustis in Virginia. He ended up being shipped to New York and Hawaii as the stage was set for the invasion of Japan and luckily he did not have to go. The last event was when his unit embarked from Seattle and headed to the Hawaiian Islands and zigzagged back and forth, to avoid enemy attack. The ship held 3,500 but Pat said, "It felt like we had 13,000 soldiers aboard. All we did was stand in line for meals." He heard the bomb had been dropped on Hiroshima and he stayed in Honolulu until he was sent back to the States and discharged in Ft. Sill, Oklahoma, in 1946. He chose to go into the reserves, being influenced by his oldest brother who, he said, "was looking out for [his] future."

He enrolled at Tech and was selected to be a cheerleader his senior year for the Texas Tech football and basketball teams (1949 and 1950) and graduated in 1950. As soon as Pat graduated in 1950, he volunteered for the Korean War. He ended up in Ft. Eustis, Virginia. He was promoted to Master Sergeant and then a commission. He decided that if he resigned as an enlisted man he would have to be an active duty officer for 3 more years, so he carried a dual rank as Master Sergeant and 2nd Lieutenant. He served in Augsburg, Germany. While on furlough in England, he saw the funeral procession of King George VI out his hotel window.

He was discharged in Germany and returned to Lubbock. He then applied for a job at Eastman Kodak in Dallas and got the job in 1953, which he stayed at for 30 years. He met and married Ethel Bloomquist in 1955, and raised one daughter, Ingrid. Ethel passed away on December 24, 2015. Pat and Ethel were married for nearly 60 years.

66

TRUETT TYLER
Following His Brothers

Truett Tyler grew up on a farm near O'Donnell, Texas, and was the youngest of four brothers. One of his brothers died in 1932 at age 8. Truett graduated early from O'Donnell High School at age 16. He watched his other older brothers, Graham and R.L., go off to war. One day, while hoeing weeds, his dad suddenly asked him if he would like to go to college and offered to pay his way for one year.

He started Texas Tech in the fall of 1942, but attended for only one year. Truett followed his brothers' examples and enlisted in the Army Air Corps in April 1944 in Lubbock. He was sent to Amarillo Army Air Field for basic training. The young man had dreamed of flying ever since a childhood experience on a carnival ride shaped like an airplane. However, by the time he was ready for flight school training, the demand for bomber pilots had declined, and he became part of a flight crew that worked on small trainer planes.

He was sent for additional training at Stockton Field in California, and then transferred to Carlsbad Army Air Base, which was a bomber training school. His assignment was to score bomb hits by the trainees. It was here that he met Leah, whom he married in 1950. He was then transferred to Lowry Field near Denver, Colorado. He was doing clerical work and reported that he "obtained the speed of 60 mistakes a minute." In spite of his "mistakes," he became a typing instructor. The military needs all kinds of skills. Truett was discharged from the service in November 1945.

He returned to Texas Tech and went into the ROTC program. He was offered a commission as a second lieutenant upon graduation in 1949. He declined the offer and went to work at Westinghouse Electric as an industrial engineer. He had a variety of jobs over his career, including a stint at General Dynamics in San Diego, and retired in 1988. As he grew older, Truett realized how much he missed West Texas and moved to Wolfforth in 2004.

Truett is a patriot who values the contribution of all veterans. The story of the service of one of his brothers, in particular, is one he wanted to tell. His brother, R.L., joined the Army Air Corps in Lubbock in 1939. He trained at March Field in California and was sent to Nichols Field in the Philippines in 1940, where he was trained to be a radio operator. However, a Japanese attack was imminent and R.L. became an infantryman to help defend the island of Luzon. He was transferred to Bataan where 74,000 Filipino and American servicemen held out for over three months against the invading Japanese. R.L. was captured on his birthday in April 1942. A few days later the men were forced to begin the grueling 90-mile journey now known as the Bataan Death March. Thousands lost their lives because of brutal physical abuse and merciless killing. R.L. survived the horrible experience but succumbed to malaria and died at the POW camp at Cabanatuan on July 19, 1942. Truett traveled to the Philippines in 2001 to pay his respects to his missing brother and his fellow missing servicemen.

Truett's son, Jeff, sent me an email concerning his uncle saying, "In May of 2017, I was contacted by the Defense POW/MIA Accounting Agency [DPAA] and asked if I thought my dad, I, and my two younger brothers might provide DNA samples via cheek swabs to aid in attempts to identify R.L.'s remains among those of unknown soldiers who died and were buried in the Philippines. Dad and I then provided samples, after which Dad died in September at age 91. The Army kept in contact with R.L.'s parents (my grandparents) about his status during and after the war. Among the correspondence I have is a letter to R.L.'s mother dated 11 October, 1949, indicating, in part, that, 'I wish to assure you that, should any additional evidence come to our attention indicating that his remains are in our possession, you will be notified immediately.' On 12 October, 2019, 70 years and one day from the date of that letter, we received official notification of identification of some of R.L.'s remains." The following release is from the Defense POW/MIA Accounting Agency, October 22, 2019: "The Defense POW/MIA Accounting Agency (DPAA) announced today that U.S. Army Air Forces Sgt. R.L. Tyler, 22, of Denton County, Texas, who was captured and died in captivity during World War II, was accounted for Sept. 10, 2019."

67

ED WARD

"If You're Not Scared, You're Lying"

Ed Ward said these were words to live by during combat duty in World War II. He had numerous close calls during his time in France and Germany. He "hit the front lines on Armistice Day, November 11, 1944, on the Siegfried Line." Here are a few examples of the "close calls" that Ward encountered. It wasn't long after he entered the war zone that he was shot at by a sniper whose bullet hit the tree next to him. Another time, after being pinned down by a sniper, he "jumped into a nearby foxhole, and as he was sliding down in the hole, he nearly set off a land mine." Once during a patrol through some woods carrying his BAR (Browning automatic rifle), he "caught something out of the corner of his eye, and it was a German holding a burp gun on him." Ward simply said "nichts" (nothing) in German and motioned for the German to lay down his weapon. Ed found himself with a prisoner. Then there was another time, also in woods, when German 88 artillery rained overhead and hit a tree right above him. He "was hit by splinters, [got a] concussion and hit the hot dirt." Miraculously, while Ed saw a lot of dead and wounded soldiers, he came through the war unscathed.

Edward Eugene Ward was born in Tahoka, Texas, on October 10, 1925. While attending high school in Woodrow, Texas, in March of 1944, Ed received his draft notice. He had asked his superintendent for a waiver, but the man would not sign off on it, so he was shipped off to Ft. Sill for indoctrination and on to Ft. Hood for basic training. After basic, he was sent to Camp Howze in Gainesville, Texas, where he was assigned to Company A, 1st Battalion, 411th Infantry Regiment, 103rd Infantry Division ("Cactus") and then on to New York, where he boarded a troop ship headed for Marseille, France.

While in action on the Siegfried Line, PFC Ed Ward and Theodore Szymanski, Maple Shade, New Jersey, were ordered to stand watch. PFC Ward pulled his shift and was relieved by PFC Szymanski. PFC Ward, dog-tired from constant combat, laid down under his raincoat and went to sleep, only to be rudely awakened by five German soldiers demanding he surrender. Ward and Szymanski were taken to a nearby pillbox for interrogation. They spent the night there. While in the pillbox, Szymanski, fluent in Polish, struck up a conversation with a Polish-speaking German. He convinced the soldier that the hills surrounding the pillboxes were full of Americans and hundreds of big tanks.

About this time, the tanks begin to fire on the pillbox, as did 105 mm howitzers. The explosions were deafening outside the pillbox door. This frightened the Germans to the extent that they agreed to surrender to Ward and Szymanski. As the American attackers neared the German concrete fortification, Ward and Szymanski jerked open the door and Ward stuck out a "white flag" indicating they were surrendering. Immediately the two American servicemen came out of the pillbox with Szymanski in front, followed by 18 Germans, and Ward trailing behind.

Ed moved up through the ranks quickly as attrition took its toll. His captain wanted to promote him to Staff Sergeant, but Ed kept refusing until the last of the sergeants had been either killed or wounded. Then he had no choice but to accept. PFC Ward was promoted to Staff Sergeant on March 25, 1945, and after V-E Day, on June 16, 1945, he transferred to the 11th Infantry Regiment, 5th Infantry Division. He was discharged March 22, 1946, in Atterbury, Indiana, and spent just 3 days short of 2 years in the Army.

When asked who his hero is, Anita's name is the first out of his mouth, since she has "put up with him for 67 years." Anita, the daughter of the man who helped construct buildings at Reese Air Force Base, met Edward on a blind date on her 18th birthday. They have four children, four grandchildren and two step-grandchildren. After their wedding Edward worked as a delivery freight line truck driver in Kansas City and Oklahoma and retired in 1987. After retiring, Edward decided to stay active by mowing yards. He eventually retired for good and went fishing at Lake Texoma.

68

WAYNE WEBB
Three Years on the Water

The USS *Gridley* (DD-380) saw a lot of action in the Pacific Theater during World War II. Lubbock resident Carl "Wayne" Webb served on the ship and was involved in six engagements with the enemy. He even has copies of the ship's logs from his stint on the *Gridley*. She was a 1,500-ton destroyer with an advanced power plant and could achieve close to 40 knots, making it one of the fastest American destroyers ever. Her main job was to escort aircraft carriers such as the USS *Enterprise* (CV-6), *Nashville* (CL-43), *Saratoga* (CV-3), *Yorktown* (CV-5), *Princeton* (CVL-23) and many others. Petty Officer Webb was a Gunner's Mate 1st Class.

Wayne Webb was born in Quanah, Texas, to Carl and Mary Webb on January 3, 1921. He attended school in Quanah and "made it through the 11th grade." He grew up in a large family. Two of his brothers, Harold in the Army and Weldon in the Seabees, also served during World War II. Harold survived the Battle of the Bulge in Europe. Wayne moved to Lubbock, Texas, in 1939 and was working at Wylie Drugstore when he received his draft notice. Electing not to go into the Army as a "ground pounder," he had a friend who was a Navy Recruiter who said he "could get [him] into that branch with no problem."

After eight weeks of basic training in San Diego, Wayne boarded the troop ship SS *Lurline* (SS for steam ship), a converted ocean liner, for the voyage to Hawaii. After a short stint loading ammunition on board the USS *Whitney* (AD-4), he spent 18 months aboard the USS *Gridley*. Recalling the bombardment of Japanese-held Kiska in August 1942, Webb said, "We shot off 535 rounds with four 5" guns." The *Gridley* also guarded the high-speed transports that rescued the survivors from the USS *Helena* (CL-50) in Pareso Bay in July 1943. Then she served as an escort for an infantry landing on Tambatuni, New Georgia, where the ship bombarded shore installations near the invasion beaches. The

Wayne Webb, USS *Gridley* print.

Gridley's logs record numerous entries of "sounding general quarters" and "commence firing" and the number of rounds fired from the 5" guns. The destroyer also assisted in the bombardment of Makin Island before heading back to Hawaii for repairs.

Webb asked for a transfer from the *Gridley* in late 1943 and attended Advanced Hydraulic School in Washington, D.C. He married Evelyn Raybon "while on a 10-day leave" in February 1944. Back in San Diego in the spring of 1944, Wayne joined the seaplane tender USS *Kenneth Whiting* (AV-14) and "became a 'plank owner' by being among the

Wayne Webb, March 14, 2018.

first crew on the ship." The ship arrived in Saipan on August 14, 1944, for operations in the Marianas. She steamed to Okinawa, arriving on April 25 and commenced combat and search operations. "We picked up 21 Japanese prisoners who came down out of the hills waving a white flag. They'd had enough." The *Kenneth Whiting* was hit by a Japanese kamikaze plane on June 21, 1945, but survived with only minor damage, continuing operations for the rest of the war. Wayne was onboard the ship when the atomic bombs were dropped on Hiroshima and Nagasaki in August 1945.

He was discharged from the Navy on November 8, 1945. "I took a train from San Francisco to Amarillo and then hitchhiked down to Plainview where my wife picked me up." He and his wife raised two boys, David and John. Back in Lubbock, he worked at W&L Manufacturing for 12 years and eventually became vice president of the company. He later started his own company, W.W. Steel, and retired in the 1990s, after working in the industry for 50 years.

The three years that the West Texas native spent out on the ocean are a distant memory. In fact, Wayne Webb says now he'd like to be remembered "just as a plain old country boy."

69

GENE WILLIAMS
A World Traveler

As I always do at the conclusion of my interviews, I hand the veteran my card and tell them to let me know if there is anything they forgot to tell me. I received the following message a short time after my interview with World War II veteran Gene Williams (no relation to the author): "Larry, I didn't tell you that I have been around the world 7 times." No, Gene, you didn't. I marveled at how a man who grew up in Anton and Lubbock, Texas, had "been around the world 7 times." A far cry from delivering auto parts on his bicycle back in the 1930s in Lubbock.

Eugene Harriel Williams ("the doctor apparently couldn't spell Harold," noted Gene) was born on October 29, 1927, in Lorenzo, Texas, to Lynn and Lela Williams. His father became an early mechanic of automobiles and opened up a repair garage in Anton, Texas. He said his dad "worked mainly on Chevrolet's, but was the first Ford factory-trained mechanic in Texas and went to school in Chicago for that." Gene started helping out around the shop at age 7. A 1944 graduate of Lubbock High, Gene played baseball and even played for a time for the Lubbock Hubbers, a minor league team that existed from 1922 to 1956. He enlisted in the Navy on November 8, 1944. When asked why the Navy, he simply said, "It was better than walking."

Basic training for Gene was at the Naval Training Center in San Diego. He was assigned to the Seabees, specifically, the 124th Naval Construction Battalion. The 124th left the states January 1, 1945, arriving at Adak in the Aleutian Islands. Arrival at Adak was a bit rough. "We were flown there, but there was no landing strip, so they literally pushed us out of the plane. I parachuted out and hit into snow up to my chest," noted Williams. "We started building runways out of corrugated metal and built docks for the ships to be able to unload. I drove a jeep and it would get as low as -56 degrees at night so I kept the jeep running all night and hooked up some coils with coal oil at night and put them under my bunk to stay warm. Later, we were loaded on ships with bulldozers and building equipment."

Gene became part of the Seabees work island hopping and would be dropped off by aircraft carriers for "clearing the beachheads on the islands in the Pacific." It was essential to clear off the landing areas before the Marines would be dropped off on shore to face the Japanese. "We were the first ones on some of these beaches such as Iwo Jima and Okinawa. While we carried an M-1 rifle, I was plenty scared. We had no Marines with us. It was just us. A couple of our guys were wounded." After the dropping of the atomic bombs on Hiroshima and Nagasaki, the war in the Pacific ended. Gene and his fellow Seabees would experience the effect of the atomic bomb themselves. As he explained, "We were on a destroyer and were close to the Bikini Atoll in the summer of 1946 when a nuclear device was detonated. We were hit with a 90-foot tidal wave and it seemed like the ship flipped over. I was radioactive for several years then it was suddenly gone. I returned to Seattle in 1946 but anyone from the Aleutian Islands had to wait 2 weeks to be discharged. Some of us went over the fence and showed up some days later. The captain said, 'Get your discharge and go home.'" It took Gene "about 3 weeks to get back to Lubbock."

Gene began doing some oilfield work and met a waitress in Anton named Winifred Johnson and they were married for 66 years until her death in July 2014. They had one daughter, Jeanetta. Gene began working as a subcontractor in the Middle East. He would bid on jobs through Lummus International Sales out of New York. His travels took him to Afghanistan, Iraq, Jordan and Syria among others. He went to work personally for Saddam Hussein supervising building projects. His wife and daughter would live in Greece for a time while he was in the Middle East and he could visit them on the weekends. Working for Saddam had its perils. Once he had to obtain his signature to be paid for a job. The banker would not accept the check and Gene had to bring back some of Saddam's personal guards. They verified that the signature was indeed Saddam's and he said it "took the bank all day to count out $1 million dollars in $100 bills. The guards took the banker out and shot him. I was scared for my life. I had them take me straight to the airport. I didn't even go back to my hotel. The only flight I could catch was to Moscow. From there I flew to Frankfurt where I could deposit the money and get a cashier's check. I was glad to be out of Iraq."

Gene spent 40 years doing subcontracting work. Gene now spends his days working a little and enjoys playing golf with a large group of buddies. When asked what he would like to be remembered for, he thought about it a bit and said, "That I tried to just be a good old boy." Mission accomplished, Gene. Thank you for your service.

70

ROBERT ELTON WILSON
"The Good Lord Was Always with Me"

West Texans are friendly folks, quick to smile, eager to help, private with their emotions and strong in their convictions. Robert Elton Wilson, Jr., was no exception. The vast Texas plains were his home, the only life he knew. That was about to change. World War II and the Army Air Corps would open a new world to this comely young man who had stayed close to his roots. Elton's new military name was Bob. And his new home was a tent shared with three guys from places he had seen only on a map. An uncommon friendship grew especially with a New Jersey man, Ted Weisse, a friendship so rich that Bob named his eldest son Ted. Their dangerous journey would take them to distant lands and challenging duties.

Bob Wilson was a long way from West Texas. He arrived in India on December 9, 1943. "The Hump" was a high-altitude military aerial supply route between the Assam Valley in northeastern India, across northern Burma, to Yúnnán province and into southwestern China. It was the primary supply line for the Chinese Army resisting the Japanese along the Burma front. Since the Japanese had control of the so-called Burma Road, this was the only way to get supplies to them.

Robert Elton Wilson, Jr., was born November 21, 1921, in the Hale County community of Snyder, the son of Robert Elton Wilson and Ollie B. White Wilson. He began farm work at an early age, but two years out of high school, his world drastically changed in ways he could never have foreseen.

Bob was visiting friends with his parents on a Sunday afternoon on December 7, 1941, when they heard the news that Pearl Harbor had been bombed. Like so many other young men at that time, Bob wanted to "do his part." He went to the recruiting office in Lubbock and joined the Army Air Corps. He was 20 years old when he passed the tests and was off to the Aviation Cadet Program at Kelly Air Field in San Antonio.

After several weeks of training, he flew his first solo flight on August 10, 1942, in a Fairchild P-19A trainer. One of the proudest days of his life was when Bob earned his wings on February 16, 1943. He went on to train on a Curtiss C-46 Commando cargo plane in Reno, Nevada, and then was assigned a crew in Buffalo, New York. From there it was a long journey to his base in the Assam province in northwest India. In Bob's words, the mission was to "deliver all kinds of supplies to the Chinese who were cut off from the east and south by the Japanese." He also "brought many Chinese back to India to be trained as soldiers."

The "Hump" was a formidable set of mountains to fly over since the planes would take off from only 90 feet above sea level and quickly climb to heights of 10,000 feet or more. Bob mentioned that "the weather was severe almost year round—winds would often exceed 100 miles per hour and it was hard to keep the plane level." He went on to say, "The General didn't believe in weather so we flew." Bob noted that "sometimes heavy rain and lightning would form an electrical charge along the edge of the wings, props and nose and would flash off like lightning"—the phenomenon known as "St. Elmo's fire." Bob felt that he was "very lucky that the good Lord was with him." He went on to fly 92 missions over the "Hump." According to official records of the operation, the airlift "expended" 594 aircraft. At least 468 American and 41 CNAC (Chinese National Airways Corporation) aircraft were known lost from all causes, with 1,314 air crewmen and passengers killed. In addition 81 more aircraft were never accounted for, with their 345 personnel listed as missing. Another 1,200 personnel had been rescued or walked back to base on their own. So many planes had crashed that this stretch came to be called the "aluminum trail." Bob had indeed been "very lucky."

Bob's time in India ended in December 1944. He returned to Dallas, Texas, and was transferred to the "Ferry Command" where he flew all types of aircraft and delivered new P51-D Mustangs to various airports around the country. He was then assigned to Special Missions in June 1945 in Washington, D.C. His primary assignment then was to "fly dignitary personnel such as generals and their families returning from other countries." He was finally discharged on November 19, 1945, and eventually took a train to Lubbock. It was January 1, 1945. Bob noted that he had "spent three Christmases away from home."

After discharge Bob wanted to go to college. He had an offer to fly for a major airline. He returned to the family he loved and the flat land he called home. His dad hugged him and said, "I'm glad you're home, son, I really need you here on the farm." So Bob laid aside his dreams, ambitions, preferences and dropped his military name, once again answering to the name Elton. He never regretted that decision.

The farm kept Elton busy so he had little social life. He was a quiet man, and a bit timid around ladies, so a friend set him up with a blind date. Her name was Anne Whorton. He lost his heart to this lovely lady. He married her and moved her into a house without running water or electricity. They shared 54 years together and brought up four children: two boys, Ted and Paul, and two girls, Sue and Jane. Elton's comment was always "I've had a good life."

Elton and Ted Weisse stayed in touch, attended Hump Pilot Reunions, exchanged Christmas letters and phone calls until Ted's death. That was a tremendous loss to Elton, but the memories they shared constantly brought him comfort.

Elton lived to be 94. He left behind 6 grandchildren, 10 great-grandchildren, 2 long-time golfing buddies, Mike Howell and Lloyd Belk, a host of friends, loving neighbors, and a yawning emptiness in the hearts that will always love and miss him.

Special thanks to Ted and Jody Boudreaux Wilson,
Elton's son and daughter-in-law, for helping with this story.

71

ANDY WINNEGAR

Naval Aviator Receives the Distinguished Flying Cross

On August 29, 2017, a crowd of friends, family, veterans and well wishers awaited the ceremony inside the Silent Wings Museum in Lubbock, Texas. Three highly decorated Navy men came to pay respects to and honor former Navy ARM2C (Aviation Radioman 2nd Class) Andy Winnegar. While all three outranked Winnegar at the time of his separation from the Navy in 1946, all were in awe of his service record. Andy was to receive the Navy's 7th highest medal, the Distinguished Flying Cross, along with six additional Air Medals awarded by the Naval Review Board. The previous year, he had been awarded several medals from his time in World War II in the Pacific. The additional medals were presented in large part to the meticulous records Winnegar kept during the war, including his flight log and own personal records. Andy received a citation in December 1944 signed off by Admiral Chester Nimitz that reads as follows:

> *For meritorious and efficient performance of duty as radioman of a torpedo-bomber during the period 15 June to 1 July 1944. During this period, Winnegar, while participating in aerial flights, carrying an Air Liaison Observer, flying at low altitudes and at slow speeds, in the face of concentrated enemy anti-aircraft fire was subjected to extreme dangers in the performance of his duties. In addition he rendered valuable aid to his pilot and observer by his own careful observations. Throughout, his courageous devotion to duty in the successful completion of these missions reflected great credit upon himself and the United States Naval Service.*

Bobbi Hanson from Congressman Jody Arrington's Abilene office helped this author in obtaining the long-overdue medals for Winnegar in 2016 and 2017. She presented a flag to him flown over the capitol in his honor and read a letter from the congressman. After each speaker read their proclamations, it was Andy's turn to speak. In typical fashion for this generation, he was humble about the awards. He said, "I don't feel like a hero. The heroes are still out there in the Pacific—the real ones that gave everything. And we had a lot of them." Andy's wife, Dolores, spoke for all of us when she said, "I'm very, very happy, and very proud of him. I call him my hero."

Andrew Jackson Winegar (the Navy had his name spelled Winnegar and he has retained that) was born to James and Ellen Winegar on November 18, 1924, in Thomasville, Missouri. His dad was a 100 percent disabled World War I veteran. Andy attended Thomasville High School and graduated in 1942. He enjoyed boxing, basketball and baseball. His hobbies included hunting, fishing and horses. He always loved the thought of flying. Still only 17 years old, his dad signed for him to join the Navy. The story of Andy's naval career can best be told in his own words from his journals from so long ago.

"I enlisted in the Navy July 23, 1942, then boot camp at Great Lakes, Radio School at Northwestern University, Evanston, Illinois; Aviation Radio and Aerial Radar School NATTC, Memphis, Tennessee; Aerial Gunners School NAS, Jacksonville, Florida. After 19 months of school I was assigned to Composite Squadron VC-4 being formed at Sand Point Naval Air Station, Seattle, Washington. Then another 6 months of training with VC-4 before we boarded the USS *White Plains* (CVE-66). April 24, 1944, we departed San Diego and passed Point Loma after 0900, bound for Pearl Harbor.

"Another month of training and we joined an invasion force of 35 ships headed for Saipan. Our crew consisted of Lt. Jg. Walter P. Owens, Maurice Hie Amm2/c and Andy Winnegar ARM2/C. We immediately started flying Anti-Sub Patrol in assigned sectors around the convoy.

"On June 8th Capt. Grady Gatlin of the Fourth Marine Division replaced Hie in the turret. Grady was an Aerial Observer and Pat and I were his volunteer crew. To get familiar with the equipment Grady flew the remainder of our ASP Missions with us as the turret gunner.

"June 15, 1944, was D-Day at Saipan and we had the second Observation Mission. My additional tasks were to take pictures and report anything significant to Grady that he might have missed. The ground troops were placing orange panels ahead of their front lines so that we could direct naval gunfire and Marine artillery ahead of their positions.

"Mortar fire was pounding the lines of Higgins Boats as they approached the beach and in spite of HQ's constant demands, we were unable to spot the guns. I soon discovered that we were being hit by small arms when some of the contents of my jungle pack spilled on the floor; a bullet had cut the zipper running down the side and there were holes in the fuselage letting in sunlight. I mentioned this to Pat and shortly after Gatlin became air sick from our evasive tactics and we had to leave the combat area by going out over the LSTs for a few minutes.

"When back on station, we were making a low pass looking for frontline panels, I leaned back to cock the K-20 Camera and a large caliber shell came through the door. Pieces of metal struck me above the right eye, broke the glass in the right goggle and imbedded in the ear cup. This brought Gatlin down from the turret and he quickly opened the first aid kit, removed my helmet and applied a large compress. My head was numb and my ears seemed to be stopped up. There was a large exit hole in the lower side of the fuselage on the left side and air was blowing everything around. Gatlin had called in and asked to be relieved from station and the standby crew was being launched. With my helmet off I had no way of knowing what was happening. I felt under the bandage and found my head was complete, no holes, and removed the bandage to replace my helmet so I would have earphones. The helmet served as well as the bandage, which could be used to wipe off the excess blood, and the bleeding soon stopped. We returned to the *White Plains* where our flight surgeon, Cmdr. Donnellson, was waiting for me. I declined sick bay, thinking they might ground me for observation and knowing we had another mission that afternoon.

"We completed our second mission without incident but after being relieved from observation we selected an airfield on Tinian as a target. After making a strafing run on some parked Japanese Betty bombers we were hit in the right elevator by a 37mm and had to return to the carrier at reduced speed.

Andy Winnegar, Navy, World War II.

"These experiences fairly well describe the remaining missions on Saipan. Some of our aircraft were totaled but when you fly low and slow over people with guns that are angry with you, it should be expected. We did total one plane from a mid-air collision with an Army L-5. The two Army officers in the L-5 were killed when they crashed behind enemy lines but we limped back to our ship where our TBM1/C was stripped and pushed over the side.

The battle for Saipan ended on July 9th. At 1615 and we headed back for Eniwetok to resupply."

Here is his entry from July 24, 1944: "D-Day Tinian—We landed on Saipan at dawn and picked up Capt. Gatlin. We were over the beach on Tinian at 0700 and it was being pounded. Everything from 20 mm to 16-inch-plus rocket-firing LCIs was hitting the landing area. Thirty minutes later the first wave started in. They were landing on two adjacent beaches; both were a solid mass of smoke. I could make out the Navy coxswain and gunner on the back of the Higgins boats. The gunners were firing over the heads of the Marines in the boats and I couldn't tell if the guns were .30 or .50s but they were pumping out the rounds. I saw a Jap running toward the beach; how he survived that shelling I don't know. Then I remembered, I am supposed to record this and I grabbed the K-20 and started taking pictures. I didn't see my Jap again; he was probably dead. It was obvious we were not taking the casualties we did on Saipan.

"After the beach head was established, we scouted inland. A few miles from Tinian Town Gatlin spotted some enemy troops and asked Owens to turn left and go back over them. As we turned we passed through a small misty-type cloud and something knocked us violently to one side. Looking back past our rudder I saw a Navy SOC going the opposite direction with about

Andy Winnegar after receiving Distinguished Flying Cross.

3 or 4 feet of their upper wing missing. The fabric of our left elevator was fluttering and the stabilizer had a large dent. I was in the turret and was the only one that knew what happened. Gatlin and I had switched places because the mic in the turret wasn't working. I came down to use the tunnel mic and tell Owens what happened; he never saw the other plane. We landed immediately on Aslito Airfield to inspect the damage. In addition to the damage to the tail section, there was a large hole in the leading edge and bottom of the left wing. There were several large nicks in two blades of the prop."

The next narrative is his entry from August 1, 1944: "We were catapulted at 0520 with instructions to land on Saipan and pick up an observer. Two other pilots and crews had flown over at the same time in a separate plane. Our observer, Capt. Gatlin, met us a few minutes after we landed on Aslito and we took off immediately. One of the other crews was Lt. (jg) Carson and his radioman Steve Walley. They were waiting for an observer when we departed.

"Around 0900 Cherokee informed us that Carson's plane had been shot down and gave us an approximate location. The plane had gone in about five hundred yards off the west side of Tinian. When we arrived a couple of Higgins boats were circling the crash location and one had pulled alongside a Destroyer Escort (DE). Cherokee had been asking us about survivors. Owens asked me to send the boats a blinker query about survivors and they replied, 'One.' I asked for a name and the reply was 'Walley.' Lost were Lt. (JG) Harold H. Carson USNR and Captain James Motley USMCR.

"With Tinian secured we headed south across the equator to Espiritu Santo for R&R or more like B and S (beer and swimming). It wasn't all fun and games. Part of our time was spent getting our planes and gear ready for the next invasion."

The next description is dated September 8: "Underway at 0700 this morning leaving Florida Island and escorting twenty-two troop and cargo ships headed for Palau by way of the North Solomons and New Guinea. The CVEs supporting this action are the USS *White Plains*, USS *Gambier Bay*, and USS *Midway*. The *Midway* is soon to have a new name, losing her name to a new CV that is being built and adding credibility to the old sailor's superstition of the bad luck that follows a name change. Her new name is to be USS *Saint Lo*.

"We had the 1500 to 1800 ASP today and testing our radar found that it only had a range of 16 miles and the SBAE procession switch didn't work either."

Here is his entry from September 16: "Strike on Peleliu today. The naval gunfire was hitting the southern end of a mountain range that had already been shelled to dust. Several OS2Us over the island directing the gun fire reminded me of our mid-air with the cruiser's SOC over Tinian. We dropped our bombs and fired our rockets into a clump of trees where Torchy directed us. I didn't see the actual target but Torchy was happy and said we hit the intended positions. We made strafing runs on installations around some buildings using up one of my 300-round canisters. I didn't see any return fire but we did find a few holes when we landed."

Here is September 17: "The morning strike was on Anguar, the neighboring island. We were given an array of pillboxes pointed out by Torchy which we bombed and fired our rockets into. I fired a few rounds before noticing my tracers were ricocheting towards our troops then Hie and I both stopped shooting; the wing gun approach was at a different angle."

This entry is September 18: "Off at 0500 this morning with smoke tanks in a three-plane formation with Lt. Flateboe and Shields flying the other two. We circled over Anguar waiting to be directed to our smoke mission while an AA battery chased an OS2U [observation floatplane] with black puffs getting dangerously close front and back of him. Our smoke tanks took up the entire bomb bay and we did not have rockets either but Flateboe asked permission to make strafing runs on the AA batteries and got it. We missed the first run because Owens didn't have his gun sight installed and I could see puffs all around Flateboe and Shields. It was easy to spot the flashes of the AA guns in the early pre-dawn light. On our pull out I was fighting the centrifugal force to bring my gun to bear, then firing until the gun was hot and the tunnel filled with smoke and struggling to clear a second position stoppage to get the gun cleared for the next run. The naval gunfire was being directed on the position as we left but they were still sending up flak."

The following is from September 21: "I was up before 0400 this morning for the early strike on Peleliu. We were catapulted at 0520 with two 500-lb bombs and 8 rockets. Our target is an area in front of our armored cars and troops along the edge of a road. We bombed, fired our rockets and strafed until the target area was clouded with smoke and dust, impossible to see. Owens and Hie saw flashes from small arms on some of our strafing runs. Leaving this area we hit targets on an island about 10 miles east of Peleliu. Flateboe made a run on a reefed ship off the coast and caused a fuel explosion that blew up the ship. We strafed a radio tower, docks and warehouse and another reefed ship before returning to the White Plains."

Here is a short entry from September 22: "We left Peleliu and headed for Ulithi, an atoll west of Yap. Tomorrow is D-Day for Ulithi. It is scheduled to be a three-day campaign."

That is followed by an even shorter entry on September 23: "Ulithi D-day. More like a 3-minute campaign. Ulithi was deserted."

The following short entries have the dates following in parentheses.

"We were supposed to have the 1100 ASP today but Owens had a sore throat. I spent the day studying physics." (September 24)

"Only one flight today and we were not scheduled. We anchored a little off Ulithi before noon awaiting orders. It didn't take long; we are underway this afternoon headed for New Guinea. We will fly ASP for a convoy as far as New Guinea then pick up another convoy and proceed to the Admiralties." (September 25)

"Worked physics problems this morning and ASP in our new plane at 1400. We crossed the equator again bound for Hollandia in New Guinea." (September 27)

"We arrived at Hombolt Harbor, Hollandia, New Guinea, at 1000. There were a lot of ships and a heavy jungle, with 6,500 ft. mountains." (September 28)

"We are underway for Manus Island in the Admiralties. Cleaning our plane and double checking equipment. They are saying it will get rough from here." (September 29)

"Arrived Manus, anchored 0830. Huge harbor, lots of shore installations and many ships. There is liberty for the fourth section this afternoon, beer and sports. I am duty petty officer tomorrow and will have to go ashore with the liberty party." (October 1)

"They sent me ashore with the liberty section as Duty Petty Officer and all went well." (October 2)

"Updated the ten transmitter frequencies on my ATC. The mail will close at noon tomorrow so I wrote mother the last letter for awhile. No mail today." (October 9)

"I helped paint part of the deck in the ready room. We expected to shove off tomorrow but I have seen tomorrow's plan of the day and it didn't mention leaving. I can't see why they closed the mail today." (October 10)

"Speed letter arrived with my flight school appointment. They hustled me off the ship without time for goodbyes and dropped me in the mud on Manus. Did I mention, they drive on the left side of the road!" (October 11)

This final description is called an epilogue in his journal: "I found a bunk in a Quonset hut barracks and introduced myself to the Master at

Arms. I told him I had a class starting Nov. 17 and needed transportation. He said he had men that had been waiting transport for 6 months and I might make it by Nov. 1945.

"My name hit the bulletin board 3 days later and I went aboard the USS *General W.F. Hase*, a troop transport that took 23 days to reach Treasure Island. They served two meals daily, cold cereal for breakfast and cold-cut sandwiches with Kool-Aid in the afternoon and you stood up at the table. I thought this was bad but per diem in San Francisco unable to get in a hotel was really bad but fortunately orders to flight school soon arrived."

* * *

Andy was discharged on March 16, 1946. He went to Cincinnati where he flew for National Air Shows. He bought a Navy SNJ (AT-6) that was already decked out with a sunburst paint job and smoke system. He met and married Susan McMahan in May 1949. They had 4 children, 2 boys and 2 girls. He opened A&L Auto Sales and was the youngest car dealer in Hamilton County, Ohio. He moved to Albuquerque in 1949 where he bought into an auto dealer selling import cars. He then sold wind chargers and flew in and out of Alpine, Texas. At one time, Andy owned four car lots. The family moved to Lubbock in 1967 where he opened Lubbock Stereo Center in 1967. The Lubbock tornado hit in May 1970 and his business was heavily damaged. He moved to Colorado Springs where he taught and towed sailplanes.

Andy and Susan divorced in 1971 and Andy worked various jobs in Wichita Falls, Corpus Christi and Lubbock. He went to work for FMC and Motors and set up tire service equipment in all of the Big O tire stores in New Mexico. Andy married Dolores Adame in September 1977. They have been married now for 41 years. Andy sold Motor Information Systems to auto repair shops and still sells occasionally to this day.

Andy went on the inaugural 2012 South Plains Honor Flight. He said, "It was one of the greatest experiences of my life—three days of action-packed bus trips that brought back all of the old memories of the service. My roommate was C.J. Solomon and we have been in almost weekly contact since the trip." When asked what he would like to be remembered for, Andy said, "My family and my time in the service. I would like to see the country reunited again like we were in World War II. It has never been the same since."

Part II
Korea

They started blowing whistles and bugles and making all kinds of noise.

—U.S. Army Sgt. Bill

72

PAUL ARCHINAL
From Airman to Admiral

So, how does one go from being an Airman 1st Class in the U.S. Air Force to an Admiral? As you might suspect, it is a long journey full of many detours along the way. This is the story of Paul Donald Archinal who seemed to be destined for just such a journey. He was born to Henry and Florence Archinal in Lockland, Ohio, on October 25, 1930. His father, a World War I veteran (he also had two uncles who fought in World War I), was a certified welder and helped build war materials for the Allied cause during World War II. Paul was interested in radio at an early age. He and his mother attended a live radio show when he was only nine years old. After the program, he told his mother, "That's what I want to do for a living." His mom said, "It's the kind of thing you can do if you set your mind to it." Attending Lockland High School where he played football and ran track, Paul graduated in 1949. His favorite classes were, of course, speech and drama, both of which would serve him well in later years.

After high school, Paul began classes at Ohio University. Paul had what's called a "golden voice," which projects well on radio and television. However, Paul's career trajectory was interrupted by the Korean War, which broke out in June of 1950. He joined the U.S. Air Force in 1951 to "keep from being drafted and I wanted to fly," noted Paul. Paul was told he was color blind and he could not be a pilot. He was assigned to the OSI (Office of Special Investigations). Once again, this seemed to be the perfect assignment for Paul. He said he "was sent undercover a lot and could easily become an enlisted man or an officer." He was still acting in a manner of speaking and said he could "always talk easily to anyone."

In 1952, Paul met his future wife, Swan Hagler, who was in nurse training in Houston. Paul said, "A friend of mine introduced us. I was stationed at Ellington Air Force Base at the time. We were married on

October 4, 1952." Swan, from Midland, Texas, was 19 and Paul was 21. Swan recalled, "He met me at 1st Baptist Church in Houston. I was in nursing school there. Our first date was on a Saturday night at the movies. Sunday we sat together in church and went out to eat. He came into town Monday night, Tuesday night, and on Wednesday night before church he proposed!" After the service, Paul and Swan moved to Cincinnati where he got a job as a producer/director at WLW. Swan noted, "It was an honor to be fired from that station. A lot of people became famous after they left that station." For example, Paul met comedian Red Skelton who had left the station years earlier. Paul and Swan went to homecoming at Ohio University and went by his old rooming house. His landlady had some mail for him. He smiled and said, "One of them was a letter from the government saying I had a college deferment. It turns out I didn't need to go in the service after all!" Paul was offered a job at television station KMID in Midland, then after brief stints in Harlingen and Beaumont, he landed a job as a weatherman at KOSA in Odessa, Texas. He had been trained as a certified meteorologist in Harlingen, Texas.

Paul recalled hearing foghorns on Lake Erie, which was only a block from his house in Cleveland, and developed a children's show that he called *Admiral Foghorn*, which aired in Odessa, Texas. A contest was held to name his ship and the winning entry was the High 'N Dry. He said that name made sense: "West Texas is high and dry!" He would dress up as an Admiral and let the kids come up and "ring the ship's bell for their birthday." The show in Lubbock featured an artist called "Salty Sam" (real name Lucio Orosco) and would go on to be the longest running children's TV show in Texas television history—15 years. Paul noted with pride that "people still come up to me to this day and say they remember me from that show. I'm very proud of that." Paul and family moved to Lubbock in 1971 where he became a sales manager for KSEL-TV and did a radio show with Bill McAlister. In later years, Paul went into the real estate business and worked for several agencies in Lubbock. Paul's love for radio work continued as he was the announcer for the Texas Tech Goin' Band from Raiderland from 1986 to 2006.

Paul and Swan moved back to Lubbock in 2010. Swan said that they "lived out on Oak Creek Lake, six miles from Blackwell, Texas, for several years. The kids said that we were getting old and should move back to town, so we moved to Lubbock in 2010." After 66+ years, 7 children (daughter Cheryl passed away at age 10 from hepatitis), 14 grandchildren, and 9 great-grandchildren and several careers including broadcasting, they moved to Ventura Place in Lubbock in 2016. Paul is now on hospice care and both he and Swan are huge fans of their hospice nurse, Kayla. Volunteers from the hospice sit with Paul so Swan can go to the store with other residents. Paul and Swan speak fondly of the numerous Kindred Hospice Veteran Volunteers, participate in pet therapy, and enjoy music volunteers who entertain and socialize with them. Two of their Veteran Volunteers are Air Force Crew Chief Welby Smith and Brigadier General Gary G. Harber. Paul Archinal has received many awards during his career, but when asked what he liked to be remembered for, he said, "My work with children as Admiral Foghorn."

73

WILLIAM BRIDGE
Korean War Vet Makes a Difference

On the wall of Bill Bridge's home were two small frames displaying the medals he earned for his service during the Korean War. "I'm proud of those," Bill stated as we concluded our interview. Bill's displays contain the Bronze Star, Purple Heart, Korean Service, United Nations Service, Good Conduct and Combat Infantry Badge for his nearly two years of service during the Korean War. He also had a photograph taken of him overlooking a river in North Korea. Just on the other side of the river was the enemy.

William L. Bridge was born on November 1, 1930, in Vernon, Texas, to Louis Simpson (L.S.) and Jesse Bridge. Bill was the youngest of 3 children with 2 sisters preceding him. The family moved to Lubbock when Bill was only 6 months old. His father worked as a salesman for Scoggin-Dickey, a long-time car dealer in Lubbock. During World War II, domestic car production ceased and Bill's dad worked at Reese Army Airfield for 5 years. Bill attended Lubbock High where he excelled in football, basketball and baseball. Texas Tech offered Bill a football scholarship to play middle linebacker in 1950. The Tech yearbook noted that the freshman team was "classed by some as one of the best freshman teams in Tech's history." Bill said, "All I wanted to do was play football." However, the Korean War interrupted Bridge's football days. He noted that "nearly the whole team was drafted in 1951."

Drafted into the Army in October 1951 and now married, Bill took his basic training in Ft. Sill, Oklahoma, and was transferred to Ft. Ord in California for what he called "mountain training." Bill said, "The first of my two sons was born when I was in Korea." Bill noted that "Korea was very mountainous and the Army knew we needed that kind of training." After stopovers in Hawaii and Wake Island, his unit landed in Seoul. After a convoy to Inchon, the unit sailed by boat to Pusan and headed north as part of the 31st Infantry Regiment, 7th Infantry Division. The regiment made their way north of the 38th parallel where they waited for orders. "We waited there for 3–4 weeks while President Truman made up his mind whether we should attack or not." Bridge recalled when the Chinese attacked: "They started blowing whistles and bugles and making all kinds of noise. We were outnumbered at least 10 to 1. I was carrying a BAR [Browning automatic rifle] at the time and I just started firing at all of these Chinese and watched them fall. I could see they were all very young. I regret killing so many young men. That bothers me to this day. I fired so many rounds that the barrel of my BAR was glowing red hot and I had to change out the barrel a couple of times. Outnumbered, we had to fall back to the 38th parallel."

On October 14, 1952, Bill's unit was part of the Triangle Hill attack, also known as Operation Showdown. The objective was to capture a row of hills occupied by the Chinese and North Koreans just north of the 38th parallel.

He noted that "out of 140 men that went up the hill, only 14 or so of us made it to the top. I had 6 hand grenades and threw them in 3 bunkers to stop the Chinese from firing down on us. That's when I was hit. I fell back down the hill and was only stopped by the bodies that littered the hill. Blood was gushing from my leg and my training kicked in and I quickly took off my belt and made a tourniquet. A medic came by and said I did a good job and he put on a proper tourniquet. I was taken to the Battalion Aid Station and then by helicopter to Seoul. I was later moved to a hospital

Bill Bridge, U.S. Army, North Korea 1952.

in Tokyo, Japan, where I stayed for 5 months. It was there that I was awarded the Purple Heart and a Bronze Star for my actions on Jane Russell Hill. If you were able to walk, you were sent back to Korea. I helped move wounded guys around the hospital. Some had limbs completely shot off. One of the doctors said, 'Bridge, get lost.' That kept me from having to go back to Korea as I only had about 4 months left in the Army. I flew back to Ft. Ord and then to Ft. Sill where I was discharged on July 14, 1953, at the rank of Sergeant.

"Back in Texas, I was offered a scholarship to Texas A&M and went there for 2 semesters. Later, I received a scholarship to the University of Texas and went there for 2 semesters. I went to work at a car dealer in Morton, Texas, and worked there for 7 years. During this time, I went to General Motors mechanics school in Greeley, Colorado. The government paid for everything. I opened up my own repair shop in Seminole, Texas, and was there about 7 years when a man named Bill Gordon from Andrews [Texas] stopped by my shop and said he was going to start up 13 vocational programs at Andrews High School and he wanted me to teach auto mechanics. Mr. Gordon budgeted $34,000 so I could set up my own vocational classes. I used the money to set up a shop and to buy tools and equipment. I sold my business in 3 months and started teaching. I had around 80 students and many of them won state awards over the years and I am very proud of that. I taught there for 21 years." Many of Bill's students went on to have successful careers and still remember him to this day.

"We moved to Ruidoso, New Mexico, and I worked as a forest ranger for 6 or 7 years. I also worked at Ruidoso Downs as security for 24 years and was a substitute teacher at Ruidoso High School. My wife, Grace Ann, and I met Joe and Kay Robbins in 1965 when we were in Andrews. Joe died in 2001 and my wife died in 2002. I went to visit Kay in Andrews and said we're both alone so we might as well get together." Kay responded, "Are you proposing?" Bill responded by saying "I guess I am!" They were married in 2006. They moved to Lubbock in August 2018 and now live in one of the cottages at the Carillon. When asked what he would like to be remembered for, Bill thought a while and said, "My work with young people and making a difference in their lives." Whether it was on the football field, the battlefield or in the classroom, Bill Bridge has made a difference in many people's lives.

74

JAMES CATHEY
The Ghosts of the Korean War

James Cathey looked at the faces of the sculptures at the Korean War Memorial and he recognized them. He also saw the "ghosts of his buddies" among them while on the 2014 Texas South Plains Honor Flight. This was his favorite memorial during the trip and one of the most somber.

James was born September 3, 1931, to William and Nena Cathey in Randolph, Texas, and attended Randolph School. While working with a buddy near Plainview, Texas, tying up bundles of hay in the West Texas sun in March 1950, he looked at his buddy and said, "Let's quit this and go join the Army." James passed the physical. His buddy did not.

He first went to Ft. Sill, Oklahoma, then Camp Stoneman in Northern California, and finally did his basic training in Hawaii. He wanted to be an engineer, but the Army sent him to infantry school at Camp Roberts in California. After training, he was sent to Okido, Japan, as part of the 45th Infantry Division of the National Guard. His division was put on a ship and made a seven-day voyage to Inchon, Korea, where they made an amphibious landing in December of 1951. He likes to say he "had Thanksgiving in Japan and Christmas in Korea" that year.

James was assigned as a sniper and his first rifle was a Springfield M1903 bolt action with a Weaver scope, and he became proficient with it. This rifle was destroyed during action and replaced with a BAR (Browning automatic rifle). He became proficient enough with the BAR to "hit his target at 750 yards." This one was also destroyed during combat and he was then issued an M2 .50 caliber machine gun on a tripod to lay down covering fire ahead of the troops.

One night James and a buddy went on patrol to spot Chinese troops. When he returned, he found his squad had been hit by mortar fire and they thought James had been buried beneath the rubble because they found his helmet. He said when he returned from his patrol, he had

74. James Cathey

a hard time convincing them he was still alive. His .50 caliber machine gun was destroyed and he went back to an M1C sniper rifle. He and another buddy decided to join the Army Rangers and they were sent for two weeks of intensive training. James made it through but his buddy did not, so James came back as a squad leader even though he was a PFC (Private First Class).

James had many close calls in Korea and was wounded twice by mortar shrapnel, earning two Purple Hearts. On one "night listening" patrol, he and another buddy heard footsteps close to their position in a ravine. First one, then two, then several steps. They made their way back to their command post and James notified his Colonel that he "had a feeling there were a lot of Chinese in that valley." The Colonel thanked him and soon an American plane flew over and "lit up the valley" and they could see "row after row of Chinese ready to attack an American position on a hill" and were able to engage the enemy successfully. James later found out that Dan Blocker ("Hoss" of the TV show *Bonanza*) was a squad leader on that hill. James said he "felt the best about that incident during the war" as he feels he probably saved numerous American lives.

While leading his squad on patrol one day, they got pinned down by Chinese fire from several yards away. On the other hand, they also had the Chinese pinned down and had settled into a stalemate. One of the men in his squad rounded up all the hand grenades and said he would "take care of the situation." He proceeded to lob numerous hand grenades at the enemy until "all was quiet." James said this guy was "quite accurate with his grenade lobbing" and later found out that before the war he had been a college football

James Cathey, U.S. Army, Korean War.

James Cathey with his faithful dog, Remington, July 2015.

quarterback. He also mentioned that he had two Native Americans in his squad—one from Oklahoma and one from Arizona—and they had "saved his life many times." In fact, one Native American from the 45th, PFC Charles George, was awarded the Medal of Honor.

James left Korea in 1952 and was assigned as a drill instructor at Ft. Bliss until his release on March 20, 1954. Once out, he spent 8 years in the National Guard and 12 years in the Army Reserve and retired from the Army after 23 years of service. He made his way back to Lubbock after he was discharged and worked as a route salesman for Bell Dairy for a short time before getting a job with Pioneer Natural Gas. He was eventually transferred to the Quitaque office and retired after 33 years.

He married Nelda Jean Bailey on May 7, 1955, after being "set up with her by her sister." They had two children, Reggie and Regina. They were married 59 years until her sudden death in September 2014, from West Nile disease. Now, James speaks to local schoolchildren about his time in the war and what the American flag means to him. He tends to his garden and plants with his faithful dog Remington by his side. He thinks back to how lucky he was to survive the Korean War as he remembers the men he fought with and who gave up their young lives for their country.

75

JEROLD DYESS
A Sixteen Year Old Sees the World

His heart raced, and he tried to quiet and slow his breathing, as he stood up all night between the panels of the lookout post wall, while listening to his enemies laugh and talk just inches away. This young American soldier's feet filled with blood; his legs threatened to buckle after many hours of holding himself upright. He didn't know how long he could physically do this or if he would be discovered; however, after the enemy finally fell asleep and awoke at dawn, he heard them shuffling about and then leave the building for good. Only then was he able to ease himself out and pull himself together enough to set out on foot to locate his own troops. This was just one incident for Jerold Booth Dyess during the Korean War.

Jerold was born on the family farm near Cone, Texas, on July 6, 1930, to O.R. (Jack) and Vergie Dyess. He grew up hunting and fishing and working hard, like most young men during the Depression era. His family moved to Melrose and Ft. Sumner, New Mexico; then to Colorado and finally to Smyer, Texas, where Booth attended school until the 11th grade. When he and his cousin saw an Army poster in 1946 that read "Join the Army and see the world," Booth said, "Boy, that's for me. I want to see the world." There was only one small problem: he was just 16 years old. He told the recruiter that he was "17 and would turn 18 in a couple of months." He was allowed to join if he could obtain his father's signature. His father said no, so Booth "forged his signature and left home." His cousin also signed up.

Dyess, who enlisted in Lubbock, took his basic training at Ft. Ord in California. He was then sent to Ft. Dix in New Jersey for six weeks and then on to Salzburg, Germany. It was here that he was taught the use of various weapons, including a 75 mm recoilless rifle (which caused him some hearing loss) and even the new M46 Patton tank, named after World War II General George S. Patton.

After spending two years in Germany, Booth was ready to leave the Army. However, he received word that a conflict had broken out in Korea, and he would be sent there. After enjoying a 60-day furlough at home, he shipped out to Korea. Landing in Korea in December 1950, his unit (Co. L, 31st Infantry Regiment) was located near the 38th parallel. He noted that he "went three months before I would take off my clothing. It was -40 degrees, and the men didn't have cold weather clothes." He spent part of his time as a jeep/truck driver and as a cook. He had to scrounge for food for 500 men, once killing a cow for meat and even shooting squirrels (for which he got reprimanded by a captain who said he might give away their position). He also "cooked up a bunch of eggs on his little Bunsen burner, and one of the men ate 27 eggs!" One night, Booth was ordered to "go retrieve a wounded soldier up the mountain behind them. Under heavy enemy fire, the Sergeant leading the group disappeared," and Booth had to take over. "We carried blankets and tied a knot on each end, put the wounded man in it and carried him down to safety while bullets were flying." Booth was discharged in El Paso and returned home to West Texas. He received the Combat Infantry Badge and the Korean Service Medal with 3 Bronze Service Stars.

Booth met his wife, Helen Smith, in Melrose, New Mexico. They were married on August 1, 1952, and have been married for 65 years. They had two children, Alan and Tammy. After a short stint as a cattleman in Missouri, Booth returned to West Texas where he worked as a carpenter and in construction. His father and his son, Alan, also worked with him.

Mr. Dyess, 87, suffered a stroke in 2009, but he learned to talk and walk again. He was able to go on the 2017 Texas South Plains Honor Flight with his son as his guardian. Alan noted that his dad "walked all the time on the trip and would not let anything or anyone slow him down. I had a hard time keeping up with him!" While visiting the National Museum of the Marine Corps in Quantico, Booth entered the Chosin Reservoir Exhibit. It was cold and had sounds like a battle, and he told his son, "I need to get out of here." The cold room had brought back too many memories for Booth. He also enjoyed the Korean War Veterans Memorial because "I was there." When asked about his military career now 66 years behind him, he simply said, "The Army was good for me." He had left home as an adolescent, "saw the world," and returned from the "Forgotten War." We should never forget the sacrifices these men made to save a country (South Korea) from oppression at the hands of a communist regime.

76

Clyde Fisher
"Finish What I Start"

These words were spoken by 86-year-old Clyde Robert Fisher, Jr. Looking back on a life well lived, Clyde had plenty of proof to back up his words. About the only thing he "didn't finish" was graduating from college. Clyde was born on April 26, 1932, in Dimmitt, Texas, to Clyde Sr. and Zetha Fisher. His dad was a carpenter and his mom ran the household of 5 children. The Fishers moved to Levelland, Texas, where Clyde would spend his grade school days during the Depression and into World War II. The family eventually migrated to Lubbock, Texas, where Clyde graduated from Lubbock High in 1951. The Korean War had started during 1950 and young men were needed.

Rather than being drafted, Clyde said he "always liked the Marine Corps and enlisted in Dallas in May 1951." He took basic and combat training at Camp Pendleton in California. During the Korean War, over $20 million was spent to update and expand the camp. By the end of the Vietnam War, over 200,000 Marines had passed through the base on their way to the Far East. Clyde was assigned to 1st Marine Division, Easy 2/11, which was a 105 mm howitzer battery. He trained for a time as a forward observer. His unit left the United States in December 1951 for the east coast of Korea. Once in Korea, Clyde found out the Marines already had too many forward observers and he was put on K.P. (kitchen police) or cooking duty. "The unit only had two full-time cooks at the time and when one guy was sent back to the States, I took over his spot." He noted that they had to cook three meals a day for about 100 guys.

Clyde recalled that "the winter in the mountains of eastern Korea was very, very cold." Fisher noted that "before we could even begin to cook, we had to thaw out the water as everything froze overnight." Being close to the 38th parallel, there was constant shelling back and forth from north to south and vice versa. Once a group of half-frozen Army men staggered into camp from fighting on the front lines and as Clyde recalled, "All the guys had these beards and they were frozen and they all looked very tired." He was ordered to "push a hot meal to these troops." He was happy to do so.

"After 6 months, we moved to the west coast of Korea. It was quite different there. There were rolling hills and sandy soil. The rats were about one foot long and the mosquitoes were quite large. We had to sleep under mosquito netting." Fisher, recalling his scariest time, said, "We were constantly getting incoming shells from North Korea and had to get out of our tents and get in our bunkers nearby. Once, when the shelling stopped, I went back into my tent and my cot was sliced down the middle by shrapnel. I might not be around to tell the story if I had been in that tent." Clyde continued, "My other job besides cooking was to unload shells for the howitzers from their crates. I carried an M-1 carbine, but had no ammunition, which made me uncomfortable. Fortunately my dad had sent me a .38 pistol for protection."

Clyde noted that he "landed in Korea on January 1st at 12 noon and left exactly one year later on January 1st at 12 noon." He returned to Camp Pendleton in California where he was assigned as an assistant police sergeant even though he was only a corporal. Fisher was assigned to the Marine Corps Training Center, 29 Palms. "There was a lot of building going on at that time expanding the camp. I was assigned as the police sergeant for HQ Battery. I had to make sure everything was ship shape and went on numerous inspection parties. I even had the authority to tell officers what to do, which they did not necessarily like."

Fisher was discharged in June 1954 at 29 Palms and took a bus back to Lubbock. He went to Texas Tech for 1 year to study as an architecture engineer. However, when told he must draw a detailed sketch of the human body, he said, "I'm out!" He moved to Midland, Texas, where he worked for A.E. Quest. There he met his future wife, Norma Nichols, at the Church of Christ. They would marry in June 1956. They had 4 daughters and now have 8 grandkids and 1 great-grandchild. Clyde worked at the Midland Post Office for a short time, then for the Midland Fire Department for 23 years and "always had a part-time job during my years on with the fire department." He figures he "had 21 different jobs over the years." He drove a school bus for Midland ISD for 24 years and retired in 2013 when he and Norma moved to Lubbock. When asked what he would like to be remembered for, Clyde thought long and hard and said, "I always tried my best. I like to finish what I start."

77

ALTON GARNER
Witness to History

Former Marine Corporal Alton Garner remembers well that day in 1953. Several Marines from the 1st Medical Battalion were chosen to go to "Freedom Village" at Panmunjom where United Nations prisoners were to be exchanged for Communist prisoners from China and North Korea. One of the prisoners being exchanged that September day was a Medal of Honor winner, Major General William Dean, who was the highest-ranking officer to be captured by North Korea. Alton's job was to talk to the prisoners and find out their names and as much as he could to identify them. Most were clothed in Russian and Chinese clothing. He noted that "all the men seemed to have been brainwashed," and one of them said he had "spent 1,001 days in captivity." The men were part of so-called Operation Big Switch, in which 12,773 United Nations POWs, including 3,597 Americans, were repatriated.

Alton was born on a farm in Terry County, Texas, in 1928 to Horace and Mabel Garner. He graduated Union High School in 1946. Here he met and then married his wife, Thalua, in 1948. Alton attended Draughon Business College in Lubbock from 1946 to 1947 and studied bookkeeping and accounting. Even though the Korean War began in 1950, Alton "escaped the draft until April 1952 when I was inducted into the Marines in Brownfield, Texas, at age 24." Even though he was married at the time, he noted that the government "started drafting married men with no children."

Garner completed ten weeks of basic training in San Diego, then ten weeks of infantry training at Camp Pendleton, and one week of cold weather training in Northern California. When he was deployed to Korea, he noted that the men were glad that a former general, Dwight D. Eisenhower, was elected president in November 1952. The trip on the troop ship USS *General John Pope* (AP-110) took 10–12 days to reach Korea. Assigned to the 1st Medical Battalion, D Company, he was

Alton Garner, U.S. Army, Korean War.

stationed on Kimpo Peninsula, west of Seoul, on the Yellow Sea. His company was "basically a Marine MASH unit." Their job was to "take the wounded, returned from the front lines, and transport them to Inchon, where they were ferried out to the hospital ship USS *Haven* [AH-12] for further medical treatment."

Alton was later transferred to Marine HQ on the Western Front. HQ was in need of men who could type; someone had come across Alton's record of being a bookkeeper. It was here that he "saw a lot of casualty lists." He recalled that they were told that "20% of the Marines sent to Korea were not going to come back." His brush with combat came in December of 1952 when his unit was sent out one night and told to bring with them the 30 and 50 caliber machine guns with tracer ammunition. This fire mission consisted of many United Nations troops and weapons. "The total number was unknown to us at that time, but it had to be in the hundreds." They stopped on the south side of a river and were told that "the enemy was on the north side and to fire when commanded." When the firing started, Alton "thought it sounded like the world was coming to an end."

Garner was discharged on April 14, 1954. He returned to Texas where he lived in Littlefield and Perryton and worked in the abstract and savings and loan business. He and his wife traveled back to Korea

77. Alton Garner

Alton Garner, return to Freedom Village, Korea, in 1990.

in 1987, so he could "show her where I was during the war." Freedom Village was still standing, barbed-wire fence and all. After retirement, he and his wife settled in Levelland to be close to their daughter, Jennifer, and her family in Lubbock. They were married for 68 years before Thalua passed away in September 2016. While on the 2017 Texas South Plains Honor Flight, Alton met up with veteran A.C. Oliver. It turned out that they had attended 1st and 2nd grade together at Union School and hadn't seen each other in 80 years. It was an unexpected addition to the wonderful experience of the Honor Flight.

Alton Garner, the young bookkeeper, became a Marine caring for wounded Marines and a witness to the high cost of war—roles that influenced him for the rest of his life.

Special thanks to Alton and his daughter, Jennifer, for their help with this article.

78

GORDON HAMBRIGHT

Naval Postmaster Wins "Best Beard Growing Contest"

Gordon Hambright served in the Navy from 1951 to 1955 as a Teleman, 3rd Class USN-1. "There was not one time [he] was ever afraid" while in the military, not even while serving in the Pribilof Islands during a 3½-day-long typhoon that spanned twelve miles in diameter. U.S. Navy veteran Gordon Hambright describes the violent weather event and eye of the storm as lasting a peaceful 8 hours. He said he remained calm aboard the USS *Electra* (AKA-4) as he assisted in communications. After the storm, with no docks constructed there, it took the Navy an entire year to load and unload supplies in landing boats.

The former farmer from Floydada, Texas, born in February 1932, to William and Ethel Hambright, worked in the post office after graduation and joined the U.S. Navy in 1951. Gordon went to Teleman School and also learned how to be a movie operator. He served in Guam for 2 years at the Naval hospital where he replaced a postmaster who had committed suicide because he could not adjust to living on the island. Gordon's pleasant outlook on life served him well as he served his country.

While in Seattle, Washington, awaiting orders, the Captain told the soldiers they could grow a beard and soon competition mounted among them, creating the Beard Growing Contest. Hambright won three first-class ribbons for the best beard. Many years later his daughter found the photo on the internet and had it made into a huge puzzle and framed it.

After retiring from the Navy in 1955, Gordon worked at the Floydada Post Office for nine years and for the Department of Transportation for twenty-seven years.

Gordon recalls one time when he was "very concerned" when his house caught on fire in 2011 in Floydada while he was inside. He thanks God and the Floydada Volunteer Fire Department that protected his

78. Gordon Hambright

house with a wall of water, working against 60-MPH winds. He survived the rescue and was able to reoccupy his home the next day.

Gordon met his wife, Darlynn, in Floydada and they were married in 1955 soon after his discharge. They settled in Floydada and had three children: Craig, Grant, and Treva.

Soon after hearing about the 2014 Texas South Plains Honor Flight, Treva got Gordon's permission and sent in their applications. She said, "At first we were very excited when he got accepted, but then I started to worry." Gordon had some health concerns that required special care and she lost sleep prior to the flight. Despite the risks, Gordon was determined to go. He said he was "going to go sometime" and he'd "rather go [pass away] while on the Honor Flight than any other way."

Gordon and Treva went on the flight on October 1, 2014, with 82 other veterans. He was able to view the memorial and helped lay the patriotic wreath at the Korean War Memorial. Another highlight from the trip was when he got to "revisit" his postmaster duties on the flight to Washington and was honored as one of two former military postal service personnel to distribute mail to the veterans.

Today Gordon is well known for his love of puzzles and his bright smile. When asked how he feels about the Honor Flight he beams, "I'd highly recommend it!"

79

FRED HARVEY
"Growing Up" on the USS Hornet

Former Yeoman 3rd Class Fred Harvey described his naval career with these sobering words: "Duty on the flight deck of an aircraft carrier was the most dangerous place to be." Fred was aboard the USS *Hornet* (CVA-12) (attack aircraft carrier) when one of the incoming AD-4 Skyraiders hit the deck and the "propeller went right through the flight deck over [his] head. This was during the transition period from prop to jet planes, and they had both on board." During his time on the Hornet, they "lost four men and saw burial at sea." Fred said that duty aboard an aircraft carrier would "make you grow up in a hurry."

Frederick Gene Harvey was born in Kearney, Nebraska, on June 23, 1935, to Porter and Alice Harvey. His father was a policeman for over 30 years. He graduated from Longfellow High School in 1953 where his favorite subjects were "girls, math and chorus." He met Norma Shafer through a mutual friend, and they married on April 10, 1954. He attended one year of college before enlisting in the Navy on May 10, 1954. He was sent to San Diego for 12 weeks of boot camp and then to ANP (Airman Apprentice School) training in Norman, Oklahoma, for eight weeks and ACA (Air Controller School) in Olathe, Kansas. He was assigned to the USS *Hornet* (CVA-12). The *Hornet* name has a long and proud naval history. The first *Hornet* was christened in 1775 and was one of the first two ships in the Continental Navy. (The other was the USS *Wasp*.) Since that time, the *Hornet* and its crews have served in numerous wars, from the American Revolution to the retrieval of Apollo 11 and 12 astronauts. Young Fred Harvey was aboard the *Hornet* in 1955 when his first child was born on his birthday, June 23.

Fred and his crewmates replaced an around-the-world crew (WESTPAC) and sailed out first to Hawaii, then to Yokosuka, Japan. The ship dry-docked for one week near Hiroshima, and Fred and his crewmates could still see the devastation from the atomic bomb dropped by the *Enola Gay* in 1945 at the end of World War II. He also recalled sailing to Hong Kong, Okinawa and then to Station Charlie where they patrolled the North and South Korean peninsula during the Cold War. During one maneuver, they "lost one of their four screws [propellers] and had to return to Yokosuka, Japan to replace it, and that took about four weeks." One of his jobs on board was working for the Air Boss, who was basically the flight deck controller in charge of planes taking off and landing. Fred would "look for the incoming planes' blinking lights on the wing which let the ship know that the hook was down that would grab the cable on deck to stop the planes." The landings weren't always perfect. He recalled that "the photographer onboard was killed when an incoming plane hit the 'Tilly' he was in while taking pictures." A Tilly can be found aboard each U.S. aircraft carrier. Its purpose is to provide support to the ship's crash and salvage team in the event of aircraft or flight deck mechanical failure.

Fred served the remainder of his time on the carrier as a chaplain's assistant. He was assigned to an attack squadron north of San Diego, then to the Admiral's Staff called COMAIRPAC (commander of all carrier and flight operations in the Pacific). He was released from service in May 1958 and received his honorable discharge in May 1962. He returned to Nebraska and attended Nebraska State Teachers College. He graduated in 1962 with a bachelor's degree in education. He taught in Lebanon and Bertrand, Nebraska, and was the superintendent at Maywood, Nebraska. He received his master's in 1965. In 1969, he received his education doctorate degree from the University of Nebraska and moved to Texas A&I at Kingsville, Texas, as a professor. He retired from there in 1992 as Professor Emeritus and moved to Bellevue, Nebraska, where he was the principal at Avery Elementary School. His son, Larry, and wife, Melinda, live in Lubbock, Texas. His daughter, Terry, and husband, Galen Gaither, live in College Station, Texas. Fred and Norma moved to Ransom Canyon, Texas, in 2007. After 58 years of marriage, Norma passed away in 2011. He later met Debbie Shelfer while working at Alderson Cadillac as a shuttle driver. They married on June 16, 2012.

Fred Harvey's four years aboard an aircraft carrier helped the young man grow up, but they also prepared him to face the trials and challenges of life. This quote by CEO John Luke, Jr., a former Air Force pilot, in an *Inc.* article called "11 Things the Military Teaches You About Leadership," describes men like Fred: "Veterans have special abilities and common traits, including discipline, maturity, adaptability, and dedication. They operate with integrity and high ethical standards in all that they do."

80

RODNEY MANNING
From a Policeman to a Preacher

Rodney Manning never started out to be a preacher. He grew up in Somerville, Massachusetts, in a "pretty rough neighborhood." It was said that in his neighborhood, "most young men either became policemen, priests or convicts." Unlike some boys he hung out with, he always had nice clean clothes because his mother worked in a laundry. His mother said, "At least you'll be the best dressed bum on the corner." His mother told him that, when pregnant with him, she was convinced she was going to have a girl and did not have a boy's name picked out. Rod was born on February 18, 1933. At the time, the British battleship HMS *Rodney* (29) was berthed at the Boston Navy Yard and his mother liked that name, so Rodney it was. The HMS *Rodney* would become famous during World War II for helping to sink the German battleship *Bismarck*.

After completing the 11th grade, Rod went to the post office in June of 1950 where he met a recruiter and told him he wanted to "join the Army." The recruiter said, "No, you don't son. You want to join the Air Force." So he did. His timing to join was not the best. The day before he was scheduled to leave for basic training at Lackland AFB, the North Koreans invaded South Korea and the war was on.

Rod began his military career as a chaplain's assistant at Sheppard AFB but applied for a three-month weapons repair school at Lowry AFB in Denver where he was taught the repair and servicing of USAF weaponry from the .45 caliber pistol to the 20 mm cannon. While attending the school in 1951, he met his future wife, Josie (Jo) Klassen, who was working in Denver for Continental Airlines. Not long after completing the weapons course, he received orders to go to Kimpo Air Base, Korea. He arrived in Korea after a two-week trip aboard the USS *General George M. Randall* (AP-115), a U.S. Navy troop ship.

Upon arrival at Kimpo, he was advised that they had an excess of weapon mechanics and was asked what else he would like to do. He had earlier applied to be an Air Policeman but did not fit the minimum height and weight requirements. Since there was a need for Air Policemen in Korea, they waived those requirements. Thus began his career in law enforcement. His duties varied. He patrolled on and off base and was assigned to a mobile strike team as an M2 .50 caliber gunner on an M-20 armored car and, on occasion, responded to sniper fire from the rice paddies around the base. He said that another of his duties was to help guard the wing's F-86 Sabre fighter aircraft on the flight line. Base personnel would count the planes returning from missions and if one was missing, they knew it had been shot down. One such plane lost in February of 1952 was that of Major George Davis, Jr., from Lubbock. He was a highly decorated pilot who would receive the Medal of Honor for his actions.

Rod was next assigned to Walker AFB in Roswell, New Mexico, providing security for nuclear-loaded aircraft. His future wife lived in Albuquerque at the time and they would be married by her father, a Methodist minister, on December 6, 1953. Rod was discharged in 1954 and returned to Boston to join the police department or state police but neither was accepting applications at the time. So, he visited Hanscom AFB near Concord and reenlisted there. He had only 90 days in which to reenlist and retain his rank and collect his reenlistment bonus. He beat the deadline by only 3 days! In 1958, he was assigned to Chateauroux Air Station in France where he worked as a Town and Highway Patrolman. He served as a patrolman and an Air Police Investigator with the 3130th Air Base Group Police Squadron (7,322nd Air Police). He was then assigned to Amarillo AFB where he was stationed for 4 years. In 1964, he was assigned to Osan Air Base in Korea where he would serve as a driver for General Billy Mitchell, Jr. Though assigned to Osan Air Base, he actually lived in an Air Force VIP hotel in downtown Seoul during his year there. He assisted in providing transportation and security for several USO shows, including one with Bob Hope. Hope informed Rod that they were trying to get clearance to go to Vietnam because he felt that the military really needed the entertainers to help them out. They did get approval and went to Vietnam in December 1964.

He was once again stationed at Walker AFB in Roswell, and then to Little Rock AFB. He received orders to go to Vietnam in May of 1968 and was stationed at DaNang, also known as "Rocket City," because of frequent rocket attacks by the Viet Cong. He flew as an observer in an O-2B Skymaster aircraft. They flew at low altitudes where, among other duties, they tried to detect enemy movement on the ground. He learned that the plane would sometimes take small arms fire and he said,

"I began using three flak jackets. One I wore, sat on another, and I placed one on the floor in front of me."

Rod next went to Birmingham, Alabama, as a recruiter in 1969. Then, after tours in Laredo AFB and Keesler AFB, he retired in May of 1974 with 24 years of active duty. Settling in Alabama, he was asked to fill in for a preacher who was to be out of town for a couple of weeks. He agreed and trained to become a Certified Lay Speaker in the United Methodist Church in 1974. While in Alabama, he served in the State Department of Corrections as Director of Investigations and Intelligence. He retired from that department in 1995 with 20 years of service. While in Alabama, he obtained a master's degree in criminal justice from Troy University.

Rod and Jo moved to Lubbock in January 2008 to be near their daughter, Kathy, who is a physician's assistant. He transferred his Disabled American Veterans membership to Lubbock and became the chapter's chaplain.

81

CLEVELAND MCMILLAN
Cooking Under Fire

"An Army marches on its stomach." Napoleon recognized in the 18th century, as did every military leader who came before and after him, that an Army needs a regular supply of food to keep fighting. In the fall of 1951, Korean War veteran Cleveland "Buzz" McMillan was "close to the front lines and had to feed 120–130 men three meals per day"—not an easy task with "incoming and outgoing artillery shells." Buzz recalled that "the 1st Sergeant was killed by a shell fragment from allied artillery." Even the task of feeding the troops was often under extreme duress.

Buzz was born in Rockwood, Texas, and graduated from high school in Melvin in 1949. He joked that his favorite subjects in school were "recess and math." The Korean War broke out in June 1950, and Buzz was drafted into the Army in October of that year. He did his basic training and Infantry training in Ft. Lewis, Washington, and also worked in the motor pool. Two volunteers were needed in the kitchen, so Buzz put in to be a cook. He eventually wound up being a mess sergeant for Co. G, 38th Regiment, 2nd Infantry Division. The 2nd Infantry, whose history can be traced back to World War I, arrived in Pusan, Korea, in July 1950. They happened to be the first unit shipped directly from the United States.

After arriving in Korea in October 1951, Buzz initially carried a BAR (Browning automatic rifle) for a short time but was soon serving on the front line as a mess cook. Later, his unit was transferred to a prisoner of war camp at Koje-do, an island off the southern coast of Korea. The prison was built into eight compounds, each designed to hold 700 to 1,200 men a piece but soon filled to five times the capacity. Buzz recalls talking to some of the prisoners: "one was only 14 and one was 15—these were just kids."

Not surprisingly, outbreaks of dissension were frequent, and control of prisoners became more and more difficult. In May 1952 and after numerous riots, the camp commandant was lured to one of the compounds on the pretense of a need to ease camp tensions. Instead, he was set upon and captured. The 38th Infantry had to sit and watch as the general was put on a mock trial on criminal charges. He was finally released after negotiations. Both General Dodd and his replacement, General Colson, were reduced in rank to colonel. The 39th Regiment, along with the 187th Airborne, were able to retake the compound in June 1952.

Buzz stayed on at Koje-do for "three to four months and made coffee for the guys on guard duty during the night at the prison camp, and they really appreciated it." He also helped feed the American troops stationed there. He returned to the front lines for a short time. The unit was assigned South Korean troops, and he remembers that they "loved sweets and would drink only sugar water a lot as their meal." Buzz left Korea in August 1952 and was discharged from the Army in September 1953.

He worked in Ft. Worth for a while and later at the New Mexico (now Navajo) Refinery in Artesia, New Mexico. There he met his future wife, Virginia Thorp, who had been married before and had a 6½-year-old daughter. They married in July 1954 and had two more daughters and a son. The family moved to Big Spring, Texas, in 1965 where Buzz worked for a welding supply store. Later, he sold figurines in the West Texas area for an Alabama company called All God's Children. Buzz "found out about the Texas South Plains Honor Flight at the Lubbock VA Clinic a couple of years ago and was finally able to go on the 2017 flight." He would have gone earlier but was caring for his wife who had dementia. He was honored to help lay a wreath at the Korean War Memorial and was especially moved by the "mail call" on the flight to Washington, D.C. He waited until he got to his room that night to read the mail because he "saw other guys crying when they read their mail on the plane" and was afraid he would do the same thing.

The former mess sergeant doesn't care if he is remembered for feeding an Army. Buzz wants others to reflect on his "love of God, family, a free country and that we should always remember those who went before us."

82

GORDON MUSICK
Near the Front Lines in Korea

Gordon Reid Musick, the youngest of three children (2 boys and 1 girl), was born in his grandfather's house at Inez, New Mexico, on April 27, 1928, to John and Josephine (Willie) Musick. He attended nearby Rogers School and played all the sports available at that time, including baseball, basketball and track. Gordon said, "I was drafted and inducted into the Army on October 24, 1950, in Albuquerque. There were 13 of us from Roosevelt County inducted. We were sent to Ft. Sill, Oklahoma, where we were issued clothing and received shots. Basic training for us was at Camp Polk, Louisiana, and 12 of us were assigned to the 45th Infantry Division [Thunderbirds], 180th Infantry, Medical Company. We were put in a barracks by ourselves and fed in a big chow hall. We were called up for medical training at Brooke Medical School, Ft. Sam Houston in San Antonio. We were trained to recognize when wounds needed to be treated at a more advanced facility."

Musick continued, "We were shipped out to Hokkaido, Japan. We were living in a tent city there for about 8 months. We finally moved into a newly built Quonset hut but shipped out for Korea the very next day which was Thanksgiving, 1951. We were put on 2½-ton troop carrier trucks and moved to the front lines. When we arrived, my feet were so cold I could hardly stand up. The Army issued us pack boots (so-called Mickey Mouse boots), which kept our feet warm with only one pair of wool socks on. Food was brought up to the front lines and we ate sitting on the ground. It was so cold that coffee soon began to freeze before one could finish eating. Eight medics were assigned to foot soldiers. I carried a first-aid waist pack for dressing wounds. I was assigned to a .50 caliber squad, which was a safer place to be.

"We lived in bunkers in the side of the hills. We had a stove made from ammo boxes at the rear wall, which knocked the chill off. Medics were not issued weapons, but I would sometimes cover the telephone console and a soldier would have me keep a pistol in case of need. We were close to the 38th parallel with two rolls of razor wire around the perimeter. Tin cans were tied to it to warn if anyone tired to cross it. The problem was, if the wind came up, the cans made a noise and you thought that it could be the enemy. During the day, one could see the enemy across the river valley. Close to our position, a forward artillery observer bunker was hit by a mortar shell, which fortunately did not detonate. All those got out with only bruises and abrasions. From one position, we had to cross open country to go to our mess hall. We were told to walk individually ten yards apart for if the enemy saw two walking together, they would fire a mortar at them. Consequently, most of us only went to one or two meals each day. In the meantime, we were given lots of candy. I ate so much chocolate during that period that I got sick of it and for a time after getting home did not eat candy.

"During my service on the front line, I had the experience of my greatest fear. It was the most scared I've ever been in my life," said former Sergeant Gordon Musick. He continued, "We were in a 12-man bunker/command post that we called a 'hootchie' near the front lines. It was dug into the side of a hill and had a sandbag outer wall with a crooked entrance. Two curtains made with ponchos were hung in the tunnel to keep light from flashing when someone entered. One was close to the outside and the other close inside. I was asked to man the phones one night and a soldier placed his pistol on the desk to use if the need arose, but said, 'Don't make any false moves for if you fire the pistol in here it will damage all our ears from the concussion.' Late that night, I heard the outside poncho rustle and in just a little while, the inner poncho began to move. I cocked my pistol and held it about chest high. The bottom of the poncho began to move a little. I just knew that if I pulled it back it would be an enemy sneaking into our area. This seemed to be a usual tactic they used to kill our soldiers. I was ready to pull the trigger when a big rat peeked in. As soon as I moved he fled and I breathed a sigh of relief. I would have shot anyone who came in for it was my duty to protect those who were sleeping. Their lives were in my hands."

Continuing, Gordon said, "After I spent 7 or 8 months in Korea, I was called up and told that I had been in the Army long enough and it was time to return home. I left the frontlines in a Jeep, then rode on a troop truck to Seoul and shipped to Osaka, Japan. I was discharged on August 20, 1952, at Ft. Sill." Gordon said he "met his wife through a newspaper article from Portales, New Mexico." His mother had arranged for the newspaper to be sent to him while he was in the service. In this particular edition, he read of the high school girls who were chosen to visit the New Mexico state offices. He picked the picture of Betty

82. Gordon Musick

Terry from the group and wrote to her. However, before he got a reply, he was rotated home and discharged. Writing again, he made a date with Betty. They would marry on August 9, 1953. Gordon said, "This was the beginning of life for me."

He attended Eastern New Mexico University in Portales and graduated with a degree in industrial arts with double minors in Bible studies and English. He began work on a master's degree but did not finish. He began preaching while in college and because he had used up all his available GI finances, he went into preaching full-time in small congregations of the Church of Christ locations for approximately 20 years. He worked for 10 years for the Child Welfare Office in Snyder, Texas. The last stop for Gordon was as a custodian at the Church of Christ in Snyder. He remained there for 5 years. After retirement, Gordon and Betty moved to Lubbock. He now writes short devotional articles, aptly called "Musick-al Notes," for South Plains Church of Christ in Lubbock. When asked what he would like to be remembered for, he said simply, "That I was a man of God. I haven't achieved much else, but all four of my adult kids are doing well."

83

ASA OLIVER

*From Family Farm to Foreign
Field to Faithful Follower*

Asa C. Oliver was "born on January 25, 1929, in Terry County, Texas, to Asa and Agnes Oliver." He graduated from Brownfield High School in 1946 and began work as a full-time farmer. World War II had recently ended, so there was not much chance of being drafted (or so he thought). Four years later, the Korean War broke out, and he was drafted into the Army on December 15, 1950. He was sent to Ft. Hood for six weeks of basic training, and after a ten-day leave, he began advanced training with the same unit to which he had been assigned in the beginning.

Asa noted that "some of the officers and non-coms [from the 1st Armored Division ('Old Ironsides')] during World War II were left as a cadre which became the nucleus of the 2nd Armored [Hell on Wheels] Division, which was being re-activated. The 2nd Armored Division was roughly 16,000 men, consisting of three Armored, three Infantry and three Artillery battalions, along with other support units." Asa was assigned to Battery B of the 14th Armored Field Artillery Battalion. During his advanced training, Asa was part of an "eight-man gun section which consisted of four cannoneers, driver, assistant gunner, gunner and section chief." Asa noted that he "had the honor of filling all eight positions of the gun section, from a #4 Cannoneer to Chief of Section" during his two years in the Battery. And he added that he "was quite proud of that."

Asa and his battalion were not sent to Korea. The United States had recently signed the North Atlantic Treaty Organization (NATO) in 1949 with several European countries to provide collective security against the Soviet Union, effectively beginning what was called the "Cold War." The term had been coined in 1947 by Bernard Baruch, who was a senior advisor to President Harry S. Truman. Asa recalled that "by signing the NATO treaty, the U.S. had obligated itself to immediately send two combat-ready divisions to Germany," one of which was his 2nd Armored Division. They were "the only combat-ready divisions the U.S. had. And so we went."

The 2nd Armored Division's Combat Command B set up at a former German Army post called Mangin Kaserne near Mainz, Germany. While the facilities were "better than anything we had in Ft. Hood," Asa said they were seldom there. The reason they were in Germany was because America "had intelligence that the U.S.S.R. kept over thirty divisions of the Red Army in their sector of East Germany, and they were 'itching' to come through the Fulda Gap [a traditional invasion route into Germany]." Asa felt like "we spent most of our time in the field doing exercises and practicing being 'cannon fodder' for them." He also felt like the "only things that kept them from coming were nuclear weapons and the U.S. Air Force."

After spending a year and a half in Germany, Asa was discharged on December 18, 1952, at Ft. Hood and "rode home with a friend to Terry County." He met his future wife, Olive Ruth Wood, in 1954 at the hospital in Brownfield where he was having minor surgery. They married in 1955 and had four children in the next five years. A.C. noted that he was happy "raising cotton, cows and kids with the light of his life—Ruth." He continued farming for a number of years until 1968, when he enrolled in Lubbock's Sunset School of Preaching. He graduated on his 41st birthday, January 25, 1970.

Since his graduation, he has preached in Flagstaff, Arizona; the three Maritime Provinces of Canada—Nova Scotia, Prince Edward Island, and New Brunswick; and Lubbock, Texas. A.C. and his wife touched many lives during his years of preaching across North America. They returned to Lubbock permanently in 1982. Ruth worked at both the Texas Tech Library and the Texas Tech Museum until she retired after 32 years of service.

When asked how he would like to be remembered, he simply said, "As a man who loved God, his family and his country." A.C. is a stellar example of someone who has demonstrated how to do all of those things well.

84

BILLY RUDD
A Case of Mistaken Identity

"I didn't know who I was until I was 70 years old." I know what you, the reader, is thinking: how is that possible? Korean War era veteran Billy D. Rudd had gone by that name for 70 years. Billy, born in 1930, went to get a passport in 2000 and was told that he "didn't exist." This came as quite a shock to Billy. His mother, Lois, was in a nursing home in Amherst, Texas, and he went by to visit her and said, "Mom, I need to know who I am." No response from Mom. Knowing he was born in Muleshoe, Texas, he went to the courthouse and in just a few minutes, he was able to obtain a copy of his birth certificate. To his surprise, his real name was Billie D. Birchfield. His mother was only 17 when he was born to Jeff and Lois Birchfield who would soon go their separate ways. Lois would meet and marry Ralph Rudd when Billy was only 2 years old. His mother would never tell Billy about his biological father.

Billy's stepfather, Ralph, was a farmer until 1946 when he moved the family to Springlake, Texas, where he bought and ran a service station. Billy said his favorite subject in school was English, but he dropped out of school in the 10th grade and "began working stuccoing and plastering houses." He was drafted into the Army on March 5, 1951. He was sent to Ft. Bliss in El Paso, Texas, for 8 weeks of basic training and 8 more weeks of advanced artillery training. He noted that a group of area men would "drive home on the weekends and would drive up to 100 miles per hour." Once they ran off the road and "all of the guys picked up the car and carried it back to the highway."

His unit, the 63rd Antiaircraft Artillery Battalion, 8th Antiaircraft Artillery Group would ship out to Germany by way of New York Harbor in July of 1951 and make the 14-day cruise onboard the USS *General C.H. Muir* (AP-142) to Mannheim, Germany. The 63rd was sent to guard the Air Force base in Wiesbaden, Germany, with four 50 mm guns mounted on an M16 turret to guard for the 90 mm antiaircraft guns. Part of Billy's job was to guard the antiaircraft weapons and help move them where ordered. He noted that at that time "the Russians wanted to take over all of Germany." He was transferred to the 1st Antiaircraft Artillery Group, 27th Antiaircraft Battalion in Mittenwald, Germany. He was able to visit the "Eagles Nest" near the town of Berchtesgaden. Built by the Nazis in 1938, it was primarily used for government and social meetings. He also recalled a 10-day trip to Paris and said he and his buddies "had a great time." They could "buy a carton of Phillip Morris cigarettes for $2 and sell them for $10." His current wife, Jo Ann, said "they were young, handsome and having a good time." Billy would return to the States in January 1953 and be discharged at Ft. Hood, Texas, on February 17, 1953, at the rank of Corporal.

Billy met Mary Walker in a Muleshoe (Texas) restaurant and they would marry in September 1954. She had a son, Richard, and she and Billy would have a daughter, Pam. Billy had various jobs over the years and began working at AAA Coffee Service in 1970 and retired in 1995. Mary passed away in 1995 and he would marry his next-door neighbor, Jo Ann Chandler, whose husband passed away in 1993. Jo Ann was the 3rd runner-up in the 1952 Miss Texas contest. Her brother, Marine Cpl. Jack Mang, was killed during the invasion of Tarawa in November 1943. He was posthumously awarded a Purple Heart.

Billy legally changed his name to Billy D. Rudd at the age of 70 years old to honor the last name of the only father he had ever known. It was not until 1975 that Billy would find out more about his biological father and was able to meet his half-sister who lived in Clovis, New Mexico, and an aunt who lived in Baird, New Mexico. He would also receive photos of his father and the family that he never knew. Billy jokingly said, "I didn't know who I was but I'm still going."

85

CURTIS RUFF
It Just Wasn't His Day

There's something about a military funeral that tugs at the heart strings. It's a wonderful mix of pride, respect, honor, sadness and a celebration of the heroism and life of another American veteran from the Greatest Generation. Sadly, as these veterans age and pass away, we lose one more from a group that perhaps did more than any other since our founding fathers to make this great country what it is today. Under a crisp, clear blue West Texas sky on January 12, 2016, the 21-gun salute was rendered by the American Legion, taps were played and the U.S. flag draping the coffin was folded with precision and respect and handed to the grieving widow, Frances. She had been married to Curtis Ruff for 61 years: 61 years that almost didn't happen.

Curtis was born on July 23, 1932, in Old Mobeetie, Texas, the next to youngest of seven children. When he was 17, his mother signed for him to join the Army. Curtis stated that "all of the five boys in our family served in the armed forces," three during World War II, one during World War II and Korea and then Curtis in Korea. After boot camp in Ft. Ord, California, he went for more training in Ft. Bliss, Texas. He insisted on going overseas, and the Army obliged him by sending him to Japan and on to Korea as part of the Army's 2nd Infantry Division known as the "Indianhead." The insignia came from an emblem that a truck driver had painted on his truck during World War I. From that early beginning, the 2nd Division would go on to become one of the most decorated units in the Army. During its illustrious history it has had 40 Medal of Honor winners and was engaged in over 20 campaigns.

When Curtis arrived in Pusan, Korea, in January of 1951, the North Koreans were making a big push into South Korea. He noted that the allies had been "pushed back about as far as they could go and it was now time to move north." He started moving north in a convoy up through mountains in the snow; as they were getting farther north, bullets started hitting the trucks. They eventually made it to their base camp. It was at this base camp that Curtis "saw his first real casualties of war." He saw behind the north wall of the mess hall "several ... uniformed soldiers stacked like firewood in the freezing cold."

His platoon marched on north from there. After arriving at the next base camp, he was called up by a captain who told him they "needed some infantry guys up front." He was to join Company G, 2nd Infantry Division. This was to be his first exposure to "this real thing called war and I didn't know what to expect." Carrying an M-1 rifle, a backpack with a sleeping bag and some rations, his company struck out to "find the enemy." Often the enemy found them by way of sniper fire, which would pin them down until they could "eliminate the problem." Besides the enemy fire, the bitter, freezing cold took its toll on both men and their equipment.

His company "got a new commander, a young Captain William Clark who was the son of the famous General Mark Clark." They thought they would "have it easy with this young guy" but soon found out he was a "fearless leader and wanted to engage and fight." Curtis said the young Captain "liked to look for action and found it." On one of their first patrols, Captain Clark had "taken things in his own hands and dropped a grenade in an enemy bunker."

Curtis said, "The living conditions were horrible and just being out in the open all day then trying to sleep at nighttime on the frozen ground, afraid to go to sleep after hearing of other soldiers with their throats cut while being helpless in their sleeping bags. Days and nights just came and went."

The winter started giving way to spring and warmer weather but then came the rain and the mud. Curtis said he "spent the next five months climbing hills and dodging bullets." His company was involved in a lot of fire fights and near misses. Since the weather had improved, they went on many more patrols and were constantly engaging the enemy. By this time, Curtis was given a 44-lb. M18 recoilless rifle to carry and had lost 22 lbs. His platoon had the lead up one particularly deadly hill. The Captain and the Lieutenant were wounded and the Sergeant had to take over the platoon. Curtis was "standing next to one of his good friends who was a machine gunner and when he stood up, he was shot and killed." He noted that he could "never forget the look on his friend's face when he was hit." A short time later, their medic was on his way to help a fallen comrade when he was also killed.

All of the action above took place on May 28, 1951. The next day, they had to return to the hill to retrieve the casualties. There were "eight or ten killed in action." As he helped carry them off the mountain, he said he had a strange feeling. It was "like he was proud that it wasn't him being carried and it also made him feel guilty that it could have been him so he guessed it just wasn't his day."

The next day, May 30, it was his day. He was going up a hill when an explosion knocked him off his feet. He wasn't sure exactly what hit him, but he remembers "the ones carrying him on a stretcher said it didn't look like he was going to make it and they had to get him out of there or he was going to die."

He also remembered being in an ambulance and not wanting to open his eyes because he was afraid that part of him was gone.

Curtis's mother received a telegram dated June 16, 1951, stating that "your son PFC Ruff was slightly wounded in action in Korea." Curtis was flown to a hospital in Japan for a couple of weeks and then on to Brooke Army Hospital at Ft. Sam Houston.

He was certainly much more than "slightly wounded." The next letter she received came from Brooke Army Hospital and the chief of medical records said that PFC Curtis "remains under treatment for wounds of the lower abdomen, the left knee, right foot and the left hand. Also, fractures of the right foot and left hand." Curtis noted that "the doctors in Japan removed 17 pieces of shrapnel from his abdomen and he has carried more in his leg all his life."

Incredibly, after months in the hospital, Curtis was kept on active duty and wasn't discharged until April 24, 1953.

He was awarded the Combat Infantry Badge, Purple Heart, Korean Service Medal, United Nations Service Medal and many more awards. He was still somewhat disabled and no longer able to do manual labor which was "all [he] had ever done." His cousin, Joe Ruff, was a court reporter and talked Curtis into attending Lippert's Business College for court reporting classes in Plainview. This was a 20-month course and he "somehow finished in 13 months." After graduation, his teacher found him a job in South Dakota where he stayed a short time. While in school, he dated Frances Wilson, who was also taking a bookkeeping course.

They soon married and had two daughters, Jo and Cindy. Curtis and Frances moved to Lubbock after a short time in South Dakota and he became the official court reporter for the 137th District Court. He then opened his own freelance firm, Curtis D. Ruff & Associates, Certified Shorthand Reporters. This business thrived under his leadership for many, many years until his retirement.

It was noted by Curtis's nephew, Harold Drake, at his funeral service that "Curtis helped many people over the years who were down on their luck and was a very giving man."

Many thanks to the Ruff family and to his daughter, Jo Kizziah, for supplying the information for this story.

86

WELBY SMITH

Crew Chief to Two of the Air Force's Fastest Bombers

Welby Smith was one of the first to join the newly named United States Air Force. The former Army Air Forces became the U.S. Air Force on September 16, 1947. Army Air fields were renamed Air Force bases and new personnel were issued new uniforms with new rank insignias. Welby was born on November 18, 1930, in Boswell, Oklahoma. He joined the Air Force at age 17 in December of 1947 and was sent to Lackland Air Force Base in San Antonio, Texas. The ambitious young man first trained in fire rescue, but couldn't get promoted very quickly, so he went into the air police. He found that he couldn't get promoted quickly there either, so he went into aircraft maintenance.

Most of his training was "on-the-job" for fire rescue and air police. He spent three years at Burtonwood AFB, England. Burtonwood was reverted to the USAF in 1948 to support U.S. European bases and it undertook the entire major servicing for the C-54 Skymaster aircraft involved in the Berlin Airlift. The Berlin Airlift Historical Foundation website documents that, from June 24, 1948, to May 12, 1949, the United States and its allies flew over 200,000 flights. They provided West Berliners over 6,700 tons of necessities, such as food and fuel, each day due to a Soviet blockade. With the airlift clearly working, the Soviets lifted the blockade.

Welby came back to the States and went into the air police at Brooks AFB in San Antonio. After a stint as an air policeman, he went into aircraft maintenance school at Amarillo AFB, Texas. After spending time at Hunter AFB in Savannah, Georgia, he was assigned to Nouasseur AFB near Casablanca, Morocco, where he was an aircraft maintenance man on the B-47 Stratojet. The B-47's distinctive swept-wing design was developed by Boeing from test results found in a German lab in May 1945. The B-47 medium bomber became the foundation of the Air Force's newly created Strategic Air Command. Boeing's website provides a statistic that, between 1947 and 1956, a total of 2,032 B-47s in all variants were built. The jet broke speed and distance records. In 1949 it crossed the United States in under four hours at an average speed of 608 MPH. The B-47 was so fast that it only needed defensive armament in the rear, because no fighter was fast enough to attack it except from the rear. B-47s were in service from 1951 until 1977.

Welby was transferred to Carswell AFB in Ft. Worth, Texas. He joked that he "could not stay out of Texas!" There he would become a crew chief on one of the Convair B-58 Hustlers, which was the first operational supersonic jet bombers capable of Mach 2 flight. The B-58 set no fewer than 19 world speed records, including coast-to-coast records, and one for the longest supersonic flight in history. On January 12, 1961, Major Henry J. Deutschendorf (singer John Denver's father) commanded a B-58 crew from the 43rd Bombardment Wing that set three world speed records. In 1963 it went from Tokyo to London (via Alaska), a distance of 8,028 miles in 8 hours, 35 minutes, 20.4 seconds, averaging 938 MPH. As of 2016, this record still stands.

Welby also did maintenance on bombers in Guam in the late 1960s that flew missions during the Vietnam War. After a nearly 21-year career, he retired as a Master Sergeant in March 1968.

As a teenager, Welby was smitten. His friend Kenneth introduced him to his sister Lajuana, whom he described as "the most beautiful girl in the world." Welby's affection for her grew, and although he did not personally get to take her to a dance, he once "arranged" for the corsage purchased by her date to come up missing, so she would have to wear the one he'd bought for her.

After both were widowed from previous marriages, Welby "married up." Lajuana would become his best friend and partner for the last half of his life. They have already spent 26 years to date in wedded bliss. With his first wife he had 4 children, and Lajuana had 3 from her first marriage. Welby and Lajuana beam with pride as they describe loving and positive family relations and communication. Even now, when they enter a store, he will walk up to a staff person and ask them, "Do you see that beautiful woman over there? That's my wife."

Welby speaks in the community about patriotism and provides hundreds of copies of Russ Murphy's "Welcome Home Soldier" on CD to his listeners and other people he meets. Welby knew Russ from Indiana Avenue Baptist Church, and the song was written in 1996 about Chad Gross, who had been involved in 120 combat missions. It has won numerous awards.

87

LAWRENCE WALKER
Triple "Service" for Lubbock Man

Lawrence (Larry) Walker of Lubbock spent nearly 50 years "serving" his country. Born in New York City on March 11, 1930, he was the only child of Harry and Lee Ann Walker. This was the Great Depression era, and Larry's father soon moved his family west to California when Larry was only a few weeks old. Harry eventually found work as the maintenance manager at the Hollywood Park Racetrack. Larry attended Hollywood High.

Volunteering for the Navy in March of 1947, Larry took his basic training in San Diego, California. He was assigned to the USS *Furse* (DD-882), a Navy destroyer, in August of 1947 and would head for the Far East in September 1947. After a one-week stopover in Honolulu, the ship sailed to its Japanese home base of Yokosuka. Acting as an occupation force after World War II, the ship cruised to Hong Kong, Midway, Wake Island, Marshall Islands, Guam, Philippines, Korea and back to Japan. Larry, a seaman, "did all duties required of him" during these voyages.

The *Furse* was transferred to the Atlantic Fleet in early April 1949 by way of the Panama Canal and arrived for duty at Newport, Rhode Island, on April 21, 1949. Assigned to the 6th Fleet, she sailed for Mediterranean duty in September 1949. Halfway through this tour of duty, things were about to change for Seaman Walker. He was transferred to Great Lakes Naval Station near North Chicago, Illinois. The Naval station was founded in 1911 and is the largest training center in the Navy. Here, Larry would embark on a 12-week medical training school. He would be assigned as a Hospital Corpsman 3rd Class to a Naval hospital in Oakland, California.

Larry married Jean Claire in 1951. They had three children, 2 girls and 1 boy. They would divorce in 1980. He was transferred to the USS *Kearsarge* (CVA 33), one of 24 Essex class aircraft carriers built at the end of World War II. In August 1952, the *Kearsarge* stopped in Hawaii for a few days. She sailed for the Far East and landed in Yokosuka, Japan, in September and joined Task Force 77 off the east coast of Korea. During the next 5 months the carrier's planes flew nearly 6,000 sorties against Communist forces in North Korea, inflicting heavy damage on enemy positions. While onboard the ship, Walker worked in sick bay and assisted during surgeries. When the ship returned to San Diego in 1954, she was used in the filming of the movie *The Caine Mutiny*. The *Kearsarge* substituted for Admiral Halsey's ship during World War II. Larry recalled watching them film the movie and seeing several movie stars such as Humphrey Bogart, Lauren Bacall, Fred MacMurray and Van Johnson. Some of the crew became extras in the movie. Larry Walker had a Hollywood connection—his uncle was the venerable actor Walter Pidgeon.

Walker transferred to Alameda Naval Air Station in 1956. Leaving the Navy in March 1957, he noted that he was "tired of being on the water and gone for long periods of time." Four days later he joined the U.S. Air Force, enlisting as an Airman 1st Class. Due to his medical training in the Navy, Larry continued his work in the medical field. His assignments took him to Norton AFB in California, Ramey AFB in Puerto Rico, then Columbus AFB in Mississippi and he was TDY to Southeast Asia for 180 days. He transferred to Laughlin AFB in Texas where he worked in the flight surgeon's office and flew as a medic aboard a Kaman HH43 Huskie search-and-rescue helicopter. He retired from the Air Force as a Master Sergeant in March 1977 after 30 years of combined military service. He was awarded numerous ribbons and medals such as the Japanese Occupation, Korean Service, United Nations, China Service, Meritorious Service, Air Force Commendation, Air Force Longevity, National Defense and Good Conduct. His service, however, was not over. He joined the Civil Service in 1974 and continued working at Laughlin for 9 years.

He met Dianna Brewer who had three children, 2 boys and 1 girl from a previous marriage. She was working at Laughlin Hospital and they married in September 1981. They moved in 1983 when Larry transferred to Reese AFB in Lubbock. His "service" to his country finally ended after 49 years when Larry retired for the final time in 1993. He continues to work on the Texas South Plains Honor Flight Committee along with his wife, Dianna.

Larry noted that he "would like to be remembered as a great husband, father and grandfather to their blended family of 6 children, 7 grandchildren and 9 great-grandchildren." He should also be remembered for his patriotism and a lifetime of service to his country.

88

FRED WATSON
Faith Helps Him through Korean War Memories

Fred Watson saw his body floating and transparent. He felt that if his spirit floated through the ceiling he would not come back. He credits the return of it to the prayers of his wife, Rebecca. A year and a half ago he had a serious leg infection and several operations. He experienced an "out-of-body experience" and he is thankful to his wife for her fervent supplications and for reading Psalms 91 and 103 aloud to him as he straddled two dimensions. The next day, he was sitting up and eating and he felt the Lord letting him know what had happened and that "someone would pray me back."

Fred Watson was born on September 19, 1928, in McKinney, Texas. He enlisted in the Marine Corps on March 4, 1952. He did his basic training in Camp Pendleton, California, and was assigned to the 3rd Marine Division. He was then shipped out to Nagoya, Japan. Fred and "seven other men were picked for a special assignment." They "were dropped into Korea close to the DMZ. Their mission was to 'look for enemy troop convoys of tanks and personnel and stop them as best they could.'" Fred was to "carry an M18 57mm recoilless rifle" and "part of his platoon would help carry the ammunition." After only one month in combat, Fred was "walking down a road and stepped on a landmine called a 'Bouncing Bettie.'" The Bouncing Bettie had a great psychological effect on U.S. and South Korean forces because of its tendency to seriously maim, rather than kill, the soldier. He was wounded and airlifted to a MASH unit where they "patched him up and sent him to the Naval hospital in Yokosuka, Japan," where he would spend several months recovering. After treatment of more than 5,800 casualties from this conflict, the facility received its first Navy Unit Commendation award. Fred was released from active duty on February 28, 1954.

Fred and his first wife, Thelma, were married almost 50 years. She passed away almost 19 years ago. He worked for Ben E. Keith Wholesale Food Distributor and delivered to 18 United Grocery Stores.

Fred has lived at a nursing home in Lubbock for 2½ years and his eyes darken with emotion as he recounts how his wife had to work with him in "baby steps" to help him face his fears of the past and the sometimes very dark times of his military service, which has led him to a place of lasting peace of mind and peace with his Creator.

Before he went on the 2013 Texas South Plains Honor Flight, he got to visit Washington, D.C., but it proved a very painful experience for him and he needed much reassurance as he came face to face with the eyes looking back at him in the statues and symbols of wartime past. His body literally froze in place as he looked at the Vietnam Memorial from a distance and he said some women visiting there (including his future wife) gently held his hand and prayed for him and eventually he was able to approach the wall and walk the length of it. Another time at the Marine Museum he physically could not watch the video and Rebecca helped walk him out and supported his decision. He "white-knuckled it" at the movie *Pearl Harbor* when it showed in theaters as he remembered the tragedy of losing a platoon battle buddy. Years later he was able to go on the Texas South Plains Honor Flight and he smiles as he describes the Vietnam Memorial, now his favorite. After forgiving himself and all that happened in earlier times, he was finally able to actually enjoy the tour of memorials and the healthy banter and camaraderie with other veterans.

This interview time proved to be a positive experience for both Fred and Rebecca. They married later in life on June 1, 2002, in a backyard ceremony in Wolfforth after meeting at church and being friends for six years. The song "In the Garden" was played at their wedding and they have both tried to encourage each other in their walk with the Lord. They both express deep grateful hearts for all the bad and the good events that have brought them closer to each other and to the Lord. They have four children, nine grand and six great-grands.

Fred is finally interested in the possibility of having some of his lost military medals restored to him, as that time in his life has taken on a positive light now and he has experienced many levels of healing both physically and emotionally. He encourages us and the younger generation to get involved, to join the military. "If something happens you won't run away." With the help of his faith, his wife and his friends, Fred no longer feels like he needs to "run away."

89

CHARLES WILLIAMS
Coming Home

My name is Larry Anderson Williams and this is a story of hope for all families of missing POWs and MIAs from our nation's wars. My uncle, Cpl. Charles Anderson Williams, was killed on November 27, 1950, at the Chosin Reservoir during the Korean War. Many people have labeled this the "Forgotten War." I can assure you that those of us who lost loved ones over there have not forgotten. Many families have waited over 50 years to find out the fate of their loved ones. Whether it was a son, brother, husband, father or even an uncle, they are still missed by their family.

My family knows all about sacrificing for our country. My mother's brother, Lloyd George, was killed in North Africa in 1942 during World War II. My wife's father, Orin Stahl, served in the Pacific Theater during World War II and her grandfather, Gust Stahl, was wounded twice in France during World War I. She also had an uncle serve in World War II and another uncle serve in the Korean War. In addition, I served in the Air Force from 1970 to 1974. No matter where I have lived over the years, I have always made a point to attend Memorial Day services to show respect and honor those who have paid the ultimate price for our freedom. To me, it is our duty to pay our respects to those who gave up their lives for their country. So each and every Memorial Day I sat through the services and wondered about the fate of my Uncle Charles in that cold, bitter winter of 1950 in North Korea.

My curiosity concerning my uncle's fate became stronger and stronger as the years went by. In early 2003, I began to research in earnest. I searched all of the internet sites pertaining to the Korean War. Through the Korean War Project website, I was able to find my uncle's name and what company he was with. He served with the Army's Co. A, 32nd Infantry Regiment, 7th Infantry Division. He trained in Ft. Knox, Kentucky, and was later shipped to Camp Haugen in Japan. From there he was part of the September landing at Inchon with General MacArthur. The 32nd was assigned to the Army's 31st Regimental Combat Team (RCT-31), later to be known as Task Force Faith (for Lt. Col. Don Faith). The Marines and Army soon swept north and ended up in the Chosin Reservoir. Conditions were brutal, with temperatures reaching -45 degrees and weapons not functioning from the cold. My uncle was in the mortar section on the east side of the reservoir. On the night of November 27, the Army's position was overrun by several thousand Chinese.

Charles A. Williams, U.S. Army, Korean War.

Thanks to the Korean War Project website, I found Bill Mattingly from Owensboro, Kentucky, who had been in Co. A at the Chosin Reservoir and he had listed many of his buddies that served with him. My uncle's name appeared on that list and I contacted this individual and found out that not only did he know my uncle but he was his best friend and assistant on 60 mm mortars. He was able to answer many of our questions about the fate of Charles. On the morning after the Chinese Intervention, my uncle was found in his foxhole with his M1911 .45 pistol in his hand and several dead Chinese around him. There were also some Chinese still alive in the foxhole with him.

Fast forward to the year 2000. The RCT-31 was finally awarded the Navy Presidential Unit Citation, and Task Force Faith received the long-overdue recognition for their sacrifices during the Chosin Reservoir battle. My 80-year-old father told me that he always had two dreams. One, that he could get Charles's Purple Heart and other medals earned, and, two, that he could bring his brother home for proper burial. After many months of research, e-mails and phone calls, my sister, Patty Lumley, and I were finally able to obtain all the medals that my uncle had earned. Dad was quite moved and unconvinced that this could be done after so many years. Fresh off the success of receiving the medals,

Charles A. Williams' remains being carried by Ft. Knox Honor Guard July 2004.

we encouraged our father to give a DNA sample in the hope that his brother's remains might someday be found and identified. In July 2003, the Army sent the Knight Group to our father's house to take the sample. He was told that it would take several months to process the sample and match it with their existing DNA database. On March 17, 2004, my father received a call from the Army Casualty Office at Ft. Knox, Kentucky, stating that they had a positive DNA match with Thomas Williams and Charles Williams. To say the least, Dad was in shock. He could not believe that after all these years his brother could finally come home and be laid to rest.

On June 30, 2014, Harry Campbell from the Army Casualty Office in Alexandria, Virginia, and Sgt. 1st Class Lisa Tartt from the Army's Casualty Area Command in Ft. Knox arrived at my father's house with all the information on Charles and how and when he was located. He was found by JPAC (Joint POW/MIA Accounting Command) during one of their digs at the reservoir in September 2003. He was found in a shallow grave with three or four other GIs from the 1st Battalion, 32nd Infantry. He still had his dog tag on, which obviously made the identification much easier. The only step remaining was to have his body flown from Hawaii to Kentucky for proper burial. Charles was the first set of remains from the Korean War to be returned to his home state of Kentucky.

On July 24, 2004, Cpl. Williams was finally laid to rest high on a hill in the veterans' section of the Carlisle, Kentucky, cemetery. Catherine DeRossett, and her family), friends, veterans, the Kentucky Dept. of Veterans Affairs and news media. The Army provided an honor guard from Ft. Knox and a full military funeral, which was impressive and quite moving. I gave the eulogy and Capt. Daryl Densford officiated as chaplain. I think Capt. Densford put it best when he said, "There's a sense of relief. Finally, the remains have come home." I closed my eulogy by saying, "I know Charles is looking down on us and smiling today. In one of his last letters to his brother, Charles said he 'couldn't wait to see old Carlisle again.' Welcome home Charles. We're sorry it took so long."

Upon returning to Louisville from the funeral, we were contacted by a reporter from the *Louisville Courier-Journal*. Patty and I answered all the questions about our uncle as best we could. My dad (who usually had something to say about everything) sat in the corner and didn't say a word, lost in his thoughts. At the end of the interview, the reporter asked my dad what he thought about all of this. He simply thought for a moment and said, "It's like I buried him twice." I'm sure that hundreds of other families across the country feel the same way when they finally bury the long-lost remains of their loved one.

Part III
Vietnam War

I'm no hero.
—Army Specialist 5 Doug Foster:
Bronze Star with "V" (for valor)

90

GEORGE BRADLEY
"Follow Your Dreams"

"They put a sack over my head and marched me to a cell. That was a scary moment." While he was not really captured by the enemy, for Sergeant George Bradley, it sure felt like it. He was taking survival training at Fairfield Air Force Base, 12 miles southwest of Spokane, Washington. George attended numerous training courses for both land and water during his 20 years in the U.S. Air Force but none as tough and terrifying as the survival training at Fairfield. Later in his career, he also attended NCO (non-commissioned officer) Leadership School at March Air Force Base, California.

George was born in New Orleans on January 19, 1946, the firstborn of four children, and was raised by his grandfather and grandmother. His grandfather, Charles, worked doing dry wall and house painting, as well as maintenance and general labor work. His grandmother, Ethel, was a domestic worker and rental property owner. The movie *The Help* reminds him of his grandmother. He recalls going to a kindergarten and grade school that was "right across from our house. On rainy days, I had no excuse not to go to school."

While George had a "good childhood" growing up in the Deep South, he was also aware of the segregation at the time. He mentioned "separate beaches, bathrooms, water fountains, diners and sitting in the back of the bus." But the young man did not allow the racism of that era to handicap him. He was a dreamer.

George graduated from Booker T. Washington High School in 1966. In 1969, he "went to sign up for the Marines, but they were out to lunch, so I joined the Air Force." He took his basic training at Lackland Air Force Base in San Antonio, Texas. When he was in high school, he had "dreamed of going to see the world and the military took me to France, England, Spain and Hawaii." He also served two tours in the Philippines as well as in Thailand, Okinawa and Japan.

His main job in the Air Force was overseeing life support and survival equipment for F4 Phantom jets. He was the NCOIC (non-commissioned officer in charge) of all survival equipment, such as parachutes, oxygen masks, and flotation devices. While stationed in Germany, he attended Supply Custodian School, and one of his best friends was a Swede named Sven Gustafson. "When we went out, people called us 'Salt and Pepper.'"

During his twenty years of service, George obtained the rank of Tech Sergeant (E-6) and completed five overseas tours. Following his dream of continuing his education, George received his associate's degree in work management in 1985 from the Community College of the Air Force.

About his time in the service, he said, "I enjoyed working with all the airmen. I learned responsibility, self-reliance, got to travel and enhance my life. I am a living testimony and encourage other people to follow their dreams."

George retired from the Air Force at Reese Air Force Base in 1989. He was married four times and jokingly said, "None of my exes live in Texas!" He worked at Lockheed Martin at Reese AFB in Tools and Parts, Texas Tech University Press in Shipping and Receiving as a tool and parts attendant, University Medical Center as an emergency room floor tech, and the Texas Health Department.

George is very animated and delights people when he sings one of his favorite songs, "Hello Dolly," in his gruff, Louis Armstrong–like voice. George has also responded to speaker requests from schools and recently spoke at the Silent Wings Museum to a large group of Lubbock schoolchildren, sharing his story and his deep but humor-filled sense of patriotism. He enjoys helping people see their cup half-full and empowering them to be who they are created to be. He lives his motto of "follow your dreams."

91

CHARLES BRIMBERRY
Danger Was Everywhere in Vietnam

Marine Corporal Charles "Joe" Brimberry and some of his buddies were "just heading to a river to get a swim and clean up when it happened." Deep in Vietnam (Joe was not sure exactly where), one of the guys near Joe "hit a trip wire that exploded a grenade." Joe was hit in the arm by shrapnel and "the two other guys were hit worse than I was." Joe was flown by chopper to the nearest field hospital to be patched up and then sent to the USS *Repose* (AH-16) hospital ship in Da Nang Harbor. The Naval Order website (navalorder.org) states that the ship would treat "over 9,000 battle casualties and 24,000 inpatients while deployed" and earned the nickname of "Angel of the Orient." Joe noted that "the best thing on the ship was the nurses onboard. They were older than us young guys and very nice to us." After two or three days, Joe was sent back to his unit. When asked what the scariest time in Vietnam was, he said, "Nighttime firefights."

Charles Joseph Brimberry was born on March 21, 1945, in Indianapolis, Indiana, to Charles and Lenna Brimberry. His father was a truck driver and later a policeman. He had two sisters. His mom and dad separated when he was a young man and "Dad picked me up from school one day and took me to Torrance, California." His mother joined them later and she and Charles stayed together until he passed away. Joe graduated from North High in Torrance in 1963. Enlisting in the Marines in July 1963, basic training was in Camp Pendleton, California. He would serve a stint in Okinawa from 1964 to 1965 and then attend cold weather school at the Mountain Warfare Training Center in Bridgeport, California, which he enjoyed. "We got to camp out, go hiking and rappel. I like all of those things." He then helped to train reserves for six months. Part of the 1st Battalion, 5th Marines, Brimberry and his unit "made an amphibious landing near Chu Lai, Vietnam, in April 1966 and headed north."

91. Charles Brimberry

Returning to his unit after being wounded, Joe would suffer from "jungle rot." Jungle rot was due to cuts or scratches that became infected and turned into painful sores. Joe was sent back to the hospital on Okinawa and then arrived in San Francisco to convalesce in December of 1966. He spent his last six months at Barstow, California, as a sergeant of the guard and was discharged on July 14, 1967. Remembering his time in Vietnam, he said his "girlfriend Patricia Hutson from back home in Torrance wrote to me every day." He also recalled that his "best friend, Cpl. Albin Baranczyk from Wisconsin, had both legs blown off and was killed in Vietnam in May 1966." He said, "The toughest part was writing to Albin's fiancée that he had been killed." Joe had introduced the couple.

Charles (Joe) Brimberry, U.S. Marines, Vietnam War.

Joe and Patricia were married on June 14, 1968. They met in church in Torrance, California, when she was 15 and Joe was 20. Joe attended El Camino Junior College where he tested for law school. He was admitted to the West Los Angeles School of Law and eventually graduated in 1975 with a Doctorate of Jurisprudence. He worked for Hughes Aircraft for nine years in the Security and Education Department. He and Pat bought a house in Simi Valley in July of 1976. After graduating from the Los Angeles County Sheriff's Academy, he worked for the Beverly Hills Police Department for six months. In 1983 he went to work at the Simi Valley Police Department and worked as a patrolman, SWAT team member and finally a detective. He said he "had several close calls and

Charles (Joe) Brimberry with Purple Heart and Police badge February 8, 2018.

an ugly homicide in 1993 led him to retire in 1995." Joe and Pat had four children, 2 boys and 2 girls.

Pat was born in Littlefield, Texas, and "wanted to move back to West Texas" as her parents lived in Lubbock. Joe amusingly noted that "Texas girls may leave Texas, but after a 35-year vacation, they want to move back home!" He wants to be remembered for his love of God, family and country.

92

Doug Foster
The Healing Wall

Doug Foster had heard about the Texas South Plains Honor Flight from some veterans in Snyder who had gone on the flight. Doug, a Vietnam veteran, didn't think he was eligible because he felt like it was mostly for World War II and Korean vets. He finally applied in 2014 and received the call in September 2016 that they "had a spot for him on the flight." It would still be a difficult decision for Doug as he had never been to Washington, D.C., and wasn't sure how he would react to the Vietnam Memorial. For him, it would be more difficult than most as he probably lost more buddies than anyone in the country whose names are etched on the long black wall.

Douglas Glenn Foster was born on March 9, 1943, in Roscoe, Texas, to Glenn and Golda Foster. Glenn and his wife were farmers near Hermleigh, Texas, and Doug would grow up doing farm work. He graduated with a class of 33 from Hermleigh High School in 1961. He would go to Texas Tech from 1961 to 1965, but regretted not finishing. He met and married Belinda on December 13, 1963. He went to work at Volker Furniture & Floor Covering in Lubbock. He received his draft notice in October of 1965 but wasn't called up until October 1966. He said he and "33 other men from the Hermleigh area were called up to the Army and sent to basic training at Ft. Bliss, Texas." Several of these men were older and were married. He was sent to Ft. Polk, Louisiana, for infantry training and would be on the list for OCS (Officer Candidate School) due to his college education. After two or three months of waiting for the school to start, he told his commanding officer to "go ahead and send me on to Vietnam."

Doug was assigned to the 2nd Battalion, 28th Infantry, 1st Infantry Division, the famed Big Red 1 unit, and left from Travis AFB on June 13, 1967, and landed in Saigon. His first assignment was to go out on night patrol. His third night out, his unit got into an ambush and three enemies were killed. Doug was an M60 machine gunner and was soon in charge of 3 other gunners. During one ambush, he ran out of ammunition and asked his ammo bearer, Joe B. Crutcher, for more and he found out he was carrying the boxes empty for a lighter load. Not a good spot to be in. Joe B. was killed in a firefight. After several of these patrols and firefights, Doug and his unit based out of Lai Khe were part of Operation Shenandoah I and then Shenandoah II, also called the Battle of Ong Thanh.

On October 16, 1967, Doug's unit was led on point by a Viet Cong defector who was killed, and a short firefight broke out as Doug saw men hit around him. He said he knew an attack was imminent as he "could always smell marijuana that the Viet Cong snipers would be smoking up in the trees." While running for cover, Doug landed at the base of a tree and looked up just in time to see a sniper dropping a small hand grenade that the men called a "half pint." He said that "while these grenades did damage, if it would have been an American grenade, I wouldn't be around to tell the story." Hit in several places by shrapnel, Doug was airlifted to the hospital in Bien Hoa where he spent a week recovering. He and other wounded were then "sent to the seaside resort Vung Tau to recover from their wounds as it was felt that the sea air would help the wounds heal more quickly." After recovering from his wounds, Doug was "reassigned to Lai Khe Base Camp to sit at a desk and a typewriter."

While Doug thought

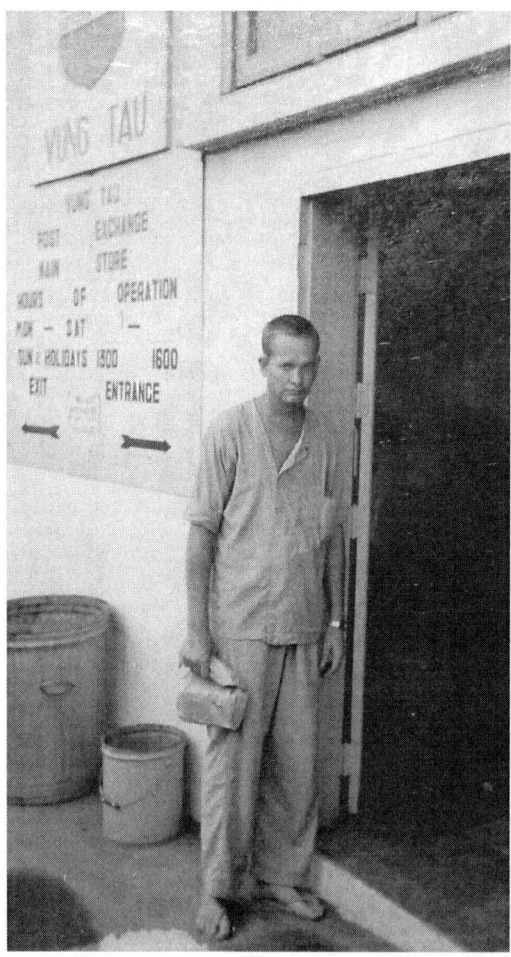

Doug Foster, U.S. Army, Vietnam War.

Doug and Belinda Foster, November 13, 2016.

his combat days were over, his unit was hit by rocket fire in the initial wave of the Tet Offensive on January 30, 1968. Doug's building was hit and the men had to "head for the bunkers." Typewriter duty was more dangerous than he thought. He noted that the "chow hall had to be closed down as it was targeted and they had to eat c-rations for 6 weeks."

Doug left Vietnam on June 14, 1968. He "came home and started farming and after the first disastrous year found a job at the Chevron Gas Plant north of Snyder in 1969 and stayed around for 25 years" until his retirement in 1995. He and Belinda continued to farm during this time and is still farming to this day with his son Rodney who was born in August 1970. Rodney didn't know a lot about his dad's days in Vietnam but was so proud of him for his service and his much-deserved trip to Washington, D.C., that he wrote a heartfelt letter to his dad expressing his admiration.

Looking at Doug's medals from his days in Vietnam, I noticed that he had earned the Bronze Star with a "V." I told him I knew that the "V" stood for valor. He immediately said, "I'm no hero." Belinda soon showed me a commendation letter that said in part, "Without hesitation or regard for his own personal safety, Specialist Foster ran through intense hostile fire to man the machine gun's location. While engaging the Viet Cong (on his own), Specialist Foster was wounded by fragments of an enemy grenade. Ignoring his wounds, he remained at his position and continued his devastating fire to cover the evacuation of his wounded comrades." Doug may not consider himself a hero, but as for the buddies he saved, he will always be considered one. By the time the battle was over, 59 soldiers were killed and 75 wounded.

While nearly backing out at the last minute, Doug would go on the 2016 Honor Flight. He wasn't sure how he would react to the Vietnam Wall. He lost so many buddies there that he "didn't have time to look them all up." It was both an emotional and cathartic time for Doug. So many good, young men lost and he had survived. He said, "They call this the 'Healing Wall' for many." I asked him, "Was it for you?" He said, "It helped, but I'm still dealing with it." He spoke for many Vietnam veterans who to this day are "still dealing with it."

93

JANNIE GREENWAY
Around the World and Back

Jannie Greenway was born during the Great Depression in 1932, in Dalton, Georgia, to R.W. and Selma Greenway and was the middle child of three children. She graduated Dalton High in 1951. She states that she had a couple of uncles who were wounded in World War II and her brother was in the Army for 2 years. She spent 21 years in the Air Force serving her country from 1954 to 1975 and was involved in both the Korean and Vietnam wars.

Jannie went to basic training in San Antonio at Lackland AFB and to Francis E. Warren AFB in Cheyenne, Wyoming, for supply school and then to Chanute Field AFB in Rantoul, Illinois. She served during the Korean War era (June 27, 1950, to January 31, 1955) and was stationed in Thailand. During her military service she lived in Puerto Rico, Thailand, Vietnam, and England. "I wasn't in combat and

Jannie Greenway swearing-in ceremony June 1950.

my base was one out of 3 that wasn't bombed," she recalls, thankfully. She remembers fondly the nickname of "Li'l Bit" she was given since she was only 5 feet 1½ inches tall. "Don't forget the half!" she jokes.

In Thailand she recalls a very emotional time where the men and women stood in a flight line watching aircraft fly in the direction of the war and then counting the few that returned. Jannie's job was NORS control (Not Operational Ready Supply) where she worked in Southeast Asia. She would call for parts and the fighter plane would touch down, drop the part, and immediately take off again. Jannie served as a Tech Sergeant, the only woman out of five Sergeants. She reached the rank of Tech Sergeant during her service. When asked how she felt about being one of the few women leaders, she states, "We were the stepping stones for women in service just as the Army WASP was for us." She someday wants to visit the WASP memorial in Sweetwater, Texas, and learn more about the courageous female pilots who helped pave the way for her and her Squadron 3743, Flight 3.

Some of her favorite times were being a part of the Francis E. Warren AFB drill team. She enjoyed the fellowship and creative formations she helped present, similar to what marching bands do today. Her first job was gathering and distributing meteorology supplies and educational materials at Chanute AFB in Illinois. At the headquarters at Offutt AFB in Omaha, Nebraska, she helped log supplies by hand using the new Univac system (the first computerized key-punch system). During the last 6–7 years she had two jobs, working supply and as the First Sergeant for the Women's Squadron in England (2 years) before being transferred to Lubbock's own Reese AFB.

Reese AFB was her home for 2–3 years when she retired in 1975. She nurtured her love of painting while working for Michaels (craft store) and recently got to hang a lot of her paintings for show at her residential community.

Jannie Greenway, U.S. Air Force Korean War.

Jannie worked for a banking company and then for 17 years at the Texas Department of State Health Services in Lubbock, Abilene, and then in Arlington where she retired.

Jannie's awards include 3 Vietnam Medals she received while stationed during a remote tour in Thailand from 1970 to 1971. She earned the Meritorious Service Medal, awarded in Lakenheath Royal AFB in Suffolk, England, while she nearly became blind suffering from cloudy vision with cataracts in both eyes. She eventually had successful cataract removal surgery in England in 1972 and 1973.

Jannie was one of two female veterans on the 2014 Texas South Plains Honor Flight. Her favorite places to visit were the Vietnam Memorial (where she helped lay the wreath), the Military Women's Memorial and seeing the Enola Gay at Udvar-Hazy Air and Space Museum in Virginia. When asked what she hopes she is remembered for, she states humbly, "That I served." When asked what she might say to encourage other veterans to go on the Honor Flight she beams, "They've GOT to go!"

94

CHARLES HANKSON
BBQ and a Slice of Sunshine

Sporting one of the brightest smiles on the South Plains, Hank beams as he leans out of his food truck serving his delicious, award-winning BBQ and striking up lively conversations. Charles Hankson loves what he does and the people that he serves.

His positive outlook in life is a big leap from where he used to be. At one time, he was familiar with the "underbelly" of the South Plains, working as a club bouncer and living on the edge; now he has settled into a more peaceful lifestyle, and uses his experiences to help people (or at least make them laugh).

He was recently asked to give the high school commencement speech in Lorenzo. His message was as simple as ABC: Avoid Bad Company. He has a passion to help young people avoid pitfalls and stay on the right path for their lives. People everywhere he goes benefit from his personal story, especially the ones at Mt. Pleasant Church (Lorenzo) where he has pastored for 32 years. The church has a summer BBQ Outreach. They are also home to a talented men's vocal group called UPG (Under God's Protection).

Charles Lee Hankson was born in 1945 in Taylor, Texas, the second of eight children. His mother worked at Ft. Hood, Texas, in the mess hall, while his father served in the Army. The youngster quickly acquired skills to help whip up meals for his younger siblings. He graduated from Roosevelt High School in 1963. At 18 he enlisted in the Army and was sent to Ft. Polk, Louisiana, for basic and AIT (Advanced Infantry Training). Two brothers and a sister followed him into the service.

The Army sent him to Korea where he spent 13 months in the DMZ. He received the EIB badge (Expert Infantryman). He was later deployed to Heidelberg, Germany, to be the driver for the school commander. In 1967, he was discharged but joined the Army Reserve in 1975. He went on to become the senior instructor for the Combat Engineers until 2000.

94. Charles Hankson

Back in 1967, Hank had met a young lady named Rose Brown at Dunbar High School in Lubbock. He was smart enough to marry her, and they raised two daughters together. Rose recently retired from the Parkway Neighborhood Center where she had worked for 25 years. She loves to sew, and has become famous for her banana bread.

Hank drove a street sweeper for the City of Lubbock from 1966 to 1972, and then became a pump designer for Goulds Pumps for 35 years. He also earned a degree in business administration and took architect and design classes at Wayland Baptist University.

Thirty years after his nightclub job, he returned to tell his former boss about the change in his life. After a long visit, the man prayed and accepted the Lord. His question to Hank was, "What took you so long [to come talk to me]?" This friend now attends Mt. Pleasant and enjoys fishing for catfish and crappie with his pastor.

The energetic 72-year-old Hankson has been a leader of the Boys and Girls Club for 18 years. "We had almost 700 kids attend the Texas Fishing Derby in 2017!" He has served on the board of 100 Black Men of West Texas for 22 years and has been on the board of The Bridge of Lubbock. "I was [even] president of the Estacado Football Booster Club for 10 years, [even though] neither I nor any members of my family went to that school."

The charismatic cook has met many celebrities, including Evander Holyfield and Jackie Joyner, as well as local personalities Calvin Lewis and sculptor Eddie Dixon. Bill Bates and Brad Sexton, who are helping with the new Lubbock VA Super Clinic, are two of his newest friends. "In the Kingdom of Heaven, it is all in who (and Who) you know. God has richly blessed me with knowing some great people in our community. I have grown to view life differently and recognize when God is bringing His light into dark situations. I am one of those stories."

95

BERNHARD T. MITTEMEYER

*A Lifetime of Service
to His Adopted Country*

Bernhard T. Mittemeyer was born October 30, 1930, in Paramaribo, Surinam, South America. His parents, Jan and Hanna, were there as missionaries from Holland. They arrived in 1926 and served there for 42 years. However, during World War II, his father went to be a chaplain for the Dutch Army in Indonesia from 1942 to 1945. Bernie, his two brothers and his mom came to the United States in 1944 and lived in Nazareth, Pennsylvania, where Bernie and his two brothers learned English. In early 1946, their father came to the States, and he and his wife planned to return to their Moravian mission work in Surinam. The plan was for Bernie and his brothers to go to Holland and live with family members there to ensure appropriate further education. However, a church family in Bethlehem, Pennsylvania, volunteered to "adopt" the three boys so they could remain in the United States, which they very much wanted to do. So Bernie was able to graduate from high school there in 1948. He then went to Moravian College in Bethlehem, Pennsylvania, as a pre-med student and graduated in 1952. Afterwards, he earned his medical degree from Temple University in 1956.

Soon after medical school and internship, he was drafted into the Army and did his basic training at Ft. Sam Houston, Texas. Although the young man was already a medical doctor, he volunteered for the airborne services, because the 101st and 82nd had liberated his home country of the Netherlands at the end of World War II. Of the 23 airborne volunteers, he was one of two to be assigned to the 101st Airborne Division. He was sent to Ft. Campbell, Kentucky, and served first as the Battle Group Surgeon and Clearing Platoon Commander. He was then assigned as Division Surgeon at the request of General William Westmoreland. At the end of his two-year tour, Bernie was going

Bernhard Mittemeyer treating a wounded soldier in Vietnam.

to leave the Army. When General Westmoreland asked him why, Mittemeyer pointed out that he "was not a U.S. citizen." Westmoreland immediately arranged for him to get his citizenship so he could become a part of the regular Army. (Bernie's older brother who had just completed his sophomore year at Lehigh University was drafted out of college and received his citizenship on the battlefield during the Korean War.) As a brand-new American citizen, Bernie accepted an Army urological residency, which he completed in 1965. Next, he was assigned as Assistant Chief of Urology at Walter Reed Army Medical Center in Bethesda, Maryland.

In April 1968, he was deployed to Vietnam. But as a volunteer who had completed his obligatory military service, he went with a promise from the Army Surgeon General Office that he would be assigned to an Army field hospital. However, after arriving at Bien Hoa, he was immediately assigned (once again) to the 101st Airborne Division as the Division Surgeon and Medical Battalion Commander, which was heavily involved in combat in the northernmost part of South Vietnam. Bernie noted that "it was a year of continuous warfare and action where movement was almost always by air ambulance and evacuation of the wounded was often during the heat of the battle." While in Vietnam, he received the Distinguished Flying Cross, the Bronze Star Medal with a V (for Valor) with Oak Leaf Cluster as well as other awards for his service.

After his 12-month Vietnam tour, Bernie seriously considered leaving the service. He elected to stay in the Army and was transferred to Ft. George Meade in Maryland as the Chief of Urology, Chairman of Surgery and Chief Professional Services. "I had three jobs at once!" he recalled. In 1971 he attended the U.S. Army War College for one year, then was again assigned to Walter Reed Medical Center. This time he served as Chief of Urology, later Chief of Department of Surgery and consultant in urology to the Army Surgeon General. In July 1977 the experienced doctor was assigned to be Commander of the U.S. Army Medical Command/Korea Surgeon, eighth U.S. Army and Commander of the 121st hospital in Seoul, Korea. Nine months later (April 1978), he was promoted to Brigadier General and assigned as Chief, Medical Corps Affairs to the Army Surgeon General. He was then promoted to Major General and served as Commander of Walter Reed Medical Center. In October of 1981 he was promoted to Lt. General and Army Surgeon General, retiring in March 1985 at which time he was awarded the Distinguished Service Medal. He was also the recipient of the Legion of Merit, Distinguished Flying Cross, Bronze Star with V device and an Oak Leaf Cluster, Meritorious Service, Air Medal, Army Commendation Medal, National Defense Ribbon, Combat Medical Badge, Vietnam Campaign Ribbon with three campaign stars, Vietnam Service, Cross of Gallantry with Silver Star (Vietnamese), Civil Action Honor (Vietnamese) and the Medical Meritorious Award (Vietnamese).

After his military service, the general was part of a group that started Health Services in California, which eventually opened up 20 HMOs and was later sold to Travelers Insurance. Not long afterward, Bernie was contacted by Dr. Lauro Cavazos and asked if he would like to "come to Lubbock, Texas, and go to work at the Texas Tech University Health Sciences Center as executive vice president." The esteemed doctor began his career at TTUHSC in November 1986. During a 10-year period, he helped establish a division of urology and later the Department of Urology. He also served as Interim Medical School Dean and Interim President of the Health Sciences Center. In 2009 he returned to the Urology Department, which is now named in his honor, and continues to work there part-time.

While in medical school Bernie married Patricia Kuhn in 1954. They raised four children: Jan, Tom, Robert and Sarah. In 1996, he married Mary Beth Smith who has two sons Brandt and Adam. Together they have eight grandchildren.

Dr. Mittemeyer remains humble and has a servant's heart, even though he holds numerous military decorations and a long list of professional rewards and honors. He remains passionate about "taking care of our veterans." He has especially enjoyed his work at the VA Clinic in Lubbock to "help care for the men and women that have served our country." After 63 years, Bernie is still serving his adopted country. When asked how he would like to be remembered, he proudly stated, "How fortunate I was to become an American citizen."

96

CHARLES SCARBOROUGH
"Recycled for a Reason"

"Lord, I can't do this anymore" were the words uttered by Charlie Scarborough after he fell face first in the mud in Vietnam. He was "on his way to take care of a problem." Little did he know that this would set the scene for a life-changing event. He noted that his whole mindset "changed in an instant and a calm came over me I had never known before. I knew everything was going to be all right." On his original discharge date, his unit was "hit by about 60 rockets and mortars. I started smoking in earnest that very day and that soon became a three-pack-a-day habit. After seventeen years of smoking, I quit cold turkey. Twenty-one days after I quit, I had a massive heart attack." Charlie spent one year, one month, and two days in Vietnam. When he was discharged in 1969 at Ft. Lewis, Washington, he was "more than ready to go home." Because of his softened heart, his life was on a different trajectory now, but not without the occasional miracle or two to remind him of his need for God.

Charles W. Scarborough's nickname growing up was "Lightning," which he acquired during his senior year of high school when he accidentally stuck an aluminum irrigation pipe in a three-phase power line. "Electricity went in my hands and out my feet. I ended up in the hospital overnight and on crutches for a month after that." Texas Tech was where he obtained a degree in agricultural economics in 1967, and he joined the Army soon after graduation.

He was born on November 27, 1944, to a Lubbock, Texas, couple, Henry and Essie B. Scarborough, and, being the eldest, has one brother. His father farmed in Petersburg, Texas. Football was a favorite pastime, and he graduated in 1963. He received his "greetings" from the Army and was inducted into the service on August 24, 1967. He broke his foot in Basic Training at Ft. Polk, Louisiana, and had to be "recycled," which extended his stay. The time served in the Army benefited him as he trained as a wireman in AIT (Advanced Individual Training), and he learned to climb poles, string communications wiring and some crypto.

After landing in Cam Ranh Bay, Vietnam, in January 1968, he went in as an individual replacement and was assigned to the HHB (Headquarters and Headquarters Battery) Americal Division, Artillery. He was put on a bus and was taken to Chu Lai Air Base. "The buses had screened wire on the windows, and we saw GIs filling up sand bags as fast as they could beside the road, and I knew this was a different world. This is not the U.S." Charlie's timing arriving in Vietnam couldn't have been any worse. The North Viet Cong were about to start the largest offensive of the Vietnam War. They attacked over 100 cities on January 30, 1968, in what was called the Tet Offensive. Arriving at the base, Charlie recalled that "a sheet was put up between our hooches [improvised living spaces] for us to watch a movie when we were attacked. We were hit with rockets and mortars. You start looking for those sandbags for cover. I had no rifle or anything. You learn to run, crawl and hide [during the attacks]. I didn't know where all the bunkers were."

In Vietnam, Sgt. Scarborough was flown to several LZs (Landing Zones) and fire bases for his cryptography work. "There would be a compromise in our signals and I had to deliver new instructions and call signs for communications. I had two flight jackets, one I wore and one I sat on. I carried an M-16 and an M-79 grenade launcher. Once, we were almost knocked out of the air by friendly fire, and the pilot had to put the helicopter in reverse and get us out of there quickly. We had sandbags all around our hooch dug into a hill, artillery, and a guard tower to watch for the

Charles Scarborough, U.S. Army Chu Lai, Vietnam June 1968.

enemy. Whenever we played poker, we would never take an IOU. There were two times that got my attention. Jumping off on one LZ, I looked down and was straddling a Claymore mine. Another time, back at our hooch, I awoke one night with a Viet Cong looking at me. I reached up and hit him right in the nose. He had sneaked into the back of our hooch, which was dug into a hill, and had come down between the hill and our dwelling. That was a little too close. On two occasions he had to escort a prisoner—both times for undesirable behavior. You always had to have two men to guard them."

One of Charlie's fondest memories in Vietnam was the time he went to Sydney, Australia, for some R&R (rest and relaxation). He went to the university there and told some students that he "wanted to go where there were no GIs." He met a girl there, and she took him home for dinner with her parents. Her mother had entertained GIs during World War II. "We went to a restaurant and the patrons paid for our supper. I had a great time in Australia, and they were all very friendly."

Charlie met his wife, Donna Snyder, on a blind date in Dallas. She was a schoolteacher in Richardson and they married in 1970. They have a daughter and a son that they adopted and now they have great-grandkids aged 3 months to 17 years old. Charlie worked at Texas Instruments for 18 years and Donna continued to teach math in both high

Charles Scarborough, wreath laying at the Vietnam Memorial, Washington, D.C. October 4, 2012.

school and college. During his time there he had a heart attack and arrested three times. He wore a nitroglycerin patch for 18 years. Charlie went into the insurance field, worked as the manager over environmental services, and finished his working career at United Supermarkets doing deliveries. He is retired and a 100 percent disabled veteran, partially due to exposure to Agent Orange. He is often reminded of the numerous miracles in his life, which helped him survive, and he has a grateful attitude.

As you know, Vietnam veterans were not treated as heroes on their home soil in America. Recalling his return from Vietnam many years earlier, Charlie said, "I was not happy when I came back and got spit on and called 'baby killer.' I buried those feelings for many years. I later chose to get involved with the Texas South Plains Honor Flight because all veterans deserve to be honored. When I went on the 2012 South Plains Honor Flight, the Vietnam Wall was very emotional and I had to walk off by myself. One of the ladies on the trip saw how I was reacting and came and sat beside me and let me know everything was ok." Charlie continues to serve as a valuable member of the Honor Flight Committee.

Charlie has waited a long time to tell his story. After serving on the Honor Flight Committee for several years, witnessing the benefits to the veterans who went, and also feeling a divine prompting in his heart, he finally knew it was time. A member of Lakeridge Methodist Church, Charlie says his "advice to anyone and everyone is to get closer to God." His faith carried him through many brushes with death over his lifetime, and now he feels he can encourage others as they sometimes get overwhelmed with life, in the same way he was comforted when he was on the Honor Flight. To meet Charlie, few would guess he had been through so much. His face is friendly and he is quick with a smile or a laugh. He is a reminder that his life was "recycled" for a reason.

Part IV
Additional Stories

I sustained paralyzing injuries in Ghazni Province, Afghanistan, which caused a lot of pain.

—Disabled Army veteran Michael Vazquez

97

VARIOUS VETERANS
"Geezers" Reunite

C.L. Lewis had an idea. He had gone on the 2012 South Plains Honor Flight to Washington, D.C., with his daughter, Vicki Hendsley. He told her how much he enjoyed the flight and how he missed visiting with other veterans from that trip, primarily the other World War II vets. Hendsley, who works at the United Supermarkets' Market Street in Lubbock, Texas, suggested he start up a weekly "coffee club" by contacting the other vets to see if they had any interest.

In July 2014, Lewis began calling the veterans and found that they, too, missed visiting with one another, and a weekly meeting was set for 9:30 a.m. (roughly) every Monday morning at Market Street.

I met with the self-proclaimed "Market Street Geezers" and it was good to see some familiar faces from the first South Plains Honor Flight, where I went along as a guardian. I am a Vietnam-era Air Force veteran and felt like the youngster around the table with a group of vets whose ages ranged from 82 to 91.

Like all veterans, we share many common bonds—such as basic training/boot camp, technical training, being away from loved ones and, for many, the first time to see parts of the United States and the world we had only read or heard about.

The memories run deep for these veterans. Most were very young at the time they entered the service, 17 and 18 years old. We can recall even seemingly small events during our service in vivid detail from 40 to 70-plus years ago but can't recall what we had for supper the night before! Such is the impression military service leaves on you.

After I met with these men, it was apparent the Texas South Plains Honor Flight mission should do everything it can to make sure as many World War II veterans as possible make this trip to our nation's capital to honor their service.

At the end of World War II, 8 million veterans returned home.

97. Various Veterans

Now, fewer than 326 thousand remain. As of this writing, the National World War II Museum estimates that 296 World War II vets die each day.

Since the World War II vets are becoming smaller in number, we are also including Korean and Vietnam War vets on our flight.

The idea of the Honor Flight came from a physician assistant and retired Air Force captain, Earl Morse. Morse wanted to honor the veterans he had taken care of for the past 27 years. Once the World War II Memorial was completed in May of 2004, it became clear that many of the veterans either could not afford the trip to Washington, D.C., to see it, or were physically unable. Being a private pilot, Morse took some of the first World War II vets to the memorial himself. Once word of this got out to other veterans, he was inundated with requests and had to charter bigger and bigger planes.

Word of his efforts quickly spread nationwide, and Honor Flight hubs were started in various states, including the South Plains in 2012. Today, several hundred veterans have been able to go see the memorials in D.C. at no charge to them.

The Texas South Plains Honor Flight has held yearlong fund-raising events during the year to ensure enough funds to take as many veterans as possible on this trip—everything from booths set up at gun shows, restaurants, tractor shows, annual ROTC campus run/walks, car shows, telethons, golf tournaments at the Texas Tech Rawls course and the support of many corporations and individuals across the South Plains.

Many veterans had attended Lubbock High School before leaving Lubbock as they answered the call to serve their nation. Many of the sweethearts and wives they left behind also did their part during World War II, with many of them working in factories or doing whatever they could to contribute to the war effort.

These veterans returned to their homes with little fanfare. They got married, rolled up their sleeves and went to work, raising their families and seldom talking about what they had done and seen during the war.

All past Honor Flight attendees are invited to be a part of the "Market Street Geezers." Just show up any Monday morning at 9:30 a.m. for coffee and fellowship. Not a bad way to start your week. Look up "Market Street Geezers" on the web and you will find they even have a Facebook page.

As we said our goodbyes after the "war stories" and coffee ran dry, veteran Chuck Cromwell, who served in the Pacific Theater, asked me, "Why did it take 60 years for us to be recognized?" I can't answer for everyone, but I do know we all owe them our deepest respect and honor and we're doing everything we can to correct that oversight.

Since 2012, the Texas South Honor Flight has made it possible for 261 World War II, Korea and Vietnam veterans to fly to Washington, D.C., to see the monuments built in their honor. Since that first flight, 25 of our veterans have passed away.

As former Supreme Court Justice Oliver Wendell Holmes once noted in a speech on Memorial Day in 1884 to a group of Union Civil War veterans, "We have seen the best and noblest of our generation pass away." The same can be said today of our area's "Greatest Generation."

For the latest news on the "Market Street Geezers," please see their website, www.marketstreetgeezers.com.

98

CHAD AND RENEE GROSS
A Simple Song about a Soldier

Chad Gross was born in Dallas and raised in Garland, Texas. From 1995 to 1999, he attended Texas Tech and graduated in 1999 with a Bachelor of Business Administration with a commission of Second Lieutenant, since he participated in Army ROTC at Texas Tech from his sophomore year through graduation. Between his sophomore and junior year at Tech, he graduated from the U.S. Army Airborne School and became the student commander of Army ROTC his senior year. As an aviation officer in the Army he attended flight school as his first assignment. Eventually, he flew Blackhawk helicopters. Subsequently, he spent most of his time with the 1st Infantry Division in Ansbach, Germany. From there he deployed twice. The first deployment was to Kosovo from October 2002 to July 2003. The second was to Tikrit, Iraq, from February 2004 to February 2005. All in all, he flew over 75 combat missions in Iraq and earned the Bronze Star Medal and the Air Medal.

The Chad and Renee Gross family includes four children: three biological sons, Corban (11), Asher (9) and Micah (6); and one daughter, Harvest (1), whom they adopted from India in 2018. Aurora, Colorado, is home base and they attend Brave Church in Denver. Chad, age 42, is going through the process of becoming an elder.

"My Christian faith is the most important thing in my life, and my number one goal in life is to bring glory to Jesus Christ. I was raised a Christian, but strayed from the faith after my parents divorced when I was 13. I kept my back turned on God until my junior year at Tech when I had a powerful conversion experience with God alone in my apartment. From that moment I trusted God with my life, yet I still needed discipleship." Chad defines discipleship as "being mentored on how to incorporate prayer into daily life, as well as the value of forming friendships with those who encourage faith and growth." Chad was drawn to a thriving college church group and met Russ Murphy and Welby Smith, two men who would gently and powerfully encourage Chad into deep commitment to Christ. Welby and Chad immediately developed a kinship through the military connection when Welby, a retired Master Sergeant in the Air Force, learned of Chad's involvement in Army ROTC. Recognizing the newness of Chad's faith, he took him under his wing. Welby invited the undergraduate to his house for a hot meal. Listening to Welby pray taught Chad how to pray in a bold, confident way, seasoned with the humility of a spirit that yields to the will of God. He and LaJuana became like grandparents, and they kept in touch after he left Tech and joined the Army. Chad's oldest son, Corban, is named after Welby, Corban Welby Gross. Welby states, "When Chad was introduced to me, I realized he was a fine, young man interested in learning about Jesus. He came to many 'watermelon and worship' times at our house. I am privileged to know this honorable soldier and have tremendous respect for Chad, his faith, and his dedication to our country." Russ Murphy, the college minister at Indiana Avenue Baptist Church at that time, adds, "It was no surprise that he became an incredible soldier. Chad did his very best as a soldier of the cross and as a soldier in our military. Chad's desire for excellence inspired me to be more committed to Christ. I know I learned more from him than he learned from me. 'Thank you, Lord, for allowing me to share in the life of Chad Gross, truly a man after your heart.'"

Chad said, "I met my wife, Renee, on a trip to Lubbock on December 26, 2000. I had just graduated from flight school at Ft. Rucker, Alabama. In Dallas, on leave, I planned to go see Welby and LaJuana while in Texas. Renee was a sophomore at Stephen F. Austin University and from Dallas. She was home for the break and wanted to visit family in Lubbock. We both showed up at the Dallas Love Field Airport and there discovered the flight was cancelled due to a Texas storm. Renee and I ended up in line at the ticket counter to rebook our flights and I noticed she had the words 'Psalm 25' on her backpack." Just as it has a recurring theme about putting our trust in God, it also describes Renee's life. Renee says, "I definitely was not looking for a boyfriend, but God used that canceled flight to introduce me to Chad."

He recalls, "Since my car was back in Alabama, Renee's mother, Linda Black, gave me a ride home." Linda remembers, "When I first met Chad, I was positively impressed with his maturity. I continue to be grateful for the blessing he is as a wonderful son-in-law, loving husband to my daughter and father to my grandchildren." Chad goes on, "I finally got to introduce Renee to Welby and LaJuana and later Russ married Renee and me in Germany in a small, 700-year-old church in the little village of Sachsen on May 24, 2002."

98. Chad and Renee Gross

Upon Chad's return from Iraq in 2005, he and Renee visited Welby and LaJuana Smith. "Welby wanted to honor me and asked Russ Murphy to write a song to welcome me home. Russ wrote 'Welcome Home Soldier' and performed it during a gathering at Indiana Avenue Baptist Church [it was a final nominee for the 2006 ICM Song of the Year] and I was overwhelmed. The emotions of being deployed, the joy of coming home and God's care through it all rushed over me. I will never forget that moment. Welby and others have given out thousands of copies of the CD to returning veterans as well as to those who have been home for years. The song amazingly brings healing to many veterans. For me it conveys a sense of earthly appreciation for military service, and reminds me of how magnificent it will be to hear my Lord say, 'Welcome home.'"

Chad remembers often the life-changing way he was mentored and whom God hand-selected to mentor him. He leans on what was modeled for him years ago as he now encourages the lost, the searching, and even the most seasoned believers. Welby Smith and Russ Murphy's legacy lives on in Chad Gross as he and his family fan the flames of faith in hearts all over the world, to the glory of God.

99

GARY HARBER
Lubbock's Southern Brigadier General

Five-year-old Gary Harber was noted publicly for boldness when he backed up traffic, as he rode his tricycle down Columbia Avenue in Centerville, Tennessee, to his parents' grocery store. As he grew, he earned respect as the youngest professional photographer in Tennessee. Gary was hired by the local funeral home to take pictures of the deceased. By age 12 he established his credentials as the photographer for the *Tennessean* and *Banner* newspapers. His "press pass" allowed him to capture images for the reporter who transported him in her car.

In 1955 after graduating from Hickman County High School in Centerville, Gary joined the Tennessee Army National Guard. General Harber served as an infantry officer at the LT level and was transferred by the U.S. Army to the Combat Engineer Branch in the Army Corp of Engineers in 1959. He achieved Army Master Aviator status and has more than 15,000 hours in military and civilian fixed and rotary wing aircraft. General Harber oversaw operations in America, Europe, and Central America. In Europe he served as the NATO Northern Regional Wartime Construction Manager and Commander of the 194th Engineer Brigade (Theatre Army). In Central America he commanded the nation-building efforts primarily focused on Panama, Honduras, and Costa Rica, building roads through the jungle and constructing schools, clinics, and support facilities. He was assigned to the Pentagon on numerous occasions including as Chief, at the Construction Branch and Army Installations Division. He also served on the Chief of Engineers General Officers' Executive Council, under Lieutenant General Henry "Hank" Hatch, which advised on matters relative to engineer-unit requirements and wartime missions. The council, comprised of five General Officer Commanders, was heavily involved in Desert Shield/Desert Storm. Harber served his beloved America for 42 years, retiring as a Brigadier General in 1997.

99. Gary Harber

General Harber never lets the injuries he suffered in a helicopter crash in the '60s affect the stalwart support he demonstrates to current and past soldiers and their families. One of the ways he chooses to stay "relevant" is by being active in volunteering with veterans who are on hospice care. Welby Smith, another vet-to-vet hospice volunteer, says, "The general is a wonderful Christian man who serves God and others, a true American hero. He still loves and serves veteran hospice patients, and it is an honor to visit [them] with him." Gary is also a member of the Daedalians (Military Pilot Organization) and is a Federal Aviation Administration (FAA) civilian flight-training instructor.

General Harber wants every reader to know that the Bible is applicable to the struggles we face today. He saw himself as a "marginal Christian" until he actually read the little Bible in his flight-suit pocket, while flying with another pilot years ago. He realized God was personally guiding him. The trajectory of his life changed, and he began to focus more on others.

Recently, General Bernhard Mittemeyer initiated the VA Super Clinic in Lubbock. Generals Walt Huffman, Edgar Murphy, and Harber combined efforts to ensure its realization. General Harber states that one of his motivations for assisting with the new Super Clinic was to "provide for those who have served this country and helped to make it the great and free nation that it is." General Huffman stated, "General Harber's expertise in developing federal projects has proved indispensable." General Mittemeyer remembers, "Brigadier General Gary Harber immediately impressed me, not only as a great man, but one who is firmly committed to the veteran population. All of the generals have lived up to exceeding the highest expectations."

Years after retirement, Gary recalls an incident that changed his life. Gary saw a film entitled *We Were Soldiers*. The war film depicted how many soldiers' lives were lost. The fighting scenes triggered his personal memories of war, and as hot tears rolled down his face, he remembered the passionate, patriotic soldiers who had served with him. He felt he should have been there with them. He exited the theater with a very heavy heart. Then he vividly remembers God flooding his heart, reassuring him that their deaths were "not your fault." A large weight lifted a yoke he did not realize he had been tied to for countless years. General Harber wants to pass that message along to other soldiers and military leaders who may not realize the emotional baggage they still carry. He knows the Lord has released him, finally, of the burden of not being with his friends who were lost in combat. Gary's prayer for current soldiers and leaders is for them to know that it's not their fault that they survived and a friend did not.

Lauren, his second-born daughter, says, "He has always been a great spiritual role model." She also shares, "He instilled in me a love of language, which has been passed on to my eldest son, who speaks German, Pashto, and French, and is currently serving in Army Special Operations."

There's another side to Gary Harber—an artistic one. He performed guitar with his brother at the Junior Grand Ole Opry in his youth, as well as absorbed the wit of his kindergarten teacher, Sarah Colley (aka Minnie Pearl).

His daughter Cathleen loves the memory of her delighted classmates as they rushed out to see her dad's UH-1 "Huey" helicopter. He was requested by the school to land on the school grounds when she was in second grade. In 2002 she introduced her dad to her next-door neighbor, Carol. After getting to know the southern gentleman whom Carol describes as a "teddy bear," the couple married 11 years ago.

Cathleen sums up the heart of her dad and all of his accomplishments with "He has the strength of a warrior and the talent of an artist. That is a rare combination."

100

GORDON MUSICK AND ERNEST SEARS

Two Love Stories from the Texas South Plains Honor Flight

The following article was written by the author upon returning from the inaugural 2012 Texas South Plains Honor Flight.

"There may not be a tomorrow for me so I should act now," thought many of the young men who went off to World War II and Korea without complaint. As many of them told me on this flight, they didn't think they "did anything special, because everyone was doing their part for the war effort." This generation was united by a common purpose. They also shared common values such as courage, duty, honor, love of country and family.

War has a way of bringing two people together that is anything but ordinary. Time gets compressed. There is a sense of urgency. The young couples of the 1940s and 1950s didn't have a lot of time for extended periods of dating or engagements. Many of these young men and women got married before the serviceman's deployment to Europe, the Pacific or Korea. These stories were told to me by two wives who recently went with their husbands on the South Plains Honor Flight.

I was fortunate enough to become acquainted with Gordon and Betty Musick from Lubbock. I was fascinated by how they met. As any military person knows, nothing is more comforting when you are thousands of miles from home than a letter from a loved one back home in the States. You hang on to that and it gives you hope that you are going to come out of the war in one piece and somehow make it home. This is the story of a young man a long way from home and the unlikely path he took to meet his future wife. Here is their story in Betty's own words.

"Gordon Musick was from Rogers, New Mexico, and went to Korea in 1951 as a medic. His mother subscribed to the Portales newspaper and sent them to Gordon in Korea. In 1952 I finished my junior year at Portales

High School and was selected to go to Girl's State in Albuquerque that summer. Gordon got the paper that had the 16 girls' pictures that went to that convention. He wrote a letter to me asking me to write to him. I received it on July 5, 1952. He was rotated home before he could receive my letter, but it followed him home to Rogers. He wrote to me again (that was before telephones were common place) and asked if he could come and see me. I wrote back and told him yes and to come on a certain Friday night.

"Before that, another boy asked me to go on an FFA–FHA hayride and I wrote to Gordon again and told him I had a 'school function' on Friday night and that he would have to come on Thursday night. I thought a bird in hand was better than one in the bush! He came to my home on September 18, 1952, and we visited for a while then went for a Coke at Mac's Drive In. The next night the boy from the hayride asked me if I wanted to get a Coke after the ride, and we pulled up under Mac's Drive Inn awning, and there sat Gordon in his car! I looked at my watch and declared that I didn't have time for a Coke. I didn't want Gordon to see me with another boy! We dated until I graduated from high school in May 1953. We celebrated 59 years of marriage this August. Four children were born to our union. I believe the marriage took!"

I also had the pleasure of visiting with Anna Sears and her husband, Ernest. After numerous requests, it took some convincing for Anna to tell me her story, so I finally handed her a piece of paper and a pen and told her I would really like her to write it down for me. Here is Anna's story in her own words.

"Ernest's ship was just off Japan when the bomb was dropped on Hiroshima in 1945. His ship was the first one into Tokyo Bay and he got to go into Tokyo. He did enjoy his visit. After we were married, he would tell me that he would take me to see Tokyo someday. Forty years to the month he took me to Tokyo. While walking in the park by our hotel, he told me that 40 years ago there was a sunken garden that he enjoyed visiting while he was there. We walked over to where he recalled it was, and the garden was still there and in good shape! It is very close to the Imperial Palace."

For Ernest, a promise made was a promise kept even if it was 40 years in coming.

Both of these stories bear witness to the love and devotion that the men and women of this generation had for each other. They can now look back and be thankful for their love for each other, their family and their country. These men returned from war to settle down, raise their families and try to make their children's lives better than theirs had been. They gave so much but asked so little. It is a lesson we should all learn from and seek to emulate.

101

FRANCES PIERCE
Gold Star Wife and Widow

The Gold Star Wives of America was established by four young widows on April 5, 1945, in New York City. When President Franklin D. Roosevelt died a week later, his widow, Eleanor Roosevelt, joined the group. According to the military.wikia.org website, the group formed to "provide support for the spouses and children of those who lost their lives while serving in the Armed Forces of the United States." During World War II, family members who had someone serving in the military would place a flag with a Blue Star in their window. If they were killed, they would then place a flag with a Gold Star in the window. The basis of the group forming was that "only a service spouse understands the sorrow and problems of another service spouse." The congressionally chartered organization has eight regions in the country and approximately 10,000 members.

The *New York Times* documented in a 2013 article that, during World War II, 12 percent of the population served in the military. Today that number is less than 1 percent. Blue and Gold Star flags hung from countless homes around the country during World War II. Everyone was involved in supporting the war effort.

Verda Frances Pierce (Turner) was born September 14, 1921, to Wheeler and Irene Turner in Lakeview, Floyd County, Texas. She went to several "community schools in Floyd County" as her father was an itinerant farmer and worked at various farms in the area. She graduated from Floydada High School in May 1939. It was there that she met her future husband, Richard Irvin Tubbs. She and Richard went to Texas Tech and would marry in December 1940. Richard volunteered for the Army Air Corps in 1941 and received his wings as part of the class of 43G in Pampa, Texas. 2nd Lt. Richard I. Tubbs was assigned to the 5th Air Force, 91st Recon. 6th Photo Group, 20th Combat Mapping Squadron. There he learned to fly F-7A and F-7B aircraft, which were simply

B-24 bombers converted for aerial photographic work. After stops in Guadalcanal, Australia, and New Guinea, his unit moved to Leyete, Philippines. Starting in November 1944, they flew missions to Formosa and China, engaged in mapping parts of Luzon and Mindanao, and provided intelligence for U.S. ground forces concerning Japanese troop movements.

Frances was pregnant with their first child when Richard left for the Pacific in August of 1944. Laney Tubbs was born on September 21, 1944. During this time, Richard went on numerous reconnaissance missions in the fall of 1944. He was on his next to last mission when his plane was struck by another B-24 in Leyete, Philippines, and 8 of the 10 crew members were killed, including Richard.

Richard's father would receive the Western Union telegram received by approximately 470,000 other families across America. The unenviable task fell to him to tell Frances that her husband had been killed and would not be coming home. Laney was four months old at the time of her father's death and would never know him. All that remained of him were stories her mother and family members told her, his letters home, and photographs. As many Gold Star wives would quickly come to realize, there is the initial shock, unbelievable pain and a tremendous sense of loss. There is also a strong determination that you must go on. Such issues as finances, raising children, survivor benefits, potential relocation and many other issues surface rapidly with the loss of a military spouse. Frances now had a four-month-old daughter to

Frances Pierce, photograph of husband, Army Air Corps pilot 2nd Lt. Richard L. Tubbs World War II.

raise and had to remain strong for her daughter and her family. Like a lot of widows during the war, Frances and Laney moved in with her parents. She and Laney would receive a small stipend from the government but not enough to cover all their expenses. Frances would also receive her husband's Air Commendation Medal after his death. Richard's remains were finally repatriated three years after his death. Richard was one of 23 servicemen who died during World War II from Floyd County, Texas.

Frances found comfort in family and friends and eventually married L.G. Pierce, Jr., on November 24, 1947. He had been a friend of her and Richard's and in fact had been the best man at their wedding years earlier. L.G. also served as a Captain during World War II in the 45th QM (Quarter Master) Group in the China-Burma-India Theater (CBI). His unit helped build the 1,072-mile-long supply route called the Ledo/Stillwell road from Burma to India. Frances and L.G. would have a son, Larry Pierce, and were married 51 years. L.G. passed away in December 1997. Larry would die of cancer in August 1998. Frances now has 3 grandchildren and 3 great-grandchildren. Frances contacted the Gold Star Wives of America and kept in touch with them for several years but found out a chapter did not exist in Lubbock. Laney would grow up and marry but noted that she "would always wonder how her life would have turned out if her father had lived." Now, Frances and Laney can only look back, remember Richard and be proud of his service and his sacrifice to his country.

Both of the author's grandmothers were Gold Star mothers. One lost a son during World War II and the other lost a son during the Korean War.

102

OPAL ROBERTS
Living Intentionally

Opal Roberts knows the importance of apparel. She remembers a uniform she wore that was made of "extremely high-maintenance fabric." While serving in the Women's Army Corps (WAC) her distinctive military attire was very thin and took much time and effort to wash, starch and iron. To keep herself looking crisp, she would force herself to stand during the bus ride to work and wouldn't sit down until lunch.

She was raised in Slaton, Texas, the daughter of C.D. and Elsie Willis. Opal was the youngest of eight children, and it seemed appropriate for her to follow her father and four brothers into serving her country. Her eyes sparkled as she explained her motive for joining the service: "I went in to finish what they started." She enlisted on August 26, 1958.

The regimented lifestyle and discipline were a good fit for young Opal as she completed 6 weeks of basic training at Ft. McClellan, Alabama. She remembered the only drawback was homesickness. "A lot of us cried at night in the beginning, and each night we girls sang 'The Lord's Prayer' for comfort. Being busy helped, and the Army kept us very busy."

After basic training, Opal served stateside in the ER at Ft. Sam Houston in San Antonio. The fast-paced tempo of that assignment forced her to learn quickly, and the autopsies she witnessed made a long-lasting impression. An opportunity arose in a different field and the young woman was transferred to Ft. Sill in Oklahoma early in 1959, where she worked as a general's receptionist at the McNair Hall headquarters building for a year and a half.

However, she had thrived in the medical field, so she was happy to go to work for several doctors at the Ft. Sill medical hospital. Opal achieved the rank of Specialist 4th Class and credits much of her success to her parents. During the three years she was away from home, not a day went by that she did not receive a letter or package from her parents.

"Mail call was the best time of the day." They supported her patriotism and prayed for the safe return of their youngest child.

After her honorable discharge in August of 1961, she met and married Ray Roberts in 1966 and raised three children in Andrews, Texas. She has six grandchildren and nine great-grandchildren.

When asked what she felt was her greatest achievement other than her service and family life, she lit up describing her time as a county librarian in Plains and Denver City.

Her most recent military experience was a trip to Washington, D.C., courtesy of the Texas South Plains Honor Flight. The veteran's eyes brimmed with tears as she recalled precious letters from family and children opened midair during the flight. Those letters warmed places in her heart that had lain dormant for years. Her memory took her back to the time when "mail call was the best time of the day."

Mrs. Roberts is occupied again with the importance of apparel. Her church sponsors a live nativity scene every year at Christmas, and this 70-something female veteran has a passion for helping make it happen. She works tirelessly behind the scenes, and stands for hours dressed in period costumes, as part of a team whose mission is to remind South Plains residents of the true meaning of the season. Just like when she was a WAC, Opal intentionally puts on a "uniform" every Christmas. She continues to show others how it looks to live intentionally. "There are so many adventures out there, and I give God the glory for everything I have done in my life."

103

WAYNE SHAWN AND JUSTIN JONES
Flight into Yesteryear

Looking to the east from Lubbock Aero, it was just a spec at first but as the shiny plane drew nearer, you could tell this one looked very different. The shape of *Maid in the Shade*, a B-25J Mitchell bomber built in 1940, came into view and the roar of its twin Wright 1700 HP engines could clearly be heard. The plane can reach a maximum speed of 275 MPH. A total of nearly 10,000 of this aircraft were produced. Only 34 are still flying.

The plane actually flew 15 combat missions over Italy in the winter of 1944. The plane was retired in 1979 and was operating in Indonesia. The home for *Maid in the Shade* is at the Commemorative Air Force in Mesa, Arizona. Restoration began in 1982. The plane was moved into a new hangar built in 1987 and thus was built in the shade, thus the name *Maid in the Shade*.

I have interviewed numerous World War II veterans. Today would be different. I contacted two Army Air Corps veterans, 97-year-old Justin Jones and 93-year-old Wayne Shawn, last week and asked them how they'd like to ride on a B-25 bomber. Their answer was an enthusiastic yes!

Jones "saw an ad to join up in the *Lubbock Avalanche-Journal* days after the attack on Pearl Harbor on December 6, 1941." He noted that he and 152 West Texas men signed up on December 12, 1941. After "getting shots and uniforms" at Ft. Sill, Oklahoma, it was back to Lubbock Army Airfield. There were only 39 enlisted men and three officers stationed there when Jones and other enlistees arrived. He worked on PT-19 (trainers), AT-6, AT-9 and AT-11 aircraft. He was part of a special unit sent to Holland to salvage as many gliders as they "could stack into 20 C-47 aircrafts, including jeeps and trailers and came under German

103. Wayne Shawn and Justin Jones

fire at one of the locations." Justin was discharged at Ft. Sam Houston on October 19, 1945, and headed back to Lubbock. He would be awarded the Bronze Star.

Wayne Shawn went to Texas Tech from 1942 to 1943. The draft was catching up to a lot of young men so he enlisted in the Army Air Corps in December 1943. After basic training at Sheppard Army Airfield in Wichita Falls, he went to Amarillo Army Airfield for flight training but the training was cancelled so he and his buddies went to aircraft mechanics school to work on Pratt and Whitney engines for a B-17 bomber. He said they "were prepared to go overseas at anytime but were sent to Nellis Army Airfield near Las Vegas, Nevada." He said, "Christmas in Las Vegas in December 1945 was something else." Still expecting to go overseas, he was sent to Selman Army Airfield in Alabama where he was discharged in March 1946.

We received word that the old bomber was ready to board. The entry for Justin, Wayne and I would be in the underbelly of the plane near the tail section. Finally aboard (with some help), we settled into our tight seats and buckled in with a thick, heavy seat belt. The large engines revved up and we were ready to go. It was at this point we each looked at each other with at least mild trepidation and wondered if this was a good idea or not. After a long taxi ride, we were airborne for the short (20- to 25-minute) flight around Lubbock. Unlike modern airliners, there was no air conditioning, so it was fairly warm inside the plane. The noise of

Justin Jones (left) and Wayne Shawn (right) in front of B25J "Maid in the Shade," September 24, 2018.

B25J "Maid in the Shade" September 24, 2018.

the engines was deafening. You couldn't even yell and hear each other so we wrote on a notepad if we wanted to converse. Once we reached our cruising altitude of 1,500 feet, the ride smoothed out and we were able to enjoy our short flight. On a perfectly clear West Texas day, we could easily see all the landmarks of Lubbock. We returned to the Lubbock International Airport and circled down for a smooth landing.

Thanks to a great crew, we had survived our flight on the 78-year-old aircraft. When we taxied in and parked, I asked Justin and Wayne what they thought of the flight. "We've come a long way in 70 years," noted Justin. Wayne was a little more pragmatic. "Nice ride. I would hate to have all day of it." Wayne cracked everyone up when he looked at the voluptuous blonde painted on the nose of the plane and said, "I think I know her!" Neither of these men had flown on a plane of World War II vintage in over 70 years. Both have gone on the Texas South Plains Honor Flight and fully enjoyed the sights of Washington, D.C. This flight on the old B-25J just might have been the frosting on the cake for these two veterans. It allowed them to return to their youth if only briefly and to recall that they were part of something bigger than themselves. We can thank them and countless other veterans for keeping America free.

104

MICHAEL VASQUEZ
From Combat Casualty to Veteran Advocate

Michael Vasquez was born in 1988 in Lubbock and graduated from Estacado High School in 2006. He joined the Army in 2005 after 9/11. He attended OSUT (One Station Unit Training) in Ft. Benning, Georgia, was an honor graduate as an Infantryman (11B) and received an honorable discharge in 2010. This is his story in his own words.

"I am totally medication-free now, but it's been a long road. After joining the Army in 2005, I sustained paralyzing injuries in Ghazni Provence, Afghanistan, which caused a lot of pain. I took 30 medications a day, masking the agony any way I could. Finding no help physically or emotionally, I went to appointments grasping for clarity, hope, and healing and [always] came home with pills, only a temporary solace. I also drank to soften the memories and medicate my broken spirit. Shrapnel damage to my abdomen and back, Traumatic Brain Injury (TBI), left-side paralysis, loss of feeling and use of legs, and partial blindness in my left eye, only magnified motives to self-medicate.

"I am grateful for the people who provided emergency medical treatment early on in the med station on our outlet post at Ghazni, then at the Army Garrison at Bagram, and at Landstuhl Regional Medical Center in Germany. From there I was flown to Brooke Army Medical Center (BAMC), where I slipped in and out of my medically induced coma and spent seven months in recovery.

"As my health plummeted and the paralysis took over, I sought help from the VA. My TBI caused me to black out sometimes 20 times a day, lose consciousness, and fall over. After numerous trips in the ambulance and many checks for concussions, I finally found a support group on social media for other vets with TBIs. This is an informal group comprised of people who were also suffering, keeping it real, and finding better ways to manage. In 2012 I was diagnosed with a Chiari Malformation, which is considered a brain disease. Most people [who have it] are born with it; however, it can be acquired also. My cerebellum was herniating into my foramen magnum, which caused stubborn brain swelling. The VA disputed the origin of the disease and refused to help me. I had a genetic test done, which ruled out genetics. My support system recommended a specialist from New York who agreed to a consultation, and I paid my own way. He examined my MRIs and advised me on surgery, stating it was better sooner than later, highly risky, and potentially deadly. In July 2013 I elected to have this surgery. I stayed two and a half weeks in the hospital afterwards, my brain and spinal cord traumatized. Overall, the surgery was a good thing, as it stopped my blackouts. However, I am now in a wheelchair permanently. I remember not being able to feel my left side and not being able to even drag my legs. I flew home and continued to seek help from the VA, and had to be sent to Amarillo, Albuquerque, and Dallas for treatments.

"Many people have helped encourage me in my struggles. I want to emphasize the word STRUGGLE. Like so many other veterans, I really struggled, often alone, with the weight of military and life experiences and opted for a quick fix of alcohol or drugs. It was only after looking at myself in the mirror one day, that I felt God pulling me back to him. I broke down and He softened my heart. He let me see how some of my actions compounded the situation and I longed to come clean and live for Him.

"My missions now include advocating for other vets. I volunteered with CVA [Concerned Veterans for America] and went to Washington to lobby for the VA Accountability Act and VA Reform Act. Vets need to be empowered with more choices, and have care provided more locally, to minimize the stresses on them and their families. Thankfully, our bills were passed almost a month ago, [ensuring] a wider range of help in civilian sectors and more costs being covered.

"I have attended Experience Life Church for many years, where I [serve] on the Safety Team. I also volunteer for HALO for Freedom Warrior Foundation. There are groups in Texas, Colorado, Wyoming, and North Carolina. I am the Media and Graphic Director. Vets who are in recovery get to come one weekend a year when [HALO] hosts 30–50 of these service personnel [with events and activities like] hog hunting from helicopters, driving NASCAR at Texas Motor Speedway, night fishing, sky diving, target shooting, observing explosives demonstrations, and attending a Western-themed gala and auction.

"I graduated from Wayland Baptist with a BAS in human services and psychology and currently I attend Texas Tech, furthering my graphic design education.

104. Michael Vasquez

"My experience being an infantry team leader, protecting military intelligence soldiers, gathering intel, [as well as] my secondary role of multimedia exploitation expert—cloning content on computers, hard drives, cell phones, and emplacing sensors on roadways and houses, behind Taliban (enemy) lines, has given me a vision for a hopeful future in fighting to end human trafficking.

"Bravo, my two-year-old service dog, was trained as a police working dog but excelled as a service dog when trained with Rebuilding Warriors Foundation. He helps me pick things up, open doors, turn off lights, and pull me in my wheelchair, if necessary.

"One of my favorite tattoos from Psalms 91:10 says, 'No harm will overtake you, no disaster will come near your tent. For he will command His angels concerning you to guard you in all your ways.' I still have occasional flashbacks to the hot July day in Afghanistan where I blacked in and out in the gunner's turret while engaging the enemy [Taliban]. I sometimes ask the Lord why I cannot fully escape these memories and retain such vivid detail and horror, and He lets me know it is His way of keeping the communication lines open with Him and me, every minute of every day."

As told to Katherine McLamore.

Veterans' Honor Roll

The following veterans interviewed or featured in this book are now deceased. We honor their memory and their service to their country.

Agee, Alvira
Allen, Marion T.
Anderson, Robert
Archinal, Paul
Bobrowski, Stanley
Boyles, William
Bradley, George
Braxton, James
Bridge, William
Britt, Roger
Brown, Claude
Cathey, James
Coon, Wilma
Cummings, Robert
Duncan, Lena Skaggs
Esparza, Thomas
Garner, Alton
Gill, Robbie
Gilly, Carl
Guyton, Jim
Haberer, Roger
Hail, Bob
Hambright, Gordon
Hamby, J.W.
Hartman, Ted
Harvey, Fred
Hendrix, Billy
Hill, Ted
Jones, Homer
Jones, Lamar
Jones, Riley David
Manning, Rodney
Martin, C.B.
McLendon, Dolphus Gene
Miller, Frank
Morgan, Horace
Owen, Wayne
Owens, R.L.
Platten, Marvin
Rich, James "Troy"
Roberts, Eugene
Robertson, Max
Robinson, Earl
Ruff, Curtis
Scheffel, Eldie
Schultze, Harold
Sears, Charles Odell
Sears, Ernest
Slaughter, J.L.
*Tarbox, Elmer
Tartaglione, Dominic
Tyler, Truett
Ward, Edward
Watson, Fred
Webb, Carl Wayne
+Williams, Charles
Wilson, Elton

*Elmer's son was interviewed for his story. Elmer died in 1987.
+Charles was Killed in Action on November 27, 1950.

BIBLIOGRAPHY

Abbe, Donald R. 2014. *South Plains Army Airfield (Images of Aviation).* Charleston, SC: Arcadia.

Ambrose, Stephen E. 1994. *D-Day June 6, 1944: The Climactic Battle of World War II.* New York: Simon & Schuster Paperbacks.

Ambrose, Stephen E. 1997. *Americans at War.* Jackson, MS: The Berkley Publishing Company.

Ambrose, Stephen E. 1998. *The Victors. Eisenhower and His Boys: The Men of World War II.* New York: Touchstone.

Ambrose, Stephen E. 2001. *Band of Brothers: E Company, 506th Regiment, 101st Airborne from Normandy to Hitler's Eagle's Nest.* New York: Simon & Schuster Paperbacks.

Appleman, Roy E. 1987. *East Of Chosin: Entrapment and Breakout in Korea, 1950.* College Station: Texas A&M University Press.

Appleman, Roy E. 1995. *Okinawa: The Last Battle—WWII.* United States. Barnes & Noble Publishers.

Atkinson, Rick. 2002. *An Army at Dawn: The War in North Africa, 1942–1943.* New York: Picador.

Atkinson, Rick. 2007. *The Day of Battle: The War in Sicily and Italy, 1943–1944.* New York: Picador.

Atkinson, Rick. 2013. *The Guns at Last Light: The War in Western Europe: 1944–1944.* New York: Picador.

Baumgarten, Harold. 2015. *D-Day Survivor: An Autobiography.* Gretna, LA: Pelican Publishing Co., Inc.

Blair, Clay. 1989. *The Forgotten War: America in Korea 1950–1953.* New York: Doubleday.

Bradley, James. 2001. *Flags Of Our Fathers.* New York: Bantam Books.

Bradley, James. 2003. *Flyboys: A True Story of Courage.* New York: Back Bay Books.

Brokaw, Tom. 1998. *The Greatest Generation.* New York: Random House.

Brokaw, Tom. 1999. *The Greatest Generation Speaks: Letters and Reflections.* New York: Random House.

Bruner, Lauren F., Edward J. McGrath, and Craig O. Thompson, 2016. *Second to Last to Leave USS* Arizona *12.7.41: The Lauren Bruner Story.* Hawaii: RMR Publishing in Association with Pearl Harbor Press.

Carlson, Elliot. 2011. *Joe Rochefort's War: The Odyssey of the Codebreaker Who Outwitted Yamamoto at Midway.* Annapolis, MD: Naval Institute Press.

Cohen, Daniel M. 2015. *Single Handed: The Inspiring True Story of Tibor "Teddy" Rubin-Holocaust Survivor, Korean War Hero, and Medal of Honor Recipient.* New York: Berkley Caliber.

Colley, David P. 2004. *Safely Rest.* New York: Berkley Caliber.

Edwards, Ted. 2018. *Seven At Santa Cruz: The Life of Fighter Ace Stanley "Swede" Vejtasa.* Annapolis: Naval Institute Press.

Frazier, Colonel Glenn D. 2012. *Hell's Guest.* Chambersburg, VA: eGenCo. LLC.

Freeman, Gregory A. 2007. *The Forgotten 500: The Untold Story of the Men Who Risked All For the Greatest Rescue Mission of World War II.* New York. Dutton Caliber.

Greene, Bob. 2002. *Once Upon a Town: The Miracle of the North Platte Canteen.* New York: HarperCollins.

Bibliography

Guarnere, William and Heffron, Edward with Post, Robyn. 2007. *Brothers in Battle, Best of Friends: Two WWII Paratroopers from the Original Band of Brothers Tell Their Story*. New York: The Berkley Publishing Group.

Halberstam, David. 2007. *The Coldest Winter: America and the Korean War*. New York: Hyperion.

Henderson, Bruce. 2015. *Rescue at Los Banos: The Most Daring Prison Camp Raid of World War II*. New York: HarperCollins Publishers.

Hervieux, Linda. 2015. *Forgotten: The Untold Story of D-Day's Black Heroes, At Home and At War*. New York: HarperCollins Publishers.

Hillenbrand, Laura. 2010. *Unbroken.: A WWII Story of Survival, Resilience, and Redemption*. New York: Random House.

Hilton, Wil S. 2013. *Vanished: The Sixty-Year Search for the Missing Men of World War II*. New York: Riverhead Books

Kershaw, Alex. 2012. *The Liberator*. New York: Broadway Books.

Kershaw, Alex. 2019. *The First Wave: The D-Day Warriors Who Led the Way to Victory in World War II*. New York: Dutton Caliber.

Kershaw, Alex. *The Bedford Boys: One American Town's Ultimate D-Day Sacrifice*. Cambridge, MA: The Perseus Books Group.

Kleiss, N. Jack. 2017. *Never Call Me A Hero: A Legendary American Dive-Bomber Pilot Remembers the Battle Of Midway*. New York: HarperCollins Publishers.

Knoblock, Glenn A. 2011. *Black Submariners in the United States Navy, 1940–1975*. Jefferson, NC: McFarland.

Kurzman, Dan. 1990. *Fatal Voyage: The Sinking of the USS* Indianapolis. New York: Atheneum Macmillan Publishing Co.

Makos, Adam. 2015. *Devotion: An Epic Story of Heroism, Friendship, and Sacrifice*. New York: Ballantine Books.

Makos, Adam. 2019. *Spearhead: An American Tank Gunner, His Enemy, and a Collision Of Lives in World War II*. New York: Ballantine Books.

Makos, Adam, with Marcus Brotherton. 2013. *Voices of the Pacific: Untold Stories from the Marine Heroes of World War II*. New York: The Berkley Publishing Group.

McManus, John C. 2015. *Hell Before Their Eyes: American Soldiers Liberate Concentration Camps in Germany, April 1945 (Witness to History)*. Baltimore, MD: Johns Hopkins University Press.

McManus, John C. 2019. *Fire and Fortitude: The US Army in the Pacific War. 1941–1943*. New York: Caliber.

Moore, Harold G., and Joseph L. Galloway. 2004. *We Were Soldiers Once... and Young*. New York: Presidio Press.

Mundy, Liza. 2017. *Code Girls: The Untold Story of the American Women Code Breakers of World War II*. New York: Hachette Book Group.

Murphy, Audie. 2002 paperback edition. *To Hell and Back*. Henry Holt and Co., LLC.

Murphy, Edward F. 1990. *Heroes of WWII: True Stories of the Men Who Earned Our Nation's Highest Award, the Congressional Medal of Honor*. New York: Ballantine Books.

Nelson, Craig. 2002. *The First Heroes: The Extraordinary Story of the Doolittle Raid—America's First World War II Victory*. New York: Penguin Group.

Nez, Chester, with Judith Avila Schiess. 2011. *Code Talker: The First and Only Memoir by One of the Original Navajo Code Talkers of WWII*. New York: Berkley Books.

Russ, Martin. 2000. *Breakout: The Chosin Reservoir Campaign, Korea 1950*. New York: Penguin Books.

Schnabel, James F. 1972. *United States Army in the Korean War. Policy and Direction: the First Year*. Washington, D.C.: U.S. Government Printing Office.

Sides, Hampton. 2001. *Ghost Soldiers: The Epic Account of World War II's Greatest Rescue Mission*. New York: Anchor Books.

Sides, Hampton. 2018. *On Desperate Ground: The Marines at The Reservoir, the Korean War's Greatest Battle*. New York: Doubleday

Sledge, E. B. 2007. *With The Old Breed*. New York: Presidio Press.

Sledge, Michael. 2005. *Soldier Dead: How We Recover, Identify, Bury, & Honor Our Military Fallen*. New York: Columbia University Press.

Snyder, Steve. 2015. *Shot Down: The True Story of Pilot Howard Snyder and the Crew of the B-17* Susan Ruth. Seal Beach, CA: Sea Breeze Publishing, LLC.

Stanton, Doug. 2001. *In Harm's Way: The Sinking of the USS* Indianapolis *and the Extraordinary Story of Its Survivors.* New York: Henry Holt and Co., LLC.

Stratton, Donald, with Ken Gire. 2016. *All the Gallant Men: The First Memoir by a USS* Arizona *Survivor.* New York: HarperCollins Publishers.

USS *Indianapolis* Survivors. 2002. *Only 317 Survived!: USS* Indianapolis *(CA-35) Navy's Worst Tragedy at Sea...880 Men Died.* Indianapolis, IN: Printing Partners.

Winters, Major Dick, with Colonel Cole C. Kingseed, 2006. *Beyond Band of Brothers: The War Memoirs of Major Dick Winters.* New York: The Berkley Publishing Group.

Zamperini, Louis, and David Rensin. 2003. *Devil At My Heels.* New York: HarperCollins Publishers.

Zuckoff, Mitchell. 2013. *Frozen In Time.* New York: HarperCollins Publishers.

Index

A&L Auto Sales 196
A–26 Invader 69
AAA Coffee Service (Lubbock, Texas) 229
Aachen, Germany 51
Abernathy, Texas 98, 102, 143; high school 98
Abilene Army Air Base 79
Abrams, Creighton 29
Academia della Farnesina 118
Adak Island 184
Adame, Dolores 196
Admiral Foghorn 199
Admiralty Islands 58
Advanced Hydraulic School 182
Advanced Individual Training 265
Advanced Infantry Training 258
Aerial Gunners School 190
Aerial Observer 190
Aerial Radar School 190
Aerographer Mate 154
Aerographer School 153
Afghanistan 185
Africa 82, 126
African Americans 22
Agape Temple (Lubbock, Texas) 104
Agee, Alvira 8
Agee, Charles 9
Agee, Charlie 8
Agee, Charlotte 9
Agent Orange 267
Air Boss (Flight Deck Controller) 217
Air Commendation Medal 283
Air Controller School (ACA) 216
Air Force Longevity Medal 237
Air Liaison Observer 189
Air Medal 59, 172, 189, 262, 273
Air Police Investigator 219
Air Policeman 219
Airman Apprentice School (ANP) 216
Airplane tender 76
AIT *see* Advanced Individual Training, Advanced Infantry Training
Alabama 174, 222
Alabama State Department of Corrections 220

USS *Alagash* (AO–97) 136
Alameda, California 58
Alameda Air Station, California 237
Alaska 76, 120, 235
USS *Alaska* (CB–1) 163
Alaska–Canadian (Alcan) Highway 120
Albuquerque, New Mexico 67, 153, 196, 223, 280, 290
Aldermaston, England 89–90
Alderson Cadillac (Lubbock, Texas) 217
Aleutian Islands 67, 76, 105, 155, 184–85
All God's Children 222
Allen, Marion T. 10
Allies 1121
Almost a Family 131
Aloma Hills 92
Alpine, Texas 196
"Aluminum Trail" 187
Alzheimer's 127
Amarillo, Texas 116, 183, 290; Air Force base 219, 234
Amarillo Army Airfield, Texas 71, 113, 177, 287
Amberley Field 138
"America the Beautiful" (song) 34
Americal Division, Artillery 265
American Campaign Medal 65, 124
American College Test (ACT) 126
American Legion 230
American Revolution 216
American Theater Campaign Medal 22, 25, 112
Ames, Iowa 73
Amherst, Texas 24, 25, 120, 228
Anchorage 105
Andersen, Arthur, LLP 114
Anderson, Iris 12
Anderson, Robert 12
Andrews, Texas 203, 285
Andrews High School 203
Angel Island 125
"Angel of the Orient" 248
Anguar 194
Anheuser–Busch 19
Ansbach, Germany 273

299

300 Index

Anti–Sub Patrol (ASP) 190
Anton, Texas 184–85
Antwerp, Belgium 13, 79, 151
Apollo 11 216
Aramco World (magazine) 81
Archinal, Paul 198
Arctic Circle 137
Ardennes, France 151
Ardennes Forest 151, 152
Arizona 55, 206
Arkansas 48
Arlington, Texas 143
Arlington Cemetery 43
Armed Forces of the United States 42, 281
Armistice Day 123, 179
Armor–piercing (AP) bombs 111
Armstrong, Louis 247
Army Casualty Office, Virginia 242
Army Commendation Medal 262
Army Installations Division 276
Army Master Aviator 276
Army National Guard 206
Army of Occupation 76, 102, 117, 152
Army ROTC 273–74
Army Special Operations 278
Army Stinson L–5 51, 71, 192
Army Surgeon General 261
Arrington, Jody 189
Artesia, New Mexico 222
Asiatic Pacific Theater Campaign Medal 22
Aslito Airfield, Saipan 193
Assam province, India 187
Assam Valley, India 186
Astronauts 216
AT–6 Texan 78, 89, 286
AT–9 "Jeep" 89, 286
AT–11 Kansan 89, 286
Atlantic City, New Jersey 22, 26, 78
Atlantic Fleet 236
Atlantic Ocean 64–65, 103, 120, 137
Atlas Obscura 72
Atomic bomb 10, 15, 21, 27, 41, 53, 76, 79, 80
Atterbury, Indiana 180
Attu Island 76, 105, 155
Augsburg, Germany 176
Aurora, Colorado 273
Austin, Texas 156
Australia 97, 282
Austria 13, 54, 169
Avery Elementary School 217
Aviation Cadet Program 186
Aviation Officer 273
Aviation Radioman 2nd Class (ARM2C) 189
Axis 96
Azores 77, 86

B–17 Flying Fortress 24, 55, 113, 139, 287
B–24 Liberator 86, 129, 150, 282
B–25 Mitchell 68–69, 105–06, 171, 172
B–25J Mitchell bomber 286, 288
B–29 Superfortress 72, 78, 147
B–47 Stratojet 234–35
Bacall, Lauren 237
Baccarat, France 123
Baffin Island 137
Bailey, K.C. 9
Bailey, Nelda Jean 206
Bailey bridge 82
Bainbridge, Maryland 83
Baird, New Mexico 229
Bakersfield, California 19
Baltimore, Maryland 109, 136, 164
Bamberg, Germany 51, 103
Band–Box Cleaners 26
Bandsman Saxophone 439, 22
Bangor, Maine 55, 86
Banner 276
Banta, Jean Ann 95
Baranczyk, Albin 249
Barin Field "Bloody Barin" 40
Barksdale Army Air Field, California 90
Barnes, Almer Doyle 43
Barnes, Bobby Skaggs 43
Barnett, Maxine M. 172
Barstow, California 249
Baruch, Bernard 226
Basic Training 264, 270
USS *Bassett* (APD–73) 101
Bastogne, Belgium 12–13, 45, 121
Bataan, Philippines 178
Bataan Death March 178
Bates, Bill 259
Battalion Aid Station 202
Battle Group Surgeon 260
"Battle Hymn of the Republic" 57
Battle of Chosin Reservoir 240–41; exhibit 208
Battle of Midway 105
Battle of Ong Thanh 252
Battle of Remagen 51
Battle of the Bulge 12, 24, 51, 53, 73, 74, 79, 90, 112, 117, 121, 123, 151, 161, 175, 181
Battle of Triangle Hill 202
Baum, Abe 29
USS *Bayfield* (APA–33) 157–58
Baylor Dental School (Waco, Texas) 272
Baytown 93
Bazooka 25
Beachum, Ralph 58, 61
Beard Growing Contest 214
Bearden, Herbert C. 15
Bearden, Leonard 15
Bearden, Ona Ruby 15
Beaumont, TX 199
Belgian pistol 161
Belgium 73, 79, 121, 151
Belk, Lloyd 188
Bell Dairy (Lubbock, Texas) 206
Bellevue, Nebraska 217
Bellflower, California 10

Ben E. Keith Wholesale Food Distributor 239
Benghazi Survivor Presentation 34
Benny, Jack 139
Berchtesgaden, Germany 229
Berkstresser, Taylor 10
Berlin, Germany 48, 112, 152; Berlin Airlift 234; West Berliners 234
Bermuda 20
Bertrand, Nebraska 217
Bethlehem, Pennsylvania 260
Beverly, Nina 154
Beverly Hills Police Department 249
Bible 103, 224–25, 238, 277
Bien Hoa 252, 261
Big O Tires 196
Big Red 1, 251
Big Spring, TX 222
Bikini Atoll 185
Bingham, Earl 166
Birchfield, Billie 228
Birchfield, Jeff 228
Birchfield, Lois 228
Birmingham, Alabama 157, 220
Birmingham Hospital, California 24
Bishop, Oklahoma 171
Bishop College 85
Bismarck (German battleship) 218
Bitche, France 123; *see also* Sons of Bitche
Black, Linda 274
Black Cat #13 55
Blackhawk helicopter 273
Blackwell, Texas 100
Blitzkrieg 151
Blocker, Dan 205
Bloodworth, Earlene 110
Blue Star Flag 72, 281
BMW (German motorcycle) 173
Board of 100 Black Men of West Texas 259
Board of the Bridge (Lubbock, Texas) 259
Bobrowski, Isobel (Susie) 19
Bobrowski, Stanley 17
Bobrowski, Stanley J., Jr. 17
Bobrowski, Susan 19
Boeing 235
Bofers 40mm gun 112, 150
Bogart, Humphrey 237
Bokchito, OK 92
Bombay, India 96, 114
Bonanza (TV show) 205
Bonaparte, Napoleon 221
Booker T. Washington High School (New Orleans, Louisiana) 246
Booker T. Washington High School (Tulsa, Oklahoma) 22
Boot Camp 99, 270
Bordeaux, France 8
Borden's (Levelland, Texas) 90
Borger, Texas 150
Boston, Massachusetts 81, 219

Boston Harbor 18, 24, 92
Boston Navy Yard 218
Boswell, Oklahoma 234
USS *Bougainville* (CVE–100) 149
"Bouncing Bettie" 238
boxcars 118
Boyles, Ellis (Pete) 21
Boyles, Henry 20
Boyles, Lillie Mae 20
Boyles, William 20
Boys and Girls Club (Lubbock, Texas) 63, 259
Bradley, George 246
Bradley, Omar 48, 51
Brady, Texas 8
Bravo (service dog) 291
Braxton, Bernice 22
Braxton, James 22
Braxton, Ruby 23
Braxton, Thomas 23
Breckenridge, Texas 125
Bremerhaven, Germany 48, 112, 118
Brest, France 121
Brewer, Dianna 237
Bridge, Grace Ann 203
Bridge, Jesse 201
Bridge, Louis Simpson (L.S.) 201
Bridge, William 201
Bridwell, J.S. 68
Brimberry, Charles (Joe) 248
Brimberry, Charles 248
Brimberry, Lenna 248
Bristol, Tennessee 42
Bristol, Virginia 42
British Columbia 120
Britt, D.L. 24
Britt, Mary 24
Britt, Ray Lynn 25
Britt, Roger 24
Brokaw, Tom 135
Broken Bow, OK 103
Bronte, Texas 118–19
Bronx, New York 134
Bronze Star 25, 54, 90, 124, 131, 201, 203, 245, 253, 261–62, 273, 287; with "V" 253; with "V" and oak leaf cluster 262
Brooke Army Hospital, Texas 123, 232
Brooke Army Medical Center (BAMC), Texas 289
Brooke Medical School, Texas 223
Brooklyn, New York 32, 105–06, 157
Brooklyn Navy Hospital 32
Brooks AFB, Texas 234
Brooks Field, Texas 172
Brown, Ann 27
Brown, J.M. 26
Brown, Lee 26
Brown, Lester C. 26
Brown, Rose 259
Brownfield, Texas 94–95, 160–61, 164, 211, 227; high school 226

302   Index

Browning Automatic Rifle (BAR) 179, 202, 204, 221
Brown's Department Store (Lockney, Texas) 27
Brownwood, Texas 168
Brussels, Belgium 112
Buchenwald Concentration Camp 48
Buffalo, New York 187
Buffalo Gap, Texas 43
Bulgaria 144
Bunsen burner 207
Burbank, California 24
Burma 96, 186
Burma Road 114, 186
Burp Gun, German 179
Burtonwood AFB, England 234
Butler College (Indiana) 78
Byers High School 89
Byrd, Richard E. 154

C–47 Skytrain 65, 90, 286
C–54 Skymaster 234
C–141 Starlifter 194
USS *C.H. Muir* (AP–142) 228
Cadet Nursing Program 13
The Cain Mutiny (movie) 237
Calcutta, India 114
Caldwell Band 116
California 10, 18, 27, 48, 83, 96, 115
Calvary Baptist Church (Lubbock, Texas) 110
Cam Ranh Bay, Vietnam 265
Cameron, James 86
"Cameron's Crew" 86
Camp Anza, California 96, 114
Camp Bouse, Arizona 160
Camp Cabanatuan, Philippines 178
Camp Chaffey, Arkansas 48
Camp Claiborne, Louisiana 96
Camp Cooke, California 73
Camp Fannin, Texas 15, 122
Camp Haugen, Japan 240
Camp Howze, Texas 179
Camp Hulen, Texas 111
Camp Joseph T. Robinson, Arkansas 117
Camp Kamcharapara, India 114
Camp Kilmer, New Jersey 64, 79, 111, 122
Camp Lejune, North Carolina 115, 157
Camp MacKall, North Carolina 166
Camp McCain, Mississippi 167
Camp Miles Standish, Massachusetts 18
Camp Peary, Virginia 10, 107
Camp Pendleton, California 209–10, 238, 248
Camp Pickett, Virginia 117
Camp Polk, Louisiana 166
Camp Roberts, California 73, 130, 175, 204
Camp Sampson, New York 136
Camp Shanks, New York 45, 50, 54, 120; "Last Stop, USA" 45
Camp Shelby, Mississippi 18

Camp Sibert, Alabama 17
Camp Stoneman, California 129, 204
Camp Tamborine, Australia 130
Camp Wheeler, Georgia 96, 151
Camp White, Oregon 120
Camp Wolters, Texas 24, 45, 128, 144, 166
Campbell, Harry 242
Camrai, France 65
Canada 120; maritime provinces of 227
"Cannon fodder" 227
Cape Gloucester 115
Carbon Arc Lamp 160
Caribbean 93
Caribbean Sea 138
Carillon LifeCare Community (Lubbock, Texas) 127, 135, 154, 203
Carlinville, Illinois 97
Carlisle, Kentucky 243
Carlsbad, New Mexico 119
Carlsbad Army Air Base, California 177
Carlsbad Caverns 38
Carson, Harold H. 193
Carswell AFB, Texas 54, 235
Casablanca 86
Catarrhal fever 32
Caterpillar Club 72
Cathey, James 204
Cathey, Nena 204
Cathey, Reggie 206
Cathey, Regina 206
Cathey, William 204
Cavazos, Lauro 262
Cawthon, Pete 171
Cawthorn, Winona 90
Cebu, Philippines 54
Centerville, Tennessee 276
Central America 276
Certified Lay Speaker 220
CG–A glider 71
CG–4A glider 90
Chablais, France 9
Chandler, Jo Ann 229
Changing of the Guard 63
Chanute AFB, Illinois 255–56
Chanute Airfield, Illinois 26
Chappell Hill, Texas 62
Chateauroux Air Station, France 219
Chemical Warfare Service 17
Cherbourg, France 12
Chetnik guerillas 87
Chevron Gas Plant (Snyder, Texas) 253
Cheyenne, Wyoming 103
Chiapas, Mexico 126
Chiari Malformation 290
Chicago, Illinois 12, 17, 53, 58; Museum of Science and Industry, 41
Chief Loadmaster 174
Chief Master Sergeant 106, 174
Chief of Chaplains Office, Army 34
Chief of Engineers 276
Chief of Section 226

Index

Chief Petty Officer 76, 98
Child Welfare Office 225
China 76, 96–97, 114, 211, 282; Yunnan province 186
China–Burma–India (CBI) 171–72, 283
China Service Medal 237
Chinese National Airways Corporation "CNAC" 187
Chittagong, India 96
Chu Lai, Vietnam 248; air base 265
Church of Christ (Midland, Texas) 210
Church of Christ (Riverside, California) 63
Church of Christ (Snyder, Texas) 225
Church of Christ Twentieth & Birch (Lubbock, Texas) 63
Cigarette Camps 24, 50, 54
Cimarron class oiler 136
Cimarron Field, Oklahoma 78
Cincinnati, Ohio 196
Cisco, Texas 141
City Bank (Springlake, Texas) 65
City of Lubbock 110, 259
Civil Action Honor (Vietnamese) 262
Civil Service 237
Claire, Jean 236
Clark, Mark 231
Clark, William 231
Claude Martin and Sons 108
claymore mine 266
Clearing Platoon Commander 260
Clemmons Ford (Comanche, Texas) 170
USS *Cleveland* 20
Cleveland, Ohio 199
Cleveland Rams 171
Clovis, New Mexico 150, 152, 229; high school 152
Coastal Defense Light (CDL) 160
Coca Cola 89–90, 148
Coeur d'Alene Mountains 58
Cohen, Hal 29
Coke Canyon Reservoir 150
Cold War 226
Colley, Sarah (AKA Minnie Pearl) 278
Cologne, Germany 78
Colorado 207, 290
Colorado City, Texas 16
Colorado Springs 196
Colson, Charles F. 252
Columbia, South Carolina 172
Columbia Air Base, South Carolina 105
Columbus AFB, Mississippi 237
Colvin, James 29
Colvin, Lon 29, 45, 47, 49
Colvin, Sally 29
COMAIRPAC 217
Comanche, Texas 130, 166
Comanche County, Texas 128
Combat Infantry Badge (CIB) 25, 124, 201, 208, 232
Combat Medical Badge 262
Commemorative Air Force 286

Community College of the Air Force 247
Composite Squadron VC–4 190
Compton, California 10
Concerned Veterans for America (CVA) 290
Cone, Texas 207
Continental Airlines 218
Continental Army 118
Continental Navy 216
Convair B–58 Hustler 235
Coon, Tom 33
Coon, Wilma 32
Cooper High School 149
USS *Coral Sea* (CVB–43) 58
Corpus Christi, Texas 114, 196
Costa Rica 276
Court reporting 232
Coxswain 66
Crenshaw, Phil 34
Crenshaw, Ruth 36
Creuzburg, Germany 48
Cromwell, Chuck 271
Crow, Norma 98
Crustbuster Mfg. 69
Crutcher, Joe B. 252
Cryptography 265
Cummings, Clara 37
Cummings, Robert C. 37
Cummings, Robert L. 37
USS *Currituck* (AV–7) 154
Curtis Candy 90
Curtis D. Ruff & Associates 232
Curtiss C–46 Commando 187
Czechoslovakia 48, 168

D–Day 10, 24, 29, 64, 157, 190
Da Nang Harbor 248; 219
Daedalians 277
Dairy Queen 116
Dalhart, Texas 45
Dalhart Field, Texas 71
Dallas, Texas 10, 39, 85, 121, 143, 187, 209, 265, 273–74, 290
Dallas Love Field 274
Dallas Metroplex Military Foundation 135
Dallas School of Mortuary 38
Dalton, Georgia 255; high school 255
Danube River 74
Danzig, Poland 93
Darnton, Barney 132
Darnton, John 132
Davis, George, Jr. 219
Dawson, Fannie Lee 62
Dayton Herald 72
Dean, William 211
DeDera, Joseph 89
Deep South 246
Defense POW/MIA Accounting Agency (DPAA) 178
Degaussed 66, 136–37
Demilitarized Zone (DMZ) 238, 258

Deming, New Mexico 55, 56
Densford, Daryl 243
Denton County, Texas 178
Denver 69, 114, 177, 218; Brave Church 273
Denver, John 235
Denver City, Texas 285
Dept. of Defense 140
Derby, Virginia 42
DeRidder, Louisiana 73
Desert Shield/Desert Storm 276
Detroit Lakes, Minnesota 139
Deutschendorf, Henry 235
Dierks, Arkansas 124
Dillard, Dorothy 45
Dimmitt, Texas 64, 209
Director of Investigations and Intelligence 220
Disabled American Veterans (DVA) 220
Distinguished Flying Cross 189, 262
Distinguished Service Cross 24
Distinguished Service Medal 262
Dixon, Eddie 259
DNA 178, 242
Doctor of Jurisprudence 249
Dodd, Francis T. 222
Dodd, Marci 106
Dodge City, Kansas 69
Dogfight 129
Donaldson, Commander 191
Douglas AD–4 Skyraider 216
Draftees 16
Drake, Harold 233
Draughon Business College (Lubbock, Texas) 211
Drew Field Air Base Chapel, Florida 80
DuLaney, Dorene 41
DuLaney, Jack 39
Dunbar High School (Lubbock, Texas) 23, 62, 85, 259
Duncan, Lena (Lyn) 42
Duncan, W.L. 43
Dunlap's Department Store (Lubbock, TX) 56
Dust Bowl 39, 68, 98
Dutch Army 260
Dutch Netherlands 93
Dyess, Alan 208
Dyess, Jerold Booth 207
Dyess, O.R. (Jack) 207
Dyess, Tammy 208
Dyess, Vergie 207

"Eagles Nest" 229
EAME Theater Campaign Medal 112
East China Sea 21
East Germany 227
Eastern Airlines 80
Eastern New Mexico 148
Eastern New Mexico University 152, 225
Eastman Kodak (Dallas, Texas) 176
Eaton, Charles 60

Edwards, Joan 102
88 gun (German) 123, 151, 158, 161, 179
88 mm gun 167
Eindhoven, Holland 90
Eisenhower, Dwight D. 48, 211
El Camino Junior College 249
El Paso, Texas 16, 114, 118, 150, 170, 208, 228
Elbe River 112, 152
USS *Electra* (AKA–4) 214
"11 Things the Military Teaches You About Leadership" 217
SS *Elk Basin* 93
Ellington AFB, Texas 198
Ellis, Garland 45
Ellis, Myrtle 45
Ellis, Rodney 48
Ellis, Val 48
Ellis, W.C. 45
"Elmer the Great" 171
Elmer's Weights 172
Endicott, Rhode Island 10
England 55, 64–65, 74, 81, 93, 167–68, 176, 246, 255
English Channel 50, 73, 78, 151, 167
Eniwetok Atoll, Marshall Islands 67
Enola Gay 217, 257
Ensley, Alabama 159
USS *Enterprise* (CV–6) 181
Esparza, Lusina 50
Esparza, Pedro 50
Esparza, Thomas 50
Espiritu Santo 193
Essayons (Army Corps of Engineers motto) 121
Essex class aircraft carrier 138, 236
Estacado High School (Lubbock, Texas) 85, 289
Estrada, Hermenejilda "Hilda" 51
USAT *Etolin* 94
Euless, Texas 141–42; high school 141
Europe 8, 15, 29, 45, 49, 50, 53, 96, 117–18, 161, 162, 276, 279
European–African–Middle Eastern Campaign Medal 65
European Campaign Medal 25
Evanston, Illinois 190
Experience Life Church (Lubbock, Texas) 290
Expert Infantryman Badge (EIB) 258
Exxon 97

F–4 Phantom jet 247
F–7A aircraft 281
F–7B aircraft 281
F–86 Sabre 219
Fairchild P–19A trainer 187
Fairfield AFB, Washington 246
Faith, Donald 241
Falmouth, England 10
Family Promise (Lubbock, Texas) 104

Index

Far East 117, 209, 236, 236–37
Farragut, David 58
Farragut Naval Training Station 58
Featherlite Block Co. 104
Federal Aviation Administration (FAA) 277
Federal Bureau of Investigation (FBI) 160
Fedhala, French Morocco 20
Ferry Command 187
50 mm gun 147, 228
52/20 work program 154
Fire Control 2nd Class 98
Fire Controlman 3rd Class 150
Firefight 252
Firestone 69
First Baptist Church (Shallowater, Texas) 41
First Sergeant 256
Fisher, Clyde 209
Fisher, Clyde, Jr. 209
Fisher, Zetha 209
Flagstaff, Arizona 59, 227
Flame throwers 36
Flateboe, Lieutenant 194
Fleming, Orville 53
Floating Reserve 147
Florida 87–88
Florida Island 193
Floyd County, Texas 58, 281, 83
Floydada, Texas 58, 60, 77, 214; high school 281; post office 214; volunteer fire department 214
Fluorescein dye 56
Flying the Hump 96
FMC Corporation 196
Focke–Wulf FW–190 90
Forest Ranger 203
"Forgotten War" 208
Formosa 282
Fort Benning, Georgia 155, 289
Fort Bliss, Texas 22–23, 50, 62, 114, 152, 206, 228, 251, 258
Fort Bragg, North Carolina 19, 122
Fort Campbell, Kentucky 260
Fort Devens, Massachusetts 82
Fort Dix, New Jersey 90, 109, 118, 121, 207
Fort Eustis, Virginia 15
Fort George Meade, Maryland 262
Fort Hood, Texas 50, 179, 229, 258
Fort Jackson, South Carolina 111
Fort Knox, Kentucky 160, 240
Fort Leonard Wood, Missouri 103
Fort Lewis, Washington 160, 221, 264
Fort Mason, California 25
Fort McClellan, Alabama 51, 284
Fort McCoy, Wisconsin 81
Fort Meade, Maryland 43, 50–51
Fort Ord, California 16, 53, 130, 201, 207, 230
Fort Polk, Louisiana 251, 258, 264
Fort Robinson, California 155
Fort Rucker, Alabama 274

Fort Sam Houston, Texas 8, 27, 48, 77, 90, 103, 109, 112, 123, 129, 145, 170, 223, 232, 260, 284, 287
Fort Scott, California 62
Fort Sill, Oklahoma 22, 62, 89, 120, 125, 160, 175, 179, 201, 204, 223–24, 284, 286
Fort Snelling 81
Fort Stockton 86
Fort Sumner, New Mexico 207
Fort Worth, Texas 31, 70, 141–42, 222, 235
Forward observer 209
Foster, Doug 251
Foster, Glenn 251
Foster, Golda 251
Foster Field, Texas 70
France 10, 24, 30–31, 96, 151, 168, 179, 240, 246
Francis E. Warren AFB 255–56; drill team 256
Frankfurt, Germany 51, 185
Freedom Village, Korea 211, 213
Fritzlar, Germany 79
Fulda Gap 227
USS *Furse* (DD–882) 236
Future Farmers of America (FFA) 280
Future Homemakers of America (FHA) 280

G.M. Diesel 69
Gaither, Galen 217
Gaither, Terry 217
Galesburg, Illinois 13
Gallups Island 92
Galveston 93
USS *Gambier Bay* (CVE–73) 193
Garland, Texas 273
Garner, Alton 211
Garner, Thalua 211
Gatlin, Grady 190–93
General Dynamics 177
General Education Development (G.E.D.) 62
USS *General George M. Randall* (AP–115) 96, 218
USS *General John Pope* (AP–110) 211
General MacArthur's Palace Guard 131
General Motors 203
USS *General O.H. Ernst* (AP–133) 115
General Officer's Executive Council 276
USS *General R.L. Howze* (AP–134) 118
General Telephone (GTE) 102
USS *General W.F. Hase* (AP–146) 196
George, Charles 206
George, Lloyd 240
George VI, King 176
USAT *George Washington* 122
Geriatric Art Society (GAS Group)—Lubbock 108
German anti–personnel bomb 159
German mines 137
German shepherd (dog) 168
German submarines 40, 111

German Tiger Tank 25
Germany 12, 18, 30, 54, 55, 73–74, 79, 103, 139, 152, 162, 168–69, 179, 208, 228–29; surrender 90
Ghazni Provence, Afghanistan 289, 291
GI Bill 14, 16, 56
Gilbert Islands 99
Gill, Rhonda 56
Gill, Robbie 55
Gill, Stacy 56
Gill, Stan 56
Gill, Stoney 56
Gill, Wanda 56
Gilly, Ann 58
Gilly, Barbara 60
Gilly, Carl 58
Gilly, Cathy 60
Gilly, Lois 59
Gilly, Vince 58
Girl's State (New Mexico) 280
GIs 109, 120, 242, 265
Glasgow, Scotland 111
Glassboro, New Jersey 163
Glasscock Drilling 114
Goat Island 99
God 3–4, 34–36, 57, 63, 72, 126, 131, 214, 222, 225, 227, 250, 259, 264, 267, 273–75, 285, 290
Gold Star Flag 72, 281
Gold Star Wives of America 281–83
Golden Eagle of China 172
Golden Gate Bridge 76
Good Conduct Medal 22, 25, 59, 65, 97, 112, 124, 201, 237
Good News Book Store (Lubbock, Texas) 126
Goodenough Island 130
Goodfellow Field, Texas 70
Gordon, Bill 203
Goree, Texas 75, 77
Gotha, Germany 48
Goulds Pumps 259
Graba, Jim 139
Grand Central Station 35
Great Depression 10, 35, 68, 92, 135, 139, 155, 166, 175, 207, 236, 255
Great Lakes Naval Training Station, Illinois 136, 190, 236
Greatest Generation 19, 91, 175, 230, 272
The Greatest Generation (book) 135
Greece 185
Green, Alberta 32
Green, Dorothy 32
Green, William L 32
Greenland 130, 137
Greenway, Jannie "Li'l Bit" 255
Greenway, R.W. 255
Greenway, Selma 255
USS *Gridley* (DD–380) 181–82
Gross, Asher 273
Gross, Chad 235, 273

Gross, Corban 273–74
Gross, Harvest 273
Gross, Micah 273
Gross, Renee 273–74
Grove, Oklahoma 144
Grovesville School 39
Grumman F4F Wildcat 40
Grumman TBF Avenger 40
Gruver, Texas 115
Guadalcanal 40, 115, 282
USS *Guadalcanal* (CVE 60) 40
Guam 37, 53, 67, 100–01, 134–35
Guantanamo Bay, Cuba 138
Gulpen, Holland 161
Gunner's Mate 1st Class 181
Gustafson, Sven 247
Guyton, Fannie 63
Guyton, Lawrence "Jim" 62
Gwinn, Wilbur 101

Haberer, Camille 65
Haberer, Davey 65
Haberer, Roger 64
Hacker, Betty 163
Hagler, Swan 198–99
Hail, Bob 66
Hail, Joyce Lea 67
Hail, Shelley 67
Hail, Stasey 67
Hale County, Texas 186
half pint (grenade) 252
half–track 25
Hall County, Texas 20
HALO for Freedom Warrior Foundation 290
Halsey, William, Jr. 237
Hambright, Darlynn 215
Hambright, Ethel 214
Hambright, Gordon 214
Hambright, William 214
Hamby, J.W. 68
Hamby Co. 69
Hamilton County, Ohio 196
USS *Hamlin* (AV–15) 76
Hamlin, Texas 57
Hammelburg, Germany 29, 47; lager 30
Hampton Roads, Virginia 51
Hancock School 113
Haney, Muriel 70
Haney, W.A. 70
Haney, Wallace 70
Haney, William 70
Hankson, Charles "Hank" 258
Hanscom AFB, Massachusetts 219
Hanson, Bobbi 189
Happy, Texas 50, 98
Happy Building 32
Hara–kiri 36
Harber, Carol 278
Harber, Cathleen 278
Harber, Gary 200, 276

Index 307

Harber, Lauren 278
Hardin–Simmons University 79
Harlingen, Texas 56, 199
Harmon Tank (Lubbock, Texas) 170
Hartman, Jean 74
Hartman, Max 59
Hartman, Ted 73
Harvey, Alice 216
Harvey, Fred 216
Harvey, Larry 217
Harvey, Melinda 217
Harvey, Norma 217
Harvey, Porter 216
Hatch, Henry "Hank" 276
USS *Haven* (AH–12) 212
Hawaii 15, 17, 20, 27, 32, 59, 95, 107, 133
Haynes Ford (Abilene, Texas) 170
Hazelwood Act 16
Headquarters and Headquarters Battery (HHB) 265
Headstream, Helen 38
"Healing Wall" 253
Hedgerows 160
Heerlen, Holland 112
Heidelberg, Germany 25
USS *Helena* (CL–50) 181
"Hello Dolly" (song) 247
The Help (movie) 246
Hendrix, Billy 75
Henry, Jason 63
Hermleigh, Texas 115, 251
Hershberger, Clarence 101
Hess, Su 133
Hi–D–Ho drive-in (Lubbock, Texas) 93
Hi–Plains Hospital (Hale Center, Texas) 80
Hickman County High School 276
Hicks Field, Texas 70
Hie, Maurice 190
Higgins, Andrew 157
Higgins, Texas 171
Higgins Boat 115, 157, 159, 190
Highland Baptist Church (Lubbock, Texas) 16
Hill, Doris 79
Hill, Ted 78
Himalayas 96
Hiroshima 10, 15, 27, 41, 53, 68, 76, 80, 116, 129, 147, 153, 163, 175, 183, 185, 216, 280
Hitler, Adolf 74, 168
Hobbs, New Mexico 82
Hobbs Daily News–Sun 82
Hockley County Courthouse 50
Hodges Elementary (Lubbock, Texas) 16
Hokkaido, Japan 223
Holcomb, Wilma 26
Holland 89, 260, 286
Hollandia 195
USS *Hollandia* (CVE–97) 102
Hollywood High School 236
Hollywood Park Racetrack, California 236
Holmes, Oliver Wendell 272
Holy Rosary Church, North Chicago 17
Holyfield, Evander 259
Homer, Maggie Ruth 147
Honduras 276
Hong Kong 217, 236
Honolulu, Hawaii 53, 143, 175, 236–37
"Hootchie" 224
Hooten, Dorothy Cox 170
Hope, Bob 32, 219
USS *Hornet* (CVA–12) 216
Hospital Corpsman 3rd Class 236
Houston, Texas 77, 114, 198
Houx, Odessa Marie 156
Howell, Mike 188
Hoye, Annie 81
Hoye, Charlie 81
Hoye, Joseph 81
Hoye, Loretta 82
Hoye, Margery 81
Hoye, Paul 81
Huffman, Walt 277
Hughes Aircraft 249
"The Hump" 186–87
Hungary 87
Hunter AFB, Georgia 234
Hunter Killers 40
Hurst, Texas 141
Hussein, Saddam 18
The Hut Camp 82
Hutson, Patricia 249
USS *H.W. General Butner* (AP–113) 141

"I bombed Japan" club 106
I–58 submarine 100
Ice Station Zebra (movie) 83
Idalou, Texas 10
SS *Île de France* 151
"In the Garden" (song) 239
Inchon, Korea 15, 129, 201, 212, 241
India 76, 126, 186
Indiana 101
Indiana Baptist Church (Lubbock, Texas) 235, 274–75
USS *Indianapolis* (CA–35) 102, 162–63
Indianapolis, Indiana 248
Indonesia 260
Inez, New Mexico 223
Infantryman (11B) 289
USS *Iowa* (BB–61) 154
Iowa State University 73
Ira, Texas 70
Iraq 185, 275
Island hopping 129, 150, 185
The Island's Last Call 34
Italy 87, 118, 121, 139
Iwo Jima 27, 37, 66, 99, 133–34, 147, 150, 185

Jacksonville, Florida 153
Jal, New Mexico 150
Jane Russell Hill (Korea) 203

308   Index

Japan 13, 20, 43, 76, 95, 109, 126, 140, 145, 170, 175, 230, 230, 232, 236, 246, 280; occupation of 21, 54
Japanese bombers 96; Betty bombers 191
Japanese Imperial Palace 280
Japanese Occupation Medal 237
Jeep, Army 118, 224, 285
Jefferson Barracks, Missouri 113
Jesus 8, 36, 61, 63, 100–01, 151–52, 186–87, 238–39, 259, 264, 273–75, 277, 291
Jodl, Alfred 90
Johnson, Lyndon B. 139
Johnson, Van 237
Johnson, Winnifred 185
Johnston Atoll 154
Joint POW/MIA Accounting Command (JPAC) 242
Jones, Clyde 89
Jones, Delma Jean 95
Jones, Don 83
Jones, Dora 89
Jones, Dorothy 85
Jones, Elizabeth Jo 95
Jones, Homer 86
Jones, Jerry 95
Jones, Justin 286
Jones, Justin T. 89
Jones, Lamar 92
Jones, R.D. 94
Jones, Rick 88
Jones, W.A. 92
Joplin, Missouri 35
Jordan 185
Joyner, Jackie 259
Juneau, Alaska 154
Junior Grand Ole Opry 278
Junior 3rd Engineer 93
Justice, Ann 114

K–rations 65
K–20 camera 190–92
Kai–shek, Chiang 114
Kaiser Shipyards 149
Kaman HH43 Huskie 237
Kamikaze 20, 94–95, 99, 126, 128, 145, 183
Kansas 69
Kansas City, Missouri 27, 35, 180
USS *Karnes* (APA–175) 95
KCBD TV (Lubbock, TX) 33
Kearney, Nebraska 216
USS *Kearsarge* (CVA 33) 236–37
Kelly Airfield, Texas 86, 113–14
Kelz, Germany 78
Kennedy, Jackie 82
Kennedy, John F. 63, 82
USS *Kenneth Whiting* (AV–14) 182
Kentucky Department of Veterans Affairs 243
Kermit, Texas 162–63
Kerrville, Texas 3
Kimpo Air Base, Korea 218

Kimpo Peninsula, Korea 212
Kindred Hospice 200
King College 42
Kingdom of Heaven 259
Kingsville, Texas 217
Kirishima 163
Kirkland AFB, New Mexico 67
Kiser, Bob 96
Kiser, Carl 97
Kiser, Jane 97
Kiser, Kurt 97
Kiser, Marna 97
Kiska, Alaska 76, 105, 155, 181
USS *Kitty Hawk* (CV–63) 27
Kizziah, Jo 233
Klassen, Josie "Jo" 218, 220
KMID TV, Midland, Texas 199
The Knight Group 242
Koblenz, Germany 24
Kodiak, Alaska 76
Koje–do, Korea 221
Korea 9, 201, 208, 210, 223, 226, 232, 236, 238, 279
Korean Service Medal 201, 208, 223, 226, 232, 238, 279
Korean Veterans Memorial 104, 204, 215, 222
Korean War 62, 110, 111, 117, 129, 141, 143, 176, 198, 201, 209, 211, 221, 226, 228, 240, 243, 255, 260, 270; Western front 212
Korean War Project (website) 240–41
KOSA–TV, Odessa, Texas 199
Kosovo 273
KP (Kitchen Police) duty 209
KSEL–TV, Lubbock, Texas 199
Kuhn, Patricia 252
Kunming, China 96, 114
Kuriles 105
Kwayalain 107
Kyle, Chris 34
Kyle, Taya 34

Lackey, Janet 59
Lackland AFB, Texas 218, 234, 246, 255
Lai Khe, Vietnam 252
Lake Charles, Louisiana 68–69
Lake Erie 199
Lake Texoma, Texas 180
Lakehurst, New Jersey 153–54
Lakenheath Royal AFB, England 256–57
Lakeridge Methodist Church (Lubbock, Texas) 267
Lakeview, Texas 281
Lal, New Guinea 129
Lamb County, Texas 25
Lambert, Miranda 156
Lamesa, Texas 113
Lamkin, Texas 128
Landing Craft, Vehicle, Personnel (LCVP) 66, 157
Landing Ship Tank (LST) 53, 73–74, 99

Index

Landing Zones (LZ's) 265–66; Landing Zone W (LZ–W) 90
Landstuhl Regional Medical Center, Germany 289
Langley, Charline 77
Laredo AFB, Texas 220
Larson Air Force Base, Washington 8
Laufenselden, Germany 18
Laughlin AFB, Texas 237
Lauterbach, Germany 48
Le Havre, France 18, 24, 46, 50, 54, 90, 117, 161
Le Mans, France 13
Le Shima 129
Lebanon, Nebraska 217
Lebow, Cleatus 98
Lebow, Elizabeth 98
Lebow, Samuel Houston 98
Ledo/Stillwell Road 283
Leek, England 111
Legion of Merit 262
Lehigh University 261
Leon, Wilson 87–88
Levelland, Texas 50, 90, 163, 209, 212
Lewis, Beverly 103
Lewis, C.L. 270
Lewis, Calvin 259
Lewis, Curtis 103
Lewis, Debbie 103
Lewis, Ester 103
Lewis, George 103
Lewis, George Lee 103
Lewis, James David 103
Lewis, Madeline 103
Lewis, Mary 103
Lewis, Pam 103
Lewis, Sherry 103
Lewis, Winnie 103
Leyte 163, 282
Liberty ship 13, 48, 64, 79
Liege, Belgium 65
Life Support and Survival Equipment 247
Light, Lattie Ellen 114
Lincoln, Nebraska 68, 86
Lingayen Gulf 126
Lion's Club 135
Lippert's Business College (Plainview, Texas) 111, 232
Little White House 155
Littlefield, Texas 212, 249
Liverpool, England 73, 79, 90, 161
L.L. Hendrix lumber yard 77
Lockheed Martin 24; PV–1 60
Lockland, Ohio 198
Lockney, Texas 26, 27, 29, 45
Lockney Co-op 31
Lockney Gin 31
Logan, New Mexico 154; high school 153
Logan, Utah 55
London, England 64, 82, 235, 245
Londonderry, North Ireland 10

Long Beach, Long Island 32
Long March 168
Longview, Texas 85
Loran Tatham Pump 51
Lord's Prayer 101; song 284
Lorenzo, Texas 109, 132, 150
Lorient, France 167
Los Angeles, California 16, 63, 116
Los Angeles County Sheriff's Academy 249
Los Angeles Times 93
Louis, Joe "Brown Bomber" 62
Louisville Courier–Journal 243
Love Field, Texas 172
USS *Lowndes* 66–67
Lowry AFB 218
Lowry Field 177
USS LSM–349 (Landing Ship Medium) 142
USS LST–569 (Landing Ship Tank) 142
Lubbock, Texas 14, 16, 19, 23, 26, 34, 38, 45, 59, 62–63, 67, 77, 85, 89–91, 98, 103, 106–07, 109, 120–21, 122, 140–41, 143, 150, 159, 160, 170, 172, 174, 176, 178, 181, 184–87, 201, 203, 206, 209–10, 219–20, 227, 249, 264, 270, 274, 283, 287–89; high school 109, 184, 201, 209, 271
Lubbock Aero 286
Lubbock Army Airfield 64, 89, 286; flying school 89
Lubbock Auto Company 172
Lubbock Avalanche–Journal 89, 286
Lubbock Christian University 69
Lubbock Hubbers 184
Lubbock Independent School District 104
Lubbock International Airport 288
Lubbock Police Dept. Canine Corps 33
Lubbock Public School System 85
Lubbock State School 104
Lubbock Stereo Center 196
Lubbock VA Clinic 222, 263
Lucky Strike, France 18, 24, 50, 54
Ludendorff Bridge 51
Luger, Connie 106
Luger, Nathan 105
Luger Scale Service 106
Luke, John, Jr. 217
Lumley, Patty 241, 243
Lummus International Sales (New York) 185
SS *Lurline* 181
Luxembourg 18
Luzon, Philippines 141, 149, 178, 282

M1 carbine 185, 231
M1 sharpshooter 121
M1C Sniper Rifle 205
M2 .50 caliber machine gun 204–05, 209, 224
M18, 57mm Recoilless Rifle 231, 238
M18 Hellcat 50
M–20 armored car 219
M–16 rifle 265

Index

M16 turret 228
M35, 2½-ton 6x6 truck 145
M46 Patton Tank 207
M-79 grenade launcher 265
M1911 .45 Pistol 241
MacArthur, Douglas 29, 144, 241
"Mae West" life jacket 55
Magee, Fibber and Magee 32
"Maid in the Shade" 286
"Mail call" 222, 285
Mainz, Germany 227
Makin Island 181
Malaysia 97
Mang, Jack 229
Mangin Kaserne 227
Manila, Philippines 50, 51, 129
Manila Bay 128
Mannheim, Germany 228
Manning, Rodney 218
Manus Island, Admiralties 194–95
Maple Shade, New Jersey 179
Marathon High School 117
March AFB, California 246
March Field, California 178
Marianas 20, 99, 183
Marine Corps Training Center, 29 Palms 210
SS *Marine Robin* 50
Mariners 92
Marion, Indiana 96
"Market Street Geezers" 270–271
Marks, Adrian 101
Marseilles, France 24, 51, 122, 200
Marshall, George 48
Marshall Islands 99, 146, 236
Martin, Byron 108
Martin, Claude B. 107
Martin, Herschel 109
Martin, Ira 109
Martin, Selena Dixon 109
Master Mason 41
Master Sergeant 176, 235, 237, 274
Matawan, New Jersey 19
USS *Matsonia* (ID-1589) 94
Mattingly, Bill 241
Maywood, Nebraska 217
McAdoo, Texas 144–45; high school 144
McAlister, Bill 199
McArthur, Douglas 129
McAuliffe, Anthony C. 13
McCowan, Ellen Larue 70–72
McCraney, Eleanor 77
McDonald, Conny 108
McDonald's Funeral Home (Lubbock, Texas) 38
McDonough, John 111
McDonough, John, Sr. 111
McDonough, Minnie 111
McDowell, Josh 34
McKinney, Texas 238
McLean, Texas 131

McLendon, Dolphus 113
McLendon, Mamie Light 113
McLendon, Oscar Folkes 113
McMahan, Susan 196
McMillan, A.A. 115
McMillan, Cleveland "Buzz" 221
McMillan, Mary Alice 115
McMillan, Teddy 115
McNair Hall 284
McVay, Charles 100, 102
Medal of Honor 24, 134, 211, 219, 230
Medical Battalion Commander 261
Medical Meritorious Award (Vietnamese) 262
Mediterranean Sea 77, 236
Melbourne, Australia 114
Melrose, New Mexico 151, 207–08
Melvin High School, Texas 221
Memorial Day 240, 272
Memphis, Tennessee 190
Memphis, Texas 37, 102
Memphis State College 32
Meningitis 166
Meritorious Service Medal 237, 257, 262
Merkel, Texas 43
Merrifield, Dorothy Jean 69
Merseburg, Germany 55
Mesa, Arizona 286
Mesa Drilling 125
Mess cook 221
Metropolitan Junior College 139
Metz, France 7, 25
Meuse River 12
Mexico 126
Miami Beach, Florida 128
Miami, Texas 124
Michigan State University 134
Mickey, Barbara 112
Mickey Mouse boots 223
Middle East 185
Middlestaedt, Marion 139
Midland, Texas 97, 199, 210
Midway 236
USS *Midway* (CVA-41) 137
USS *Midway* (CVB-41) 193
Miel, Wallie Rose 156
Mihailovich, Draza 87
Military History Now 91
Military Women's Memorial, Virginia 257
Miller, Frank 117
Miller, George 118
Miller, Givens 117
Miller, Jewel 117
"Million–dollar wound" 53
Mindanao 282
Mineral Wells, Texas 24, 29, 45
Minglewood, Tennessee 32
Minneapolis, Minnesota 139
Mirecourt, France 135
Miss Texas, contest 229
Missing in action (MIA) 5–6, 46, 87

Index

USS *Missouri* (BB–63) 54
USS *Mitchell* (AP–114) 160
Mitchell, Billy, Jr. 219
Mittemeyer, Bernhard 260–62, 270
Mittemeyer, Jan 262
Mittemeyer, Robert 262
Mittemeyer, Sarah 262
Mittemeyer, Tom 262
Mobile Army Surgical Hospital (MASH) 212, 238
Monahans, Texas 125
Monroe, Louisiana 157
USAT *Monterey* 130
Montgomery Ward 143
Moore Field, Texas 78
Moravian College 260
Moravian Missionaries 260
Moreeall, Ben 107
Morgan, Horace 120
Morgan, Jennifer 213
Morgan, Velma 121
Morotoi, Southeast Asia 59
Morse, Earl 271
Morse code 4, 35, 86, 105, 125
Morton, Texas 203
Moscow 185
Moselle River 18, 25
Mote, Virginia 150
Motley, James 193
Motor Information Systems 196
Mt. Baker, Washington 60
Mt. Pleasant Church (Lorenzo, Texas) 258
Mt. Pleasant, Texas 146–47; high school 146
Mt. Suribachi, Iwo Jima 67, 99, 135
Mt. Vernon United Methodist Church (Lubbock, Texas) 23
Mt. Vernon, New York 133
Mountain Warfare Training Center, California 248
Muleshoe, Texas 65, 228–29
Muncy, Texas 26
Munich, Germany 51, 103
Murphy, Audie 24
Murphy, Doris 163
Murphy, Edgar 277
Murphy, Russ 235, 273–75
USS *Murray* (DD–576) 43
Musick, Betty 279
Musick, Gordon 223, 273
Musick, John 223
Musick, Josephine "Willie" 223
Mustard gas 37
USS *Mustin* (DD–413) 76
"My Country 'Tis of Thee" 135
My Desk Is a Pulpit 34
Myrtle Beach, South Carolina 105

Nab Zab, New Guinea 129
Nagasaki, Japan 10, 15, 27, 68, 76, 80, 147, 153, 183, 185

Nagoya, Japan 238
"Name Enough" 46
Namur, Belgium 118
Naples, Italy 158
NASCAR 290
USS *Nashville* (CL–43) 181
National D–Day Museum 157
National Defense Medal 25, 124, 237, 262
National Football League 171
National Museum of the Marine Corps 164, 208, 239
National Weather Service 154
National WWII Museum 69, 83, 134, 157, 270
Native Americans 206
Naval Academy 85
Naval Air Station (NAS), Florida 190
Naval Air Station Alameda, California 58–59
Naval Air Station Kaneohe Bay, Hawaii 58
Naval Air Technical Training Center (NATTC) 190
Naval Aviation Museum 40
Naval Base San Diego 66
Naval Hospital (Yokosuka, Japan) 238
Naval Order (website) 248
Naval Review Board 189
Naval Station Great Lakes, Illinois 58
Naval Station Newport, Rhode Island 136
Naval Training Center 39, 184; California 75
Navy Bombing Squadron VB–146 58
Navy Fifth Fleet 150
Navy 97th Construction Battalion 10
Navy Occupation Service Medal, Pacific 85
Navy Presidential Unit Citation 241
Navy Reserve 143
Navy Sixth Fleet 236
Navy SNJ (AT–6) 196
Navy SOC (Scout Observation Plane) 192
Navy Third Fleet 150
Navy Unit Commendation 238
Navy WAVES 42
Nazareth, Pennsylvania 260
Nazis 47, 48, 89, 162, 229; war souvenirs 152
NCO Leadership School 246
Nebraska 69, 217
Nebraska State Teacher's College 217
Nellis Army Airfield, Nevada 287
Netherlands 260
Nevada 143
New Brunswick 227
New Deal, Texas 129
New Delhi, India 172
New Guinea 94, 126, 128, 130, 193–95, 282
New Jersey 112, 121, 173, 186
New London, Connecticut 83
New Mexico 69, 196
New Mexico Refinery 222
New Orleans, Louisiana 18, 26, 32, 95, 157, 246

New York 103, 151, 175, 179, 290; harbor 48, 73, 81, 228; navy yard 163
New York City 22, 42, 117–18, 122, 173, 236
New York Times 132, 281
Newfoundland 86
SS *Newton* 37
Nichols, Norma 210
Nichols Field, Philippines 178
Nimitz, Chester 189
90 mm anti–aircraft gun 228
Nissen hut 82
Norden bombsight 55
Norfolk, Virginia 77, 136; naval station 37
Norman, Oklahoma 142
Normandy, France 10, 29, 64–65, 73, 111, 157–59, 176
North Adams Transcript 82
North Africa 20, 240
North America 227
North Andover, Massachusetts 78
North Atlantic Ocean 77
North Atlantic Treaty Organization (NATO) 226–27, 276
North Carolina 16, 27, 290
North Island, California 154
North Korea 201, 210, 211, 217, 230, 237, 240; Communist forces 237
North Sea 48, 55
North Solomons 193
North Viet Cong 265–66
Northern California 211
Northern Regional Wartime Construction Manager 276
Northwestern University 190; medical school 74
Norton AFB, California 237
Not Operational Ready Supply (NORS) 256
Nouasseur AFB, Morocco 234
Nova Scotia 227
Nuclear weapons 227
Number 4 Cannoneer 226
Nuremburg, Germany 51

O–2B Skymaster 219
O.L. Slaton Junior High (Lubbock, Texas) 126
Oak Creek Lake, Texas 199
Oakland, California 144, 236
Obar, New Mexico 153
Oberporlitz, Germany 18
Odell, Texas 92
Odessa, Texas 143
Odom, Florence 122
Odom, Frank 122
Odom, Henry 125
Odom, John 122
Odom, Murlin 125
Odom, Vernon 125
O'Donnell, Jimmy 102
O'Donnell, Texas 113, 177
Office of Special Investigation (OSI) 198

Officer Candidate School (OCS) 251
Offutt AFB, Nebraska 256
Ogden, Utah 81
Ohio University 198
Ohrdruf Concentration Camp 47
Okido, Japan 204
Okinawa, Japan 10, 15, 21, 27, 35–36, 37, 53–54, 95, 115–16, 129, 147, 150, 163, 183, 185, 217, 246, 248–49
Oklahoma 69, 180, 206
Oklahoma Baptist University 126
Olathe, Kansas 216
Old Ironsides 46
Old Mobeetie, Texas 230
Oliver, A.C. 213, 226
Oliver, Agnes 226
Olton, Texas 163
105 mm howitzer 167, 180, 209
120 mm B1 anti–aircraft gun 62
137th District Court (Lubbock, Texas) 232
155 mm gun 167
Operation Big Switch 211
Operation Frostbite 137
Operation Market Garden 90
Operation Overlord 64
Operation Shenandoah I 252
Operation Shenandoah II 252
Operation Showdown 202
Operation Varsity 90
Orangetown, NY 45
Orly Field, Paris, France 118
Orosco, Lucio 199
Osan, Korea 54; air base 219
OS2U Kingfisher 194
Otara River 48
Overseas Service Bar 112
Owen, Ben 128
Owen, Lois 129
Owen, Wayne 128
Owens, Oleta 131
Owens, R.L. 130
Owens, Walter P. 190, 193
Owensboro, Kentucky 241
Owi, Dutch East Indies 129
Oxford University 74

P–47 Thunderbolt 78–79, 150
P–51 Mustang 87, 114, 121
P–51D Mustang 187
Pacific Ocean 27, 95, 163
Pacific Theater 15, 18, 37, 51, 53, 76, 79, 83, 106, 116, 125, 128–29, 141, 146–47, 150, 164, 167, 181, 185, 240, 271, 279
Palau 99, 101, 193
Pampa, Texas 281; airfield 69
Panama 276
Panama Canal 37, 51, 109
Panmunjom, Korea 211
Panola County, Texas 83
Parachute Rigger and Repairman (620) 26
Paramaribo, Surinam, South America 260

Index

Paratrooper 144
Pareso Bay 181
Paris, France 13, 65, 79, 103, 112, 118, 161, 229
Paris, Texas 103
Parkinsonism 172
Parkway Neighborhood Center (Lubbock, Texas) 259
Parris Island, South Carolina 115, 133
Parsons, New Mexico 151
Pasewark, Bill 133
Pasewark, Jean 134
Pasewark, Scott 135
Patrol Bombing Squadron VPB–146 58, 60
Patton, George S. 12, 24, 29, 47–48, 62, 73, 75, 173, 207
PBY plane 76
PBY-5A 101
Pearl Harbor 22, 37, 61, 66, 78, 81, 83, 95, 98–99, 107, 150, 155, 186, 190, 286; movie 239
Pecos, Texas 143
Peleliu 115, 194
Penicillin 13
Penn Relays 17
Pennington Gap High School 42
Pensacola, Florida 39
Pentagon 34
Pepsi Canteen 43
Perryton, Texas 212
Petersburg, Texas 264; high school 111
Petroleum Engineering School 96
Philadelphia, Pennsylvania 22
Philippine Liberation Ribbon 59
Philippine Sea 149
Philippines 9, 22, 37, 100, 109–110, 126, 236, 246
Phoenix, Arizona 160
Pidgeon, Walter 237
Pierce, Frances 281–83
Pierce, L.G., Jr. 283
Pierce, Larry 283
Pillbox, German 180
Pioneer Natural Gas 206
Plains, Texas 285
Plainview, Texas 68–69, 92, 111–12, 131; high school 68, 92; flying club 68
Platten, Beverly 137
Platten, Chuck 139
Platten, Marvin 136
Plumb, Charlie 27
Point Loma, California 190
Poland 168; language 180
Pontoon Bridge 73
Pope, Elsie 141
Pope, Leon 141
Pope, Thomas 141
Port Adelaide, Australia 130
Port Hueneme, California 10
Port–en–Bessin–Huppain, France 111
Portales, New Mexico 224, 279; high school 279–80; Mac's Drive–In 280

Post Exchange (PX) 27, 64
Post–Traumatic Stress Disorder (PTSD) 147
Prairie View A&M College 62, 83
Pratt & Whitney engines 287
Presidential Unit Citation 131
Presidio, California 62
Pribilof Islands 214
Price, Albert 89
Priestley, Mildred 159
Prince Edward Island 227
USS *Princeton* (CVI–23) 181
prisoners of war (POWs) 25, 30, 35–36, 46, 51, 87, 109–10, 116, 118, 121–23, 141–42, 167–68, 211
Pruitt, Jo 87
PT–19 (Primary Trainer) 70, 86, 89, 286
Puerto Rico 27, 255
Pulitzer Prize 132
Purdue University 17, 96–97
Purple Heart 25, 38, 54, 56–57, 131, 152, 159, 172, 201, 205, 229, 232, 241
Pusan, Korea 201, 221, 230
Pyle, Ernie 129

Quanah, Texas 181
Quantico, Virginia 164, 208
RMS *Queen Elizabeth* 10, 46, 167
RMS *Queen Mary* 10, 111
Queensland, Australia 126
Quest, A.E. 210
Quitaque, Texas 20, 206
Quonset hut 10, 82, 195, 223

Radioactive 185
Raider Ranch (Lubbock, Texas) 148, 174
Ralls, Texas 45, 48, 126
Ramey AFB, Puerto Rico 139, 237
Randolph, Texas 204
Randolph Field, Texas 172, 189
Range–finder operator 99
Ransom Canyon, Texas 217
Ratliff, Anne Merle 156
Rawls Course, Texas Tech 271
Raybon, Evelyn 182
Razor wire 224
Rebuilding Warriors Foundation 290
Red Army 227
Reese AFB, Texas 106, 110, 180, 237, 247, 256
Reese Army Airfield, Texas 201
Reese Technology Center 34
Regenauer, Lee 121
Reid, Norma Grace 126–27
Reims, France 90
Remington 206
Reno, Nevada 187
Repo Depot 109
USS *Repose* (AH–116) 248
Rest and Relaxation (R&R) 265
Rhine, Wanda Mae 16

Rhine River 45, 73, 89, 112, 123
Ribble, Mona 152
Rich, Ada 144
Rich, Ezra 144
Rich, James Troy 144
Rich, Libby 145
Richardson, Texas 265
Ridgway, Hank 121
Rix Funeral Home (Lubbock) 38
Robbins, Joe 203
Robbins, Kay 203
Roberts, Eugene 146
Roberts, Opal 284
Roberts, Ray 285
Roberts, Roy 23
Robertson, Estel 149
Robertson, Esther 149
Robertson, Max 149
Robertson, Max, Jr. 150
Robertson, Nannie Mae 150
Robinson, Earl 151
Rock of Gibraltar 77
"Rocket City" 219
Rockwood, TX 221
Rodewald, James 153
Rodewald, Monetta 153
Rodewald, Otto 153
HMS *Rodney* (29) 218
Rogers, New Mexico 279–80; high school 223
Romania 87
USS *Ronquil* (SS–396) 83–84
Roosevelt, Eleanor 318
Roosevelt, Franklin D. 8, 67, 70, 82, 129, 155, 281
Roosevelt County, New Mexico 223
Roosevelt High School (Lubbock, Texas) 258
Ropesville, Texas 53, 184
Roscoe, Texas 251
Rosie the Riveter 121
Roswell, New Mexico 87; Air Force base 8
Royal Gorge 145
Rudd, Billy 228
Rudd, Pam 229
Rudd, Ralph 228
Ruff, Curtis 230
Ruff, Frances 230
Ruhr Pocket 51
Ruidoso, New Mexico 203
Ruidoso Downs 203
Rush Springs, Oklahoma 8
Russell Islands 115
Russia 17, 34, 43

Saale River 48
Saalfeld, Germany 18
Saar–Moselle Triangle 167
Sachsen, Germany 274
Safeway Stores 131
Saigon 251

St. Elmo's fire 187
St. John's Methodist Church (Lubbock, TX) 172
USS *Saint Lo* (CVE–63) 193
St. Lo, France 111
St. Louis, Missouri 19, 74
St. Mary's College 171
St. Nazaire, France 167
St. Nazaire Pocket 51
USS *Saint Paul* (CA–73) 136
St. Paul, Minnesota 136
St. Petersburg, Florida 12
Saint–Raphael, France 158
Saipan 37, 67, 95, 99, 146, 183, 190, 192
Saloniki, Greece 86
Salween River, China 171
Salzburg, Germany 207
Sam Houston State 62
San Antonio, Texas 48, 77, 78, 186, 223, 234
San Diego, California 20, 94, 99, 102, 116, 147, 150, 153, 162, 181, 184, 190, 211, 216, 217, 236; naval training station 141
San Francisco, California 53, 76, 95, 99, 143, 154, 183, 196, 249
San Francisco Bay 125
San Marcos, Texas 68
San Pedro, California 109, 150
Sand Point Naval Air Station, Washington 190
Santa Ana, California 55
Santa Fe Railroad 50
SS *Santa Maria* 18
Santa Monica, California 59
USS *Saratoga* (CV–3) 181
Sasebo, Japan 76, 95, 142
USS *Saugatuck* (AO–75) 37
Saunders, Joy 65
Savannah, Georgia 234
SB2C Helldiver 71
Scarborough, Charles "Lightning" 264
Scarborough, Essie 264
Scarborough, Henry 264
Scheffel, Eldie 155
Scheffel, Gustav William 156
Schleiz, Germany 18
Schmeling, Max 62
Schultze, Harold 157
Schutzstaffel (SS) 152
Scoggin–Dickey 201
Scotland 46, 81, 151, 167; northern region 24
Scott Field, Illinois 86, 125
Sea Biscuit 139
Seabees 10, 107–08, 181
Sears, Anna 280
Sears, Charles Odell 160
Sears, Ernest 280
Sears, Joe 161
Sears, Louise 161
Sears, Susan 161

Index 315

Seattle, Washington 72, 109, 185, 214
2nd Class Electrician 141
2nd Lieutenant 176, 273
Selective Service 83
Selma Army Airfield, Alabama 28
Seoul, Korea 15, 201–02, 212, 219, 224, 259
75mm recoilless rifle 207
Shallowater, Texas 39, 41, 150
Shallowater Co–op Gin 41
Shallowater ISD 41
Shamrock Station 129
Shanghai, China 142
Shawn, Wayne 286
Sheepshead Bay, New York 92
Shelfer, Debbie 217
Shellback 76
Sheppard, J.W. 68
Sheppard AFB, Texas 8, 218
Sheppard Army Airfield, Texas 26, 68, 113, 125, 287
Sherman tank 30, 74, 147
Shields, Lieutenant 194
Sibert, William L. 17
Siegfried Line 89, 167, 179
USS *Sierra* (AD–18) 154
Sierra Blanco, Texas 117
Silent Wings Museum (Lubbock, Texas) 91, 189, 247
Silver Star 172
Simi Valley, California 249
Simi Valley Police Department 249
Sims, Barry 164–65
60 mm mortar 241
Skaggs, Carrie Kirk 42
Skaggs, Grover Cleveland 42
Skelton, Red 199
Skinout Mountain, Jones County, Texas 113
Slaton, Texas 72, 86, 284
Slaughter, Bruce 164
Slaughter, Dola 162
Slaughter, J.L. 161
Slaughter, James 162
Slaughter, Jody 165
Smith, Adam 262
Smith, Ann 142
Smith, Betty 48
Smith, Brandt 262
Smith, Helen 208
Smith, LaJuana 274–75
Smith, Lee R. 141
Smith, Mary Beth 262
Smith, Welby 200, 234, 273–75, 277
Smyer, Texas 50, 207
Smyrna Airfield, Tennessee 125
Snyder, Donna 265
Snyder, Shirley 116
Snyder, Texas 15, 116, 119, 225; high school 15, 70
Snyder Laundry 116
Social Security Administration 104
Sofia, Bulgaria 87
Solomon, C.J. 166–170, 196
Solomon, Clifford 166
Solomon, Pearl 166
Solomon, Ples 166
Somerville, Massachusetts 218
Sonar 83
Sons of Bitche 123; *see also* Bitche, France
Sophie B. Wright School for Girls 32
Sousa, John Phillip 77
South America 27
South Carolina 55, 70, 103, 166
South Dakota 55, 232
South Korea 208, 217, 218, 230
South Pacific 21, 35, 58, 109
South Plains, Texas 68, 69, 108, 258; kennel club 33
South Plains Army Airfield, Texas 71, 106
South Plains Church of Christ (Lubbock, Texas) 225
South Pole 154
South Vietnam 261
Southampton, England 22, 46, 50, 151
Southaven Assisted Living (Lubbock, Texas) 67
Southcrest Baptist Church (Lubbock, Texas) 34
Southeast Asia 237
Southern Pacific Railroad 117
Southwestern Bell Telephone Co. 141, 43
Soviet blockade 234
Spain 246
Special Missions 187
Specialist 4th Class 284
Spitfire (British airplane) 90
Spokane, Washington 9
SPQ 3 Specialist (Communication) 42
Springfield M1903 204
Springlake, Texas 228
Spur, Texas 16, 145
Sri Lanka 76
Stahl, Gust 240
Stahl, Orin 240
Standard Oil 114
Stars and Stripes 82
Station Charlie 217
Stephen F. Austin University 274
Steward 83
Stockigt, Germany 19
Stockton Field, California 177
USS *Storm King* (AP–171) 107
Strategic Air Command 235
Submarine Combat Patrol Insignia 84
Sudan, Texas 20; high school 20
Suez Canal 77
Suffolk, England 292
Sul Ross State University 118–19
Sunset School of Preaching (Lubbock, Texas) 227
Supply Custodian School 247
SWAT team 249
Sweetwater, Texas 256

316 Index

Switzerland 118
Sydney, Australia 94, 125, 265
Syria 206
Szymanski, Theodore 179

T.G. & Y. 104
Tacloban, Philippines 128
Tahoka, Texas 179
Taliban 290
Tambatuni, New Georgia 181
Tampa, Florida 80
Tank Driver 73
Tarawa 229
USS *Tarawa* (CV-40) 138
Tarbox, Elmer 171
Tarbox, Emma May 171
Tarbox, J.E. 171
Tarbox Parkinson's Disease Institute 172
Tartaglione, Dana 173
Tartaglione, Dominic 173
Tartaglione, Joanne 173
Tartaglione, Josephine 173
Tartt, Lisa 242
Task Force Baum 29, 47, 49
Task Force Faith 241
Task Force 38 149–50
Task Force 58 150
Task Force 99 163
Taunton, Massachusetts 81
Taunton Daily Gazette 81
Taylor, Texas 258
Taylor, Virginia 116
TBM1/C 192
Teague, Dalton 39
Teague, Norman 41
Tech Sergeant 247, 255
Technical training 270
Ted Jay Combo 116
Teleman 3rd Class 214
Temple, Texas 146
Temple University 260
Tennessean 276
Tennessee Army National Guard 276
Tennessee Maneuvers 111
Terrell, Texas 162
Terry, Betty 224–25
Terry County, Texas 211, 258
Tet Offensive 253, 265
Texas 290
USS *Texas* (BB-35) 150
Texas A&I University 217
Texas A&M University 92, 203
Texas Christian University 95
Texas College 85
Texas Department of State Health Services 257
Texas Department of Transportation 214
Texas Health Department 247
Texas Instruments 265
Texas Motor Speedway 290
Texas Panhandle Honor Flight 2011, 88

Texas South Plains Honor Flight 33, 161, 164–65, 270–272, 285, 288; Committee 237; 2012 flight 60, 157, 196, 267, 279; 2013 flight 21, 34, 43, 57, 110, 175, 239; 2014 flight 33, 204, 215, 257; 2016 flight 9, 63, 104, 251, 254; 2017 flight 208, 213, 222
Texas State Legislature 172
Texas Tech 14, 16, 19, 39, 62, 70, 77, 85, 87, 89, 93, 94, 113, 125–26, 128, 135, 140, 148, 149, 171, 175–77, 201, 210, 251, 264, 273, 281, 287, 290; athletic hall of fame 172; band 199; library 227; medical school 172, 247; museum 227; press 247; ROTC 177
Texas Wesleyan College 141
Thailand 246, 255, 257
Thatcham, England 82
Theuma, Germany 18
Thionville, France 7
Third Class Petty Officer 107
38th parallel 202, 208–09, 224
"This Is My Father's World" (song) 135
Thomasville, Missouri 190
Thompson Implement Co. (Abernathy, Texas) 143
Thompson Junior High 16
Thorp, Virginia 222
Three Rivers, Texas 150
Thurman, Pat 175
Tikrit, Iraq 273
Tilly 217
Tinian 37, 100, 147, 163; D–Day 192
Tinsing, China 116
Tirishima Japan 105
Tokyo 129, 235; Bay 280; Harbor 54
Toledo Scale 106
Tomb of the Unknown Soldier 33, 104
Tommy's Machine Shop (Levelland) 51
Torpedo boat 95
Torpedoes 98, 100
Torrance, California 249
Toul–Rosières Air Base, France 8
Tourniquet 202
Traumatic brain injury (TBI) 289
Travis AFB, California 251
Treasure Island, California 196
Trench foot 123
Tres Ritos, New Mexico 127
Trier, France 18
Trier, Germany 13
Trip wire 248
Tripler Army Hospital, Hawaii 143
Troy University 220
Truax Field, Wisconsin 125
Truman, Harry S. 82, 129, 147, 202, 227
Truth or Consequences, New Mexico 82
Tubbs, Laney 282–83
Tubbs, Richard Irvin 281
Tucson, Arizona 86
Tulane University 126
Tulsa, Oklahoma 22, 23, 114

Index 317

Turkey 168
Turner, Janice 124
Turret gunner 190
Tuskegee Institute (University) 22
21-gun salute 230
2006 ICM Song of the Year 275
Tye Company 31
Tyler, Graham 177
Tyler, Jeff 178
Tyler, R.L. 177
Tyler, Truett 177
Tyler, Texas 85

U-boats 18, 40, 81; U-505 41
Udvar-Hazy Air and Space Museum, Virginia 257
UH-1 Iroquois "Huey" 278
Ulithi 194
Under God's Protection (UPG) 258
Union, Texas 94, 149; high school 211, 213
Union Civil War veterans 272
Union of Soviet Socialist Republics (U.S.S.R.) 227
United Grocery Stores, Lubbock, Texas 239
United Methodist Church 220
United Nations 212; service medal 232, 237
United States 260
U.S. Air Force Reserve 110, 173
U.S. Air Force 8, 173, 198, 217-18, 227, 234-35, 237, 246, 274
U.S. Army 12, 22, 29, 35, 45, 50, 53, 62, 78, 81, 93, 103, 109, 111, 117, 120, 122, 144, 151, 155, 160, 173, 181, 204, 207, 218, 221, 223, 226, 228, 230, 240-41, 251, 258, 260, 264, 273, 276, 289
U.S. Army Air Corps 26, 54-55, 64, 68, 70, 75, 78, 86, 92, 105, 113, 125, 133, 144, 166, 170, 177-78, 186, 281, 287
U.S. Army Air Forces 172, 234
U.S. Army Airborne School 273
U.S. Army Band 22
U.S. Army Battery A, 9th AAA 62
U.S. Army Battery B, 14th Armored Field Artillery Battalion 226
U.S. Army Combat Engineers 50, 121, 258, 276, 289
U.S. Army Garrison at Bagram 289
U.S. Army, Infantry Replacements 15
U.S. Army Paratrooper 50
U.S. Army Quartermaster Corps 118
U.S. Army Rangers 205
U.S. Army Reserve 128, 175, 206, 258
U.S. Army 31st Regimental Combat Team (RCT-31) 241
U.S. Army War College 262
U.S. Army Women's Auxiliary Ferrying Squadron (WASP) 256
U.S. Coast Guard 157, 159
U.S. Company A, 32nd Infantry Regiment, 7th Infantry Division 240
U.S. Company G, 2nd Infantry Division

("Indianhead") 231
U.S. Congress 102, 118
U.S. Defense Department 100
U.S. Marine Corps 40, 66, 1088, 115-116, 133, 141, 146, 185, 209, 238, 241, 246, 248
U.S. Marine Corps 1st Medical Battalion 211
U.S. Marine Corps, 2nd Marine Division 67
U.S. Maritime Service Training Station 92
U.S. Merchant Marine 92-93, 109
U.S. Navy 20, 32, 37, 39, 58, 66, 75, 83, 92-94, 98, 101, 136-37, 141, 149, 153, 162, 184, 189, 214, 218, 226
U.S. Post Office 63
U.S. Postal Inspection Service 143
U.S. Quartermaster Q177 118
U.S. Squadron 3743, Flight 3 256
U.S. War Department 87
United Supermarkets 267; Market Street 270
Units, U.S.:
U.S. 1st Allied Airborne 89
1st Antiaircraft Artillery Group 229
1st Armored Division (Old Ironsides) 226
1st Battalion, 5th Marines 248
1st Battalion, 32nd Infantry 242
1st Infantry Division 273
1st Marine Division, Easy 2/11 209
1st Mobile Photo Supply and Maintenance Division 64
2nd Armored Division (Hell on Wheels) 226-27
2nd Battalion, 5th Marine Regiment 115
2nd Battalion, 28th Infantry, 1st Infantry Division 251
2nd Infantry Division (Indianhead) 221, 230-31
2nd Marine Division, 2nd Tank Battalion 146
3rd Army 18, 24, 51, 75
3rd Army, 108th Evacuation Hospital 173
3rd Bomb Group, 64th Squadron 128
3rd Marine Division 238
4th Armored Division 45-47, 49
4th Marine Division 190
5th Air Force 4
5th Air Force, 91st Reconnaissance Squadron 281
5th Fleet 154
7th Armored Division 51
7th Army 13, 51, 123
8th Air Force 55
8th Antiaircraft Artillery Group 228
8th Army Medical Command/Korea 262
9th Air Force 64
10th Armored Division 12
10th Armored Infantry 45-47; company A 29
10th Mountain Division 139
11th Air Force 77th Bomb Squadron 105
11th Airborne Corps ("Angels") 166

Index

11th Airborne Division 144
11th Armored Division 73
11th Infantry, 5th Infantry Division 180
14th Air Force 96, 113
14th Armored Division 30
15th Army 18
18th Infantry Division 155
21st General Hospital 123
27th Antiaircraft Battalion 229
29th Infantry Division 111
31st Infantry Regiment, Company L 208
31st Infantry Regiment, 7th Infantry Division 201
32nd Infantry Division, 128th Infantry, company G 130–31
35th Engineer Combat Battalion 120–21
38th Infantry Regiment 221–22
43rd Bombardment Wing 235
43rd Calvary Reconnaissance Squadron 51
45th Infantry Division (Thunderbirds) 123, 204, 223
45th Quarter Master Group 283
47th Bomb Group 68
50th Squadron 55
59th Finance Group 152
63rd Antiaircraft Artillery Battalion 228
68th AACS (Army Airwaves Communication System) 126
69th Depot Repair Squadron 113
77th Infantry 53–54
82nd Airborne 260
84th Infantry Division, "Railsplitters" 151–52
87th Infantry Division 18, 24
93rd Chemical Mortar Battalion 17
94th Air Depot Group 65
94th Infantry 167
100th Bomb Group 55
100th Infantry Division 122
101st Airborne 13, 121, 260
107th Mechanized Calvary Recon Squadron 51
112th Field Artillery HD (Horse Drawn) 105
124th Naval Construction Battalion 184
150th Signal Company 712
180th Infantry, Medical Co. 223
187th Glider Infantry Regiment 166
194th Engineer Brigade 276
301st Air Depot Group 113
311th Troop Carrier Squadron 27
404th Fighter Group 79
408th Airborne Quartermaster Co. 145
411th Infantry Regiment, 103rd Infantry Division (Cactus) 179
444th Engineer Base Depot Company 81
458th Air Service Squadron 89
506th Battalion 19
554th Anti-Aircraft Battalion 111
739th Tank Battalion 160
750th AAA (Anti-Aircraft) Battalion 175
1017th Guard Squadron 64
1382nd Engineering Petroleum Distribution Co. 96
3130th Air Base Group Police Squadron 219
3458th Quartermaster Truck Company 103
7322nd Air Police 219
Univac (computer system) 256
University of Alabama 39, 96
University of Arkansas 124
University of Chicago 14
University of Georgia 12
University of Michigan 74
University of Minnesota 139–40
University of Nebraska 23, 217
University of Oklahoma 85
University of Pennsylvania 17
University of Southern California 63
University of Tennessee 113
University of Texas 39, 118, 203
Urban warfare 173
USO 43; shows 22, 219
Utah 129
Utah Beach 10, 158, 167, 173

V–E Day (Victory in Europe) 112, 180
V–J Day (Victory over Japan) 144
V–1 rocket 90
V–2 rocket 82, 90
Vallejo, California 99
Van Nuys, California 25
Vancouver, Washington 150
Vazquez, Michael 289
Venezuela 97
Venona Project 43
Ventura Place, Lubbock, Texas 199
Ventura PV–1 58
Vernon, Texas 201
Verviers, Belgium 51
Veterans Administration (VA) 289; Accountability Act 290; Lubbock, Texas Super Clinic 277; Reform Act 290
Veterans Day 163
Vézelay, France 161
Victory ship 31, 65
Viet Cong 27
Vietnam 27, 142, 174, 219, 235, 248–49, 251, 255, 261–62, 264–66
Vietnam Campaign Ribbon 262
Vietnam Veterans Memorial, "The Wall" 63, 239, 251, 254, 257
Vietnam War 111, 143, 209, 255, 270; era 270; snipers 252
Vietnamese Service, Cross of Gallantry w/ Silver Star 262
Vogue Dress Shop (Lubbock) 93
Vung Tau, Vietnam 252

W&L Manufacturing (Lubbock, Texas) 183
W.W. Steel (Lubbock, Texas) 183

Index

Wahiawa Naval Radio Station 143
Wake Island 201, 236
Walker, Harry 236
Walker, Larry 236
Walker, Lee Ann 236
Walker, Mary 229
Walker, Richard 229
Walker, Samuel 161
Walker AFB, New Mexico 219
Walley, Steve 193
Walter Reed Medical Center 261–2
War Admiral 139
"War Stories" 271
Ward, Anita 180
Ward, Ed 179
Warfare History Network 149
Warm Springs, Georgia 155
USS *Washington* (BB–56) 162–63
Washington (state) 58, 126
Washington, D.C. 24, 42–43, 104, 162–64, 182, 187, 215, 239, 251, 253, 270–71, 285, 290
Washington University (St. Louis, Missouri) 32
USS *Wasp* 216
Waters, John K. 29
Watson, Fred 238
Watson, Rebecca 238–39
Watson, Thelma 239
Wayland Baptist University 259, 290
"We build, we fight" 107
We Were Soldiers (movie) 277
Weaver scope 204
Webb, Carl Wayne 181
Webb, Carl 181
Webb, David 183
Webb, Harold 181
Webb, John 183
Webb, Mary 181
Webb, Weldon 181
Weisse, Ted 186, 188
"Welcome Home Soldier" (song) 235, 275
Wellman, Texas 124
Wellman Gin 87
Wellman ISD, Texas 87
Wendover Army Air Base, Utah 78–79
Wesel, Germany 90
Wessel River 152
West Indies 136
West Los Angeles School of Law 249
West Nile Disease 206
USS *West Point* (AP–23) 87
West Texans 186
West Texas 70, 116, 132, 143, 148, 177, 183, 208, 222, 230, 287
Westbrook, Carol 118
Western Caroline Islands 37
Western Union telegram 282
Westex Document 34
Westinghouse Electric 177
Westmoreland, William 260–61

WESTPAC 216
"When the Roll Is Called Up Yonder" (song) 156
White House 43
USS *White Plains* (CVE–66) 190–91, 193
USS *Whitney* (AD–4) 181
Whorton, Ann 188
Wichita Falls, Texas 26, 75, 196
Wickes, Arkansas 122–23
Wickett, Texas 125
Wiesbaden, Germany 18, 228
Wiley Collegians 23
Will Rogers Field, Oklahoma 89
Williams, Charles A. 240
Williams, Eugene 184
Williams, Jeanneta 185
Williams, Larry A. 240
Williams, Thomas 242
Williams, Wanda 60, 61
Willis, C.D. 284
Willis, Elsie 284
Wilson, Jane 188
Wilson, John W. 63
Wilson, Mary Jo 23
Wilson, Ollie B. 186
Wilson, Paul 188
Wilson, Robert Elton 186
Wilson, Robert Elton, Jr. 186
Wilson, Sue 188
Wilson, Ted 188
Wilson, Texas 87
Winnegar, Andy 189
Winnegar, Ellen 190
Winnegar, James 190
Winters, Texas 120
Winthrop, Arkansas 124
Wisconsin 249
Wisdom, Bernice 82
WLW News Radio, Cincinnati, Ohio 199
Wolfforth, Texas 177, 239
Women in Military Service for America Memorial 33, 43
Women's Army Corps (WAC) 284–85
Women's Royal Naval Service (WRENS) 82
Wood, Olive Ruth 227
Woodrow, Texas 149, 179
Worms, Germany 46
Wright 1700HP engines 286
Wuemberger, V.L. 35
World War I 37, 64, 77, 96, 144, 221, 230, 240
World War II 52, 91, 128, 201, 207, 209, 217–18, 226, 230, 237, 244, 255, 260, 265, 279, 283, 288; victory medal 25, 65, 97, 124
World War II Memorial 164–65, 271
Wylie College 23
Wylie Drugstore (Lubbock, Texas) 181
Wyoming 290

Yap 99, 194

Yates, Ester Yates 103
Yellow Beach 115
"The Yellow Rose of Texas" (song) 156
Yellow Sea 212
Yeoman 3rd Class 216
Yokohama, Japan 76
Yokosuka, Japan 76, 216–17, 236, 237
Yokota Air Base, Japan 140

USS *Yorktown* (CV–5) 181
Yugoslavia 86–87
Yuma, Arizona 86
Yunnanyi, China 96

Zigzag 175
Zon, Holland 90